==

To my father

(Late) Shree. JAYANT NANDE

who dedicated much of his life to the education of others
and always encouraged me in all my endeavours

PRAJAKTA NANDE

==

FITNESS EVALUATION TESTS FOR COMPETITIVE SPORTS

For

M.Sc. (Food Science and Nutrition) students, Sports Nutritionists, Physical Education students (B. P. Ed and M. P. Ed), Coaches, Fitness Instructors and Players

Prajakta J. Nande

M.Sc., Ph.D.

Food Science and Nutrition

Visiting Faculty

Rashtrasant Tukadoji Maharaj Nagpur University

Nagpur, Maharashtra

Sabiha A. Vali

M.Sc., Ph.D.

Food and Nutrition

Professor and Head

Rashtrasant Tukadoji Maharaj Nagpur University

Nagpur, Maharashtra

Himalaya Publishing House

MUMBAI • NEWDELHI • NAGPUR • BANGALORE • HYDERABAD • BHUBANESHWAR • CHENNAI • PUNE • LUCKNOW • AHMEDABAD • ERNAKULAM • INDORE

First Edition : 2010

Published by : Mrs. Meena Pandey
for **HIMALAYA PUBLISHING HOUSE PVT. LTD.,**
"Ramdoot", Dr. Bhalerao Marg, Girgaon, **Mumbai - 400 004.**
Phones: 2386 01 70/2386 38 63, Fax: 022-2387 71 78
Email: himpub@vsnl.com
Website: www.himpub.com

Branch Offices:

New Delhi : "Pooja Apartments", 4-B, Murari Lal Street, Ansari Road, Darya Ganj, **New Delhi - 110 002.** Phone: 23270392, 23278631, Fax: 011-23256286

Nagpur : Kundanlal Chandak Industrial Estate, Ghat Road, **Nagpur - 440 018.** Phone: 2738731, 3296733 Telefax : 0712-2721215, **E-mail:-nagpur@himpub.com**

Bangalore : No. 16/1 (Old 12/1), 1st Floor, Next to Hotel Highlands, Madhava Nagar, Race Course Road, **Bangalore - 560 001.** Phone : 22281541, 22385461, Telefax: 080-22286611, **E-mail:-hphblr@himpub.com**

Hyderabad : No. 3-4-184, Lingampally, Besides Raghavendra Swamy Matham, Kachiguda, **Hyderabad - 500 027.** Phone: 040-27550139. **E-mail:-hphhyd@himpub.com**

Chennai : No. 85/50, Bazullah Road, T. Nagar, **Chennai - 600 017.** Phone: 044-28144004/28144005

Pune : First Floor, "Laksha" Apartment, No. 527, Mehunpura, Shaniwarpeth, (Near Prabhat Theatre), **Pune - 411 030.** Phone: 020 - 24496323/24496333, **E-mail:- pune@himpub.com**

Lucknow : C-43, Sector - C, Ali Gunj, **Lucknow - 226 024.** Phone: 0522-2339329

Ahmedabad : 114, "SHAIL", 1st Floor, Opp. Madhu Sudan House, C.G.Road, Navrang Pura, **Ahmedabad – 380 009.** Phone: 079-26560126, Mobiles: 09327324149,09314679413

Ernakulam : 39/104 A, Lakshmi Apartment, Karikkamuri Cross Rd., Ernakulam, **Cochin – 622011**, Kerala. Phone: 0484-2378012, 2378016, Mob- 09344199799

Bhubaneswar : 5 Station Square, **Bhubaneswar (Orissa) - 751 001.** Mobile - 9861046007, **E-mail:- orissa@himpub.com**

Indore : Kesardeep Avenue Extension, 73, Narayan Bagh.Flat No. 302, IIIrd Floor, Near Humpty Dumpty School, Narayan Bagh, **Indore (M.P.)** Mob-09301386468

Printed by : Geetanjali Press Pvt. Ltd. **Nagpur.**

PREFACE

Sports performance is the central concept in competitive sports. Sport training aims at improving the performance of athletes. Knowledge of sports performance is therefore a starting point for talent selection, formulation of sports training schedule and its assessment and evaluation.

Theory of sports performance is a relatively new addition to the general and specific methods of training. The sports performance depends upon physical fitness, technique and tactics which are interrelated and interdependent. Physical, physiological, psychological and nutritional factors also affect performance. For proper control and regulation of the improvement of physical fitness, periodical measurement and assessment of physical fitness components is needed. Performance evaluation is essential to grade the athlete. These tests form essential criteria for selection of sportspersons for various sports disciplines.

For interpretation of sportsmen's performance, several researchers have attempted and developed normative data. With the help of these norms or standards, one can easily assess the level of sportsmen's performance and categorize them accordingly. A number of physical fitness tests have been formulated in various countries but are hardly available in one literature. With the increasing involvement of youth in the area of sport there is a need for evaluation of physical performance so as to ascertain their suitability for training and future performance. Nutritional and health status are key factors influencing the performance. Besides physical fitness, mental and emotional stability in competitive sports is of dire importance.

Strength and conditioning professionals spend a great deal of time and effort trying to improve athletic performance. Coaches can evaluate each athlete by using the results of a vast battery of tests.

This book is an earnest effort to compile and present various physical fitness, psychological and talent evaluation tests which we feel would serve as a guide to all those involved in sports and competitive games.

Dr. Prajakta J. Nande

Dr. S. A. Vali

CONTENTS

Part I	**Introduction to Physical Fitness**	***1-3***
	Components of Physical Fitness	
	Motor Fitness	
	Specific Fitness	
Part II	**Performance Evaluation**	***4***
1	**Performance Evaluation to Monitor Athletic Development**	***5-8***
	Evaluation Process	
	Requirements of a Test	
	Benefits of Testing	
	Factors Influencing Test Results	
	Need to Record Information	
	Performance Evaluation Categories	
	Maximal and Submaximal Tests	
2	**Aerobic Fitness**	***9-18***
	VO_2max, Aerobic Power and Maximal Oxygen Uptake	
	Factors Affecting VO_2max	
	VO_2max for Various Age Groups	
	Athletes	
	Non Athletes	
	VO_2max Assessment	
	Normative Data for VO_2max	
Part III	**Performance Evaluation Tests**	***19-20***
3	**Aerobic Endurance-VO_2max Evaluation Tests**	***21-44***
	Run/Jog Tests	
	Treadmill Tests	
	Step Tests	
	Cycle Test	
	Run and Treadmill Test	
	Swim Test	
	Multistage Fitness Test	
4	**Heart Rate Tests**	***45-46***
	Orthostatic Heart Rate Test	

Resting Heart Rate

5	**Anaerobic Endurance Evaluation Tests** Cunningham and Faulkner Test Running-based Anaerobic Sprint Test (RAST)	*47-50*
6	**Agility Evaluation Tests** Run/Change of Direction Tests Obstacle Test Quick Feet Test	*51-60*
7	**Balance Evaluation Tests** Standing Stork Tests – Static and Blind Balance Test – Motion	*61-64*
8	**Event Time Predictors** Run Tests	*65-69*
9	**Fitness (General) Evaluation Tests** Physical Fitness Tests - General	*70-77*
10	**Flexibility Evaluation Tests** Flexion Tests – Hip and Trunk Sit and Reach Tests Static Flexibility Tests	*78-87*
11	**Reaction Time Evaluation Tests** Reaction Time and Quickness Assessment Tests	*88-93*
12	**Strength (Core) Evaluation Tests** Core Muscle Strength and Stability Test	*94-95*
13	**Strength (Elastic) Evaluation Tests** Jump Tests Leg Strength (Elastic) Tests	*96-102*
14	**Strength (General) Evaluation Tests** Upper Body/Abdominal Strength Tests Lower Body/Leg Strength Tests Hand/Arm/Shoulder Strength Tests Burpee Test	*103-120*
15	**Speed and Power Evaluation Tests** Run Tests Cycle Tests Power and Run Test Rowing Test	*121-140*
16	**Psychology Evaluation Tests** Anxiety, Task and Ego Orientation Tests	*141-146*
17	**Talent Evaluation Tests** Evaluation of Male and Female Physical Talent	*147-149*

SECTION - I

Cycle Test

Treadmill Test

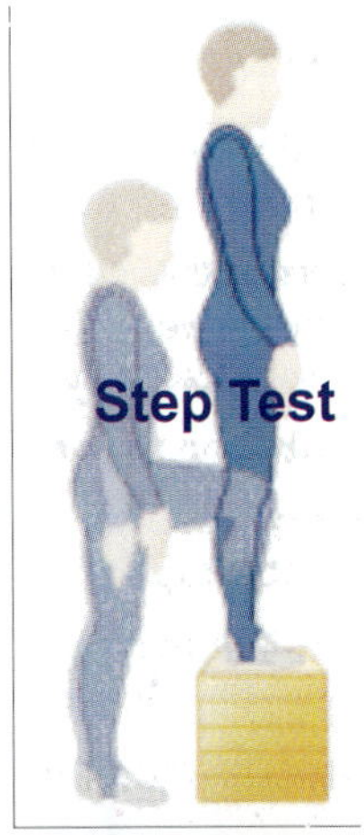
Step Test

Walk Test

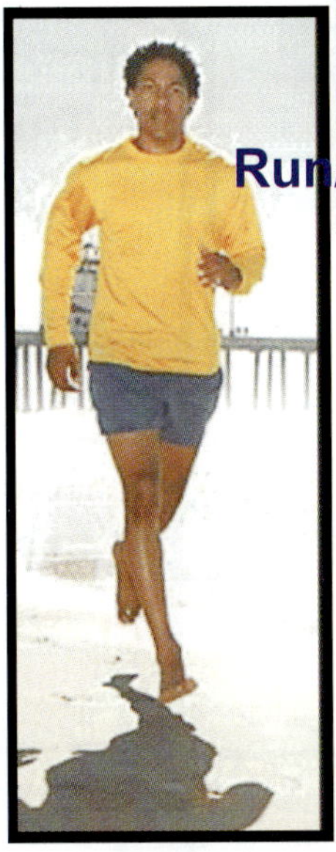

Run/Jog Test

Standing Stork
Test

Hip Flexion
Test

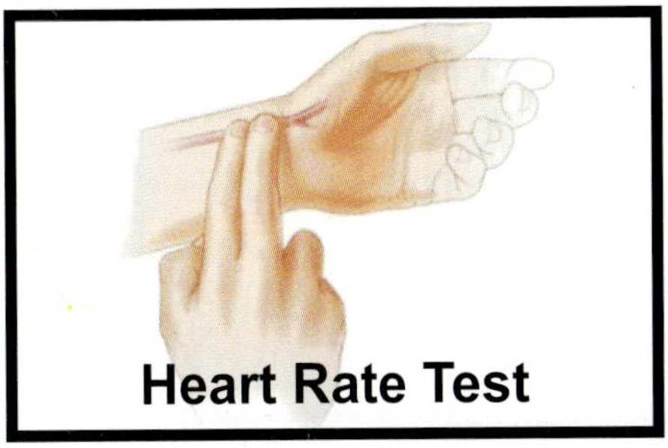
Heart Rate Test

Swim Test

Balance Beam
Test

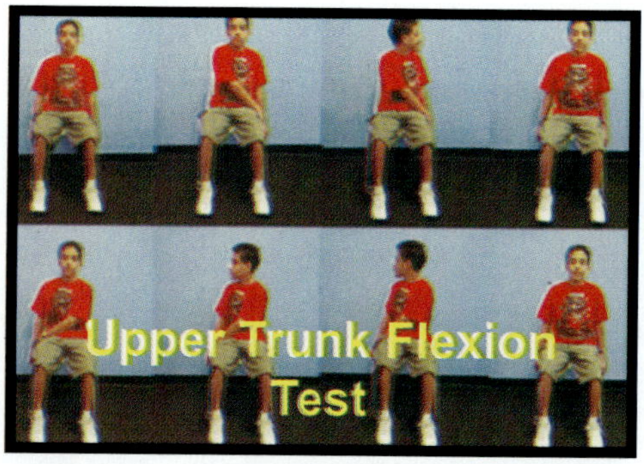
Upper Trunk Flexion
Test

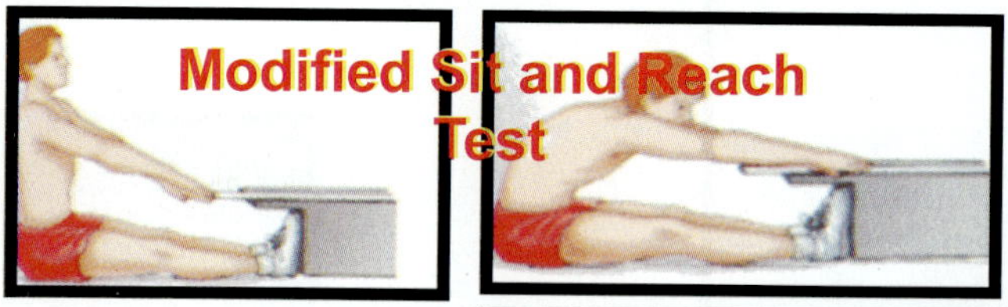
Modified Sit and Reach
Test

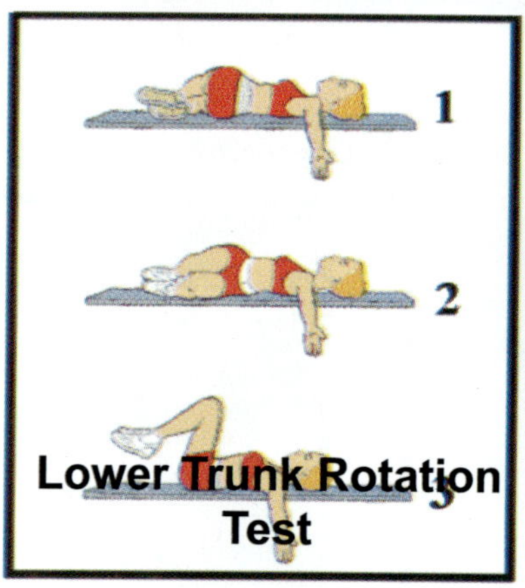
1
2
3
Lower Trunk Rotation
Test

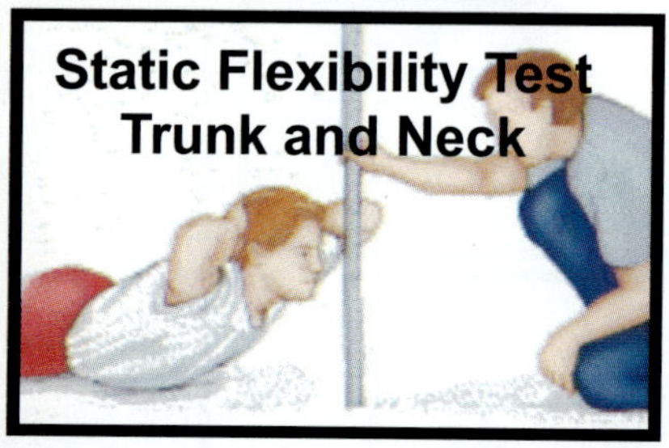
Static Flexibility Test
Trunk and Neck

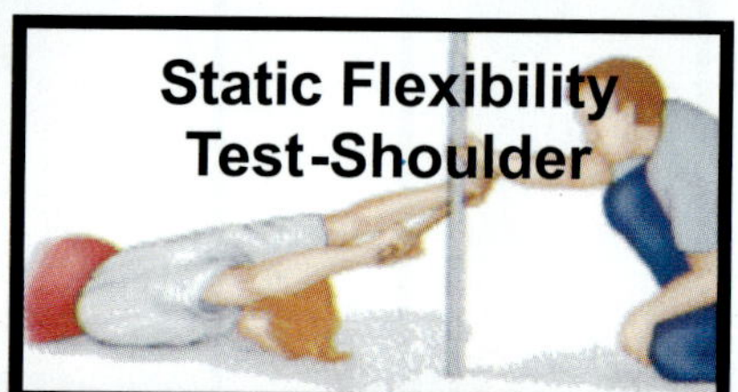
Static Flexibility
Test-Shoulder

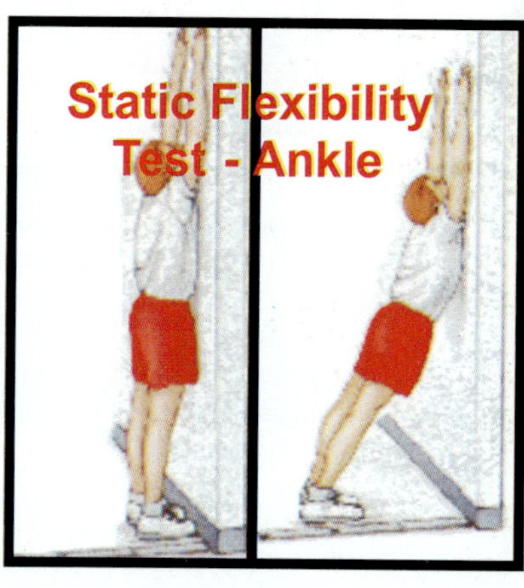
Static Flexibility
Test - Ankle

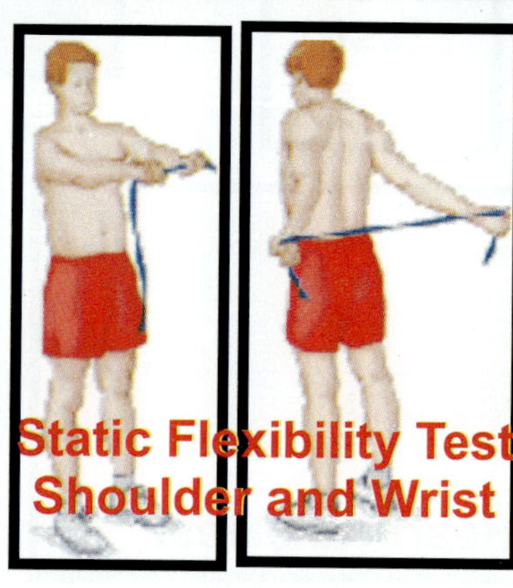
Static Flexibility Test
Shoulder and Wrist

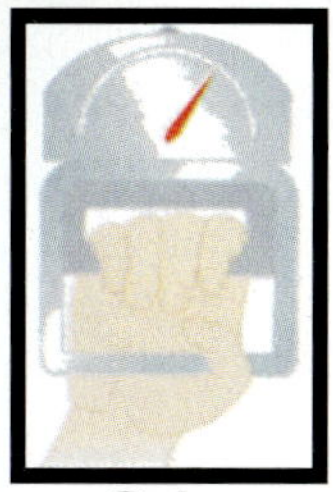

Grip Strength Test

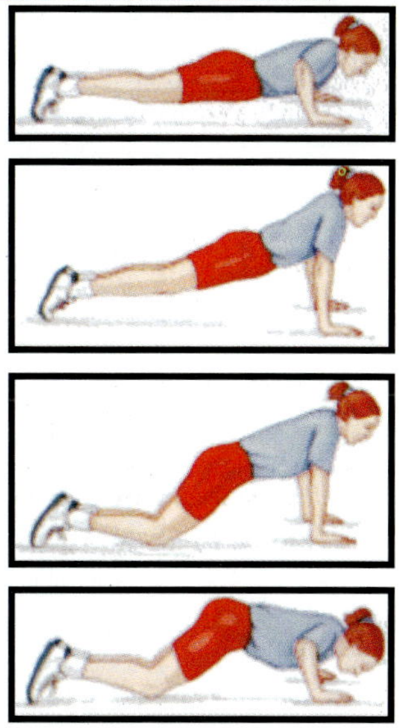

Overhead Press Up Test

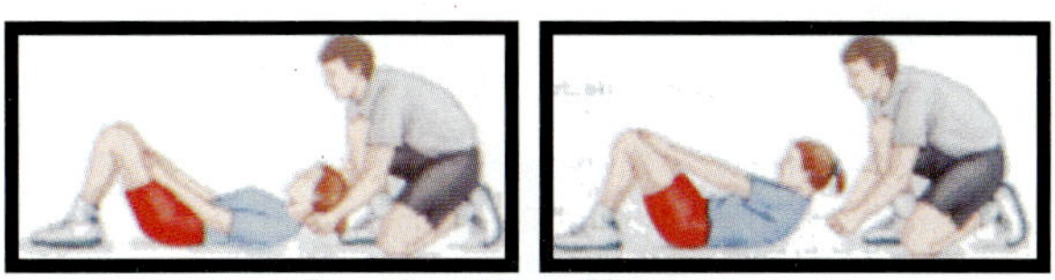

Curl - Up Test

Bench Press Test

Leg Strength Elasticity Test
Sergeant Jump Test
M1
M2
Upper Body/Abdominal Strength Tests
Leg Press Test
Flexed Arm-Hang Test
Wall Squat Test
Chin Up Test
Knee Extension Test
Concept 2 Rowing Step Test
Biceps Curl Test
Burpee Test

SECTION - II

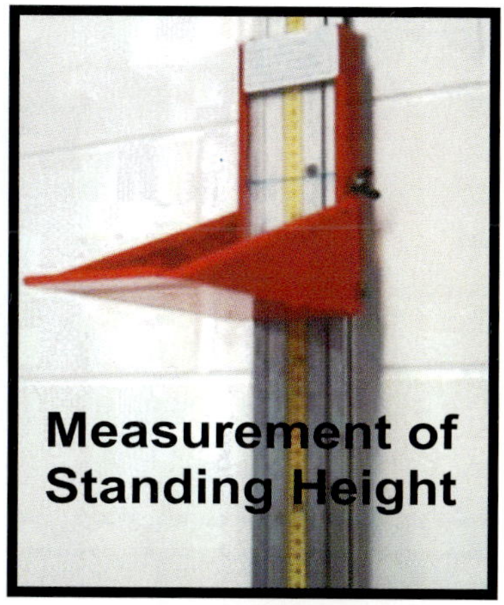

Measurement of Standing Height

Body Weight

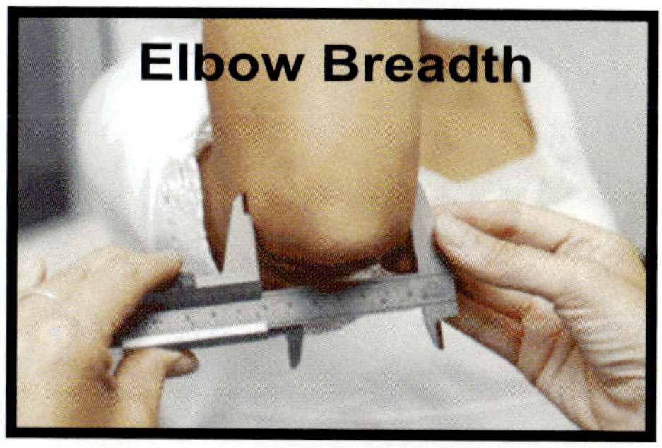

Elbow Breadth

Head Girth

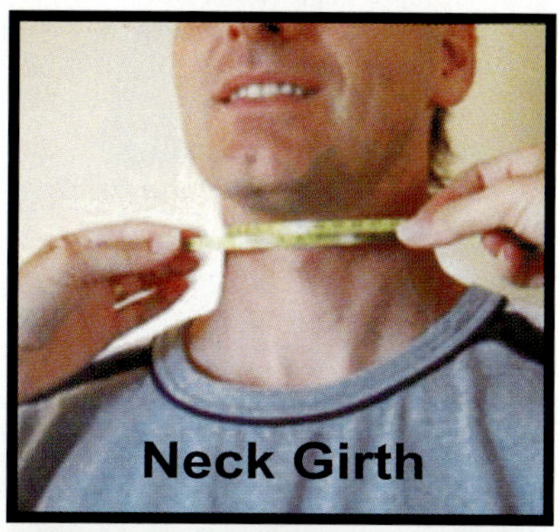

Neck Girth

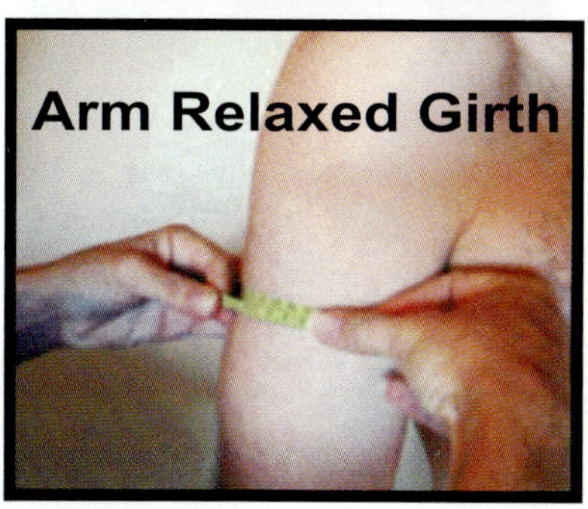

Arm Relaxed Girth

Arm Flexed Girth

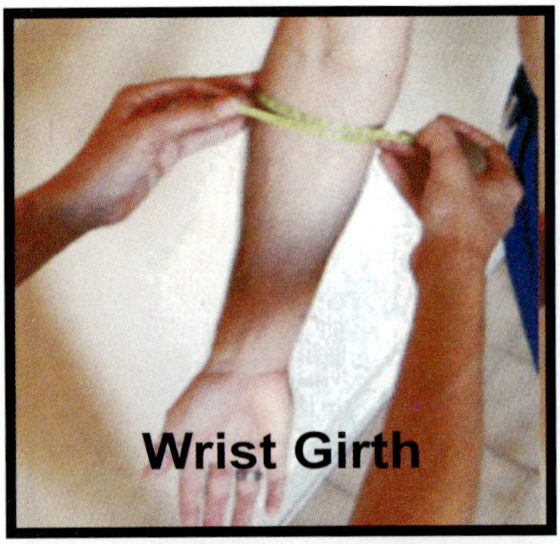
Wrist Girth

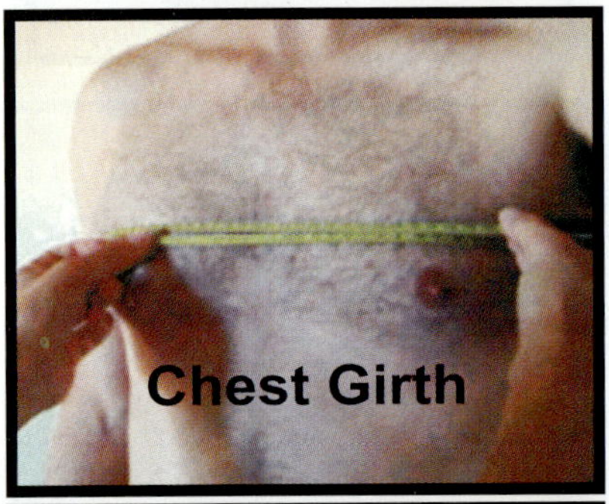
Chest Girth

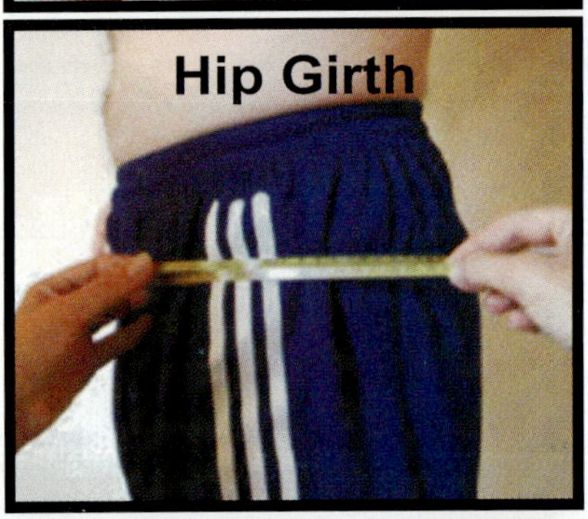
Hip Girth

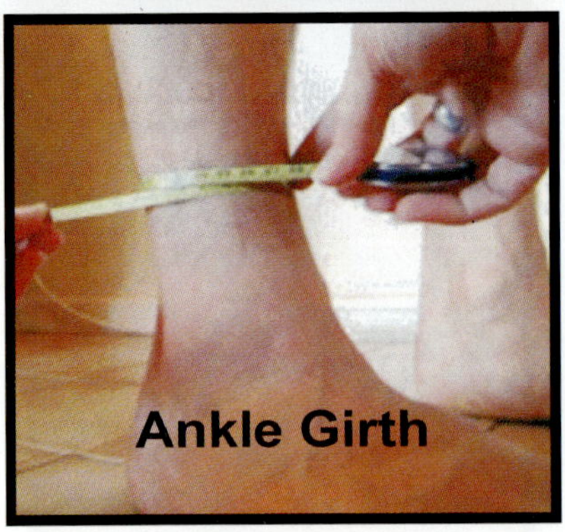
Ankle Girth

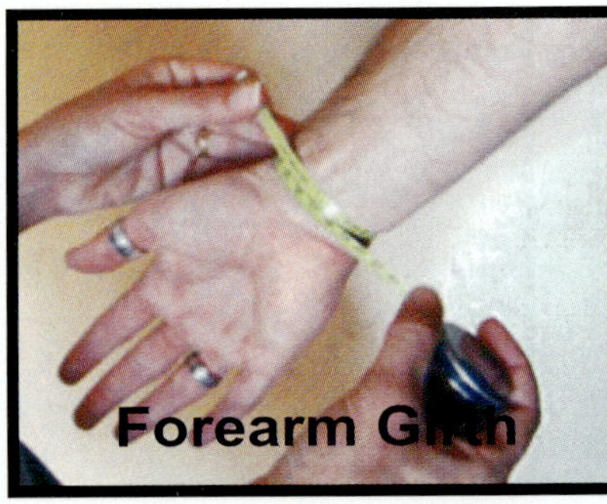
Forearm

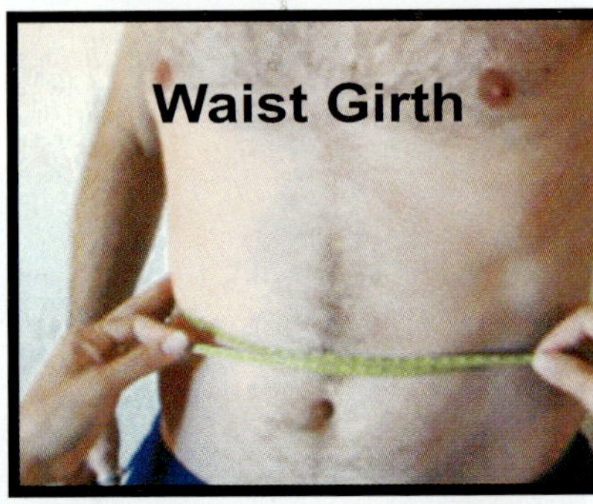
Waist Girth

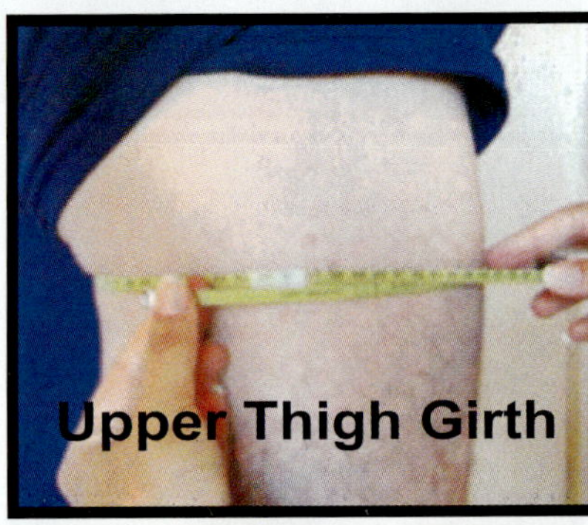
Upper Thigh Girth

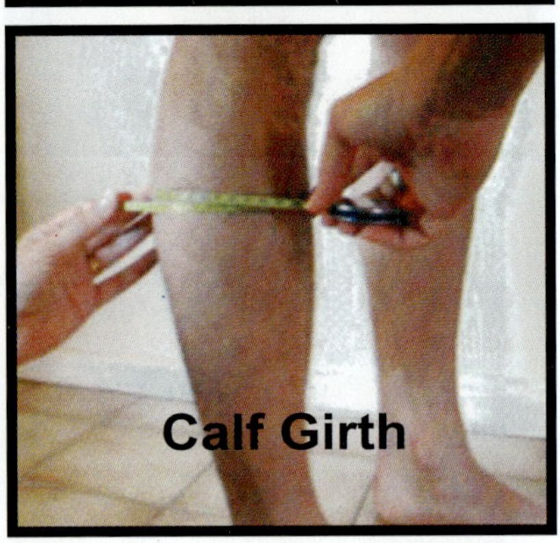
Calf Girth

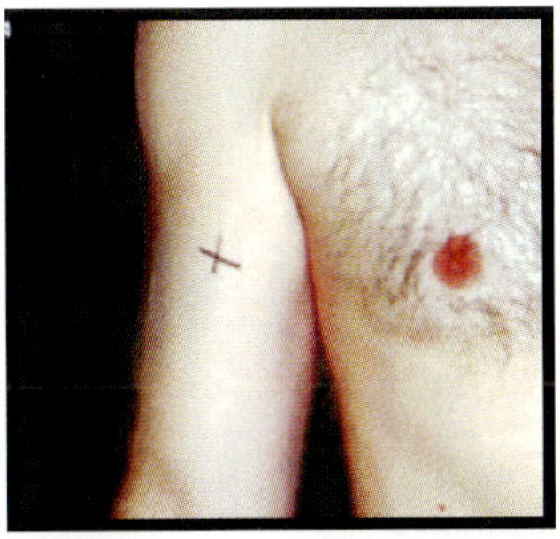
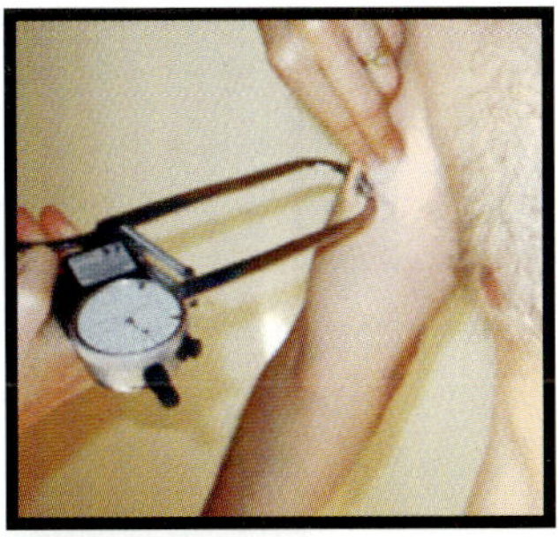

Bicep Skinfold Site and Measurement (topendsports.com)

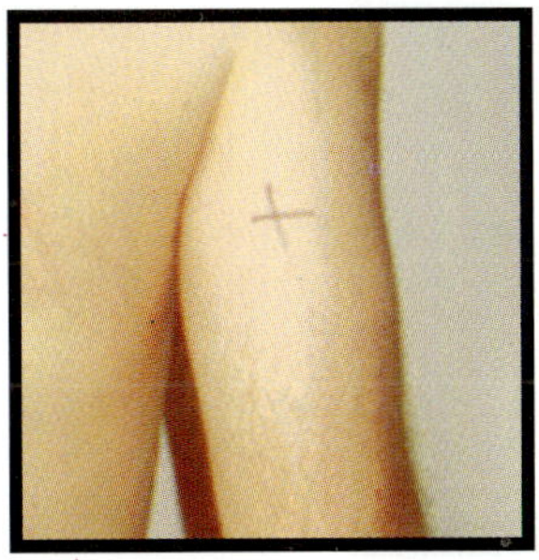
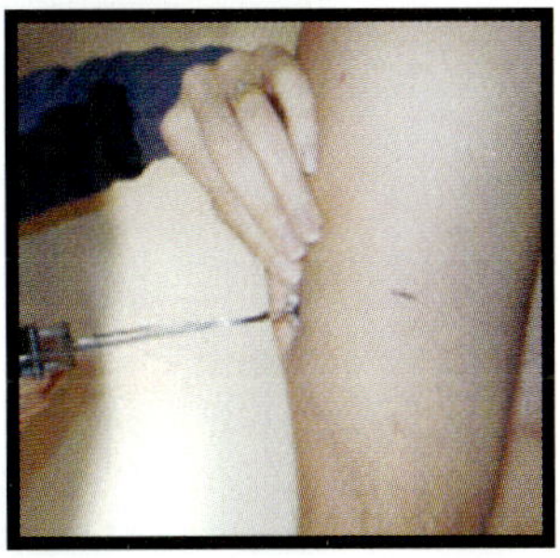

Tricep Skinfold Site and Measurement (topendsports.com)

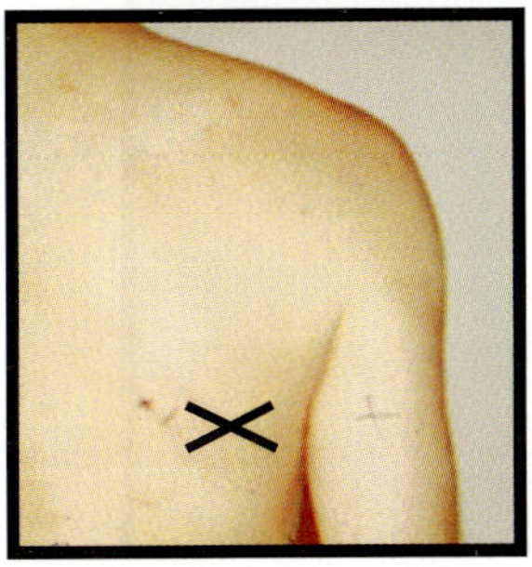
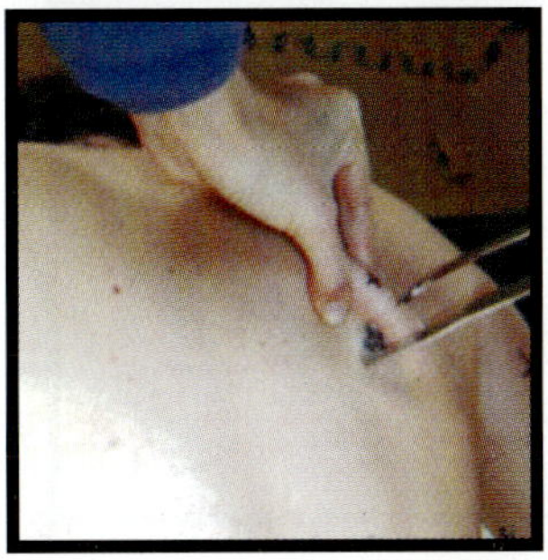

Subscapular Skinfold Site and Measurement (topendsports.com)

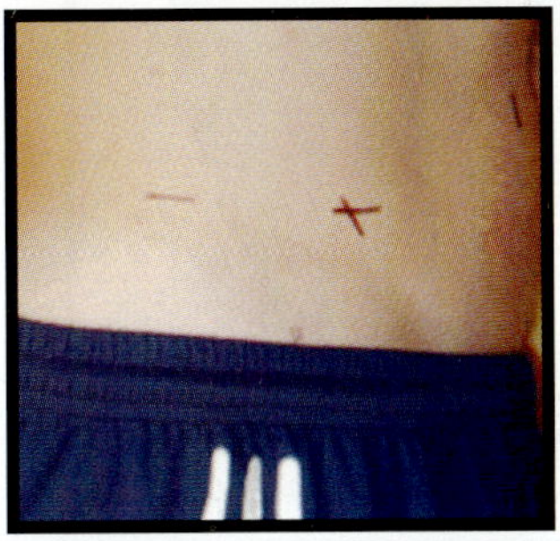
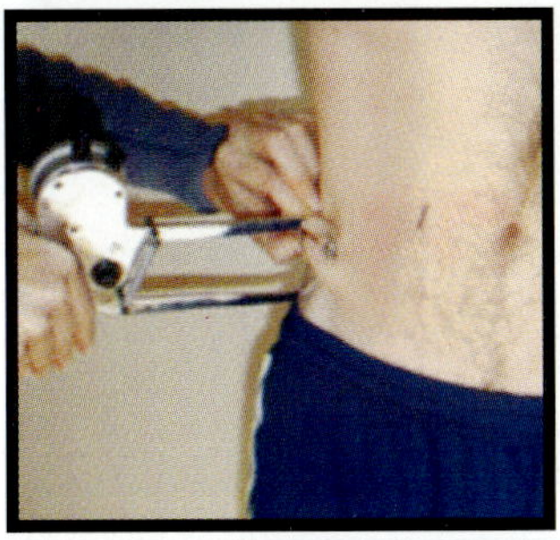

Suprailiac Skinfold Site and Measurement (topendsports.com)

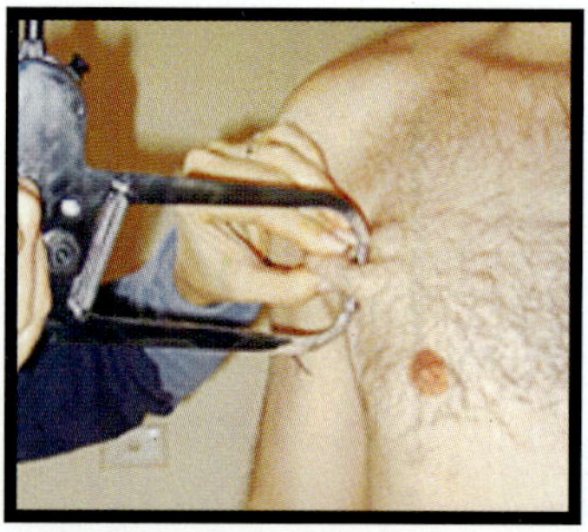

Chest Skinfold Measurement (topendsports.com)

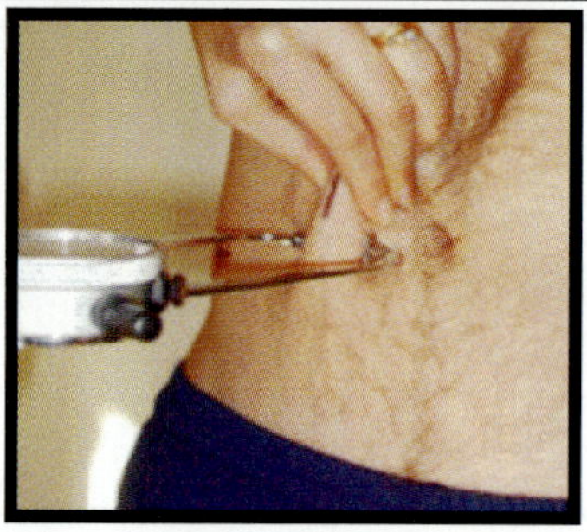

Abdominal Skinfold Measurement (topendsports.com)

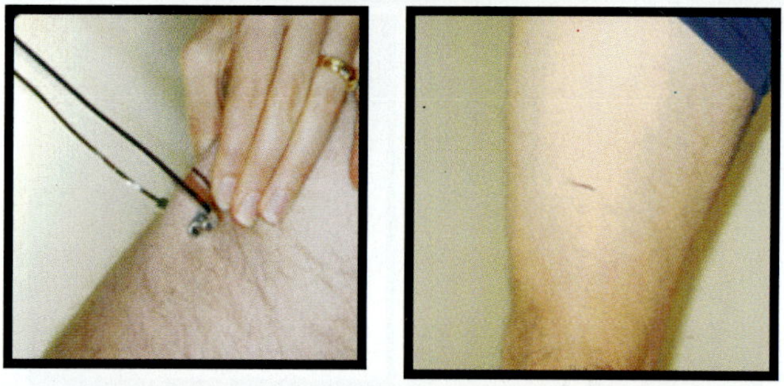

Thigh Skinfold Site and Measurement (topendsports.com)

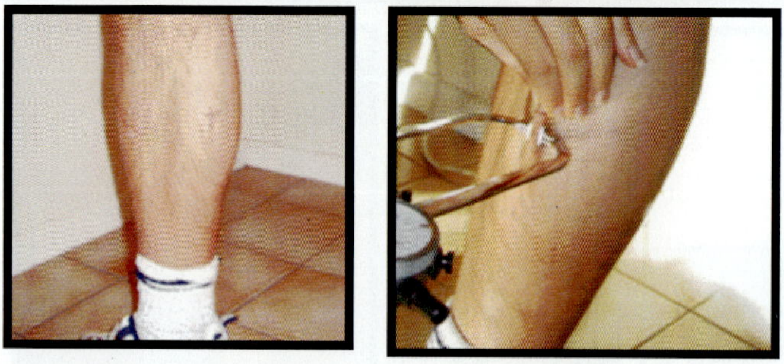

Calf Skinfold Site and Measurement (topendsports.com)

Part IV	**Body Composition Assessment**	***150-151***
18	**Anthropometric Tests**	***152-167***
	Measuring Somatotype	
	Endomorphy	
	Mesomorphy	
	Ectomorphy	
	Standing Height	
	Body Mass/Weight	
	Chart - Weight for Height and Age	
	Estimations of Ideal Body Weight in Adults	
	Equations for Prediction of Ideal Body Weight	
	Sitting Height	
	Arm Length	
	Hand Span	
	Arm Span	
	Shoulder Width	
	Elbow Breadth	
	Body Girths/Circumferences	
	Body Mass Index (BMI)	
19	**Arm Fat Distribution**	***168-174***
	Equations for Prediction of Arm Fat, Arm Muscle Circumference, Body Frame Size and Segments and Trunk Frame Size and Index	
20	**Skinfold Measurement**	***175-182***
	Skinfold Measurement – the Most Economical way to Calculate Body Fat	
	Advantages of using Skinfold Calipers	
	Disadvantages of using Skinfold Calipers	
	Use of Good Quality Calipers	
	Top 5 Body Fat Calipers	
	How to take Skinfold Measurements	
	Skinfold Measurement Sites	
	Tips when using Body Fat Calipers	
Part V	**Prediction of Body Density, Body Fat and Lean Body Mass Based on Skinfolds, Body Mass and Circumferences**	***183***
21	Equations for Estimation of Body Density	***184-196***
22	Equations for Estimation of Percent Body Fat	***197-204***
23	Equations for Estimation of Lean Body Mass	***205-210***

Part VI **Other Methods for Estimation of Body Fat Content** *211-219*

Body Volume Determination
Hydrostatic Weighing
Bioelectric Impedance Analysis (BIA)
Dual-Energy X-Ray Absorptiometry (DEXA)
Near Infrared Interactance
Total Body Potassium (TBK)
Total Body Protein (TBP)
Whole Body Air Displacement Plethysmography
Magnetic Resonance Imaging (MRI)
Total Body Electrical Conductivity (TOBEC)
Computed Tomography (CT Scan)

Appendices *220-247*

Appendix I *220-222*
RM-1 (1- RM) Assessment

Appendix II *223-224*
Acceptable Weight Range for Height to find Weight Corresponding to BMI Levels

Appendix III *225-228*
Percentiles of Upper Arm Fat Area in Square Millimeters
Percentiles of Upper Arm Circumference in Millimeters
Percentiles of Triceps Skinfold (Millimeters)
Percentiles of Upper Arm Muscle Area in Square Millimeters

Appendix IV *229-236*
Conversion Constants to Predict Percent Body Fat for Young and Older Women and Young and Older Men

Appendix V *237-238*
Relative Fat Values in Male and Female Athletes

Appendix VI *239-240*
Skinfold Caliper Types

Appendix VII *241-246*
Equipments

Appendix VIII *247*
Approximate Conversions to and from Metric Measures

References *248-257*

Part I

INTRODUCTION TO PHYSICAL FITNESS

One of the misconceptions in the sports world is that a sports person gets in shape by just playing or taking part in his/her chosen sport. If a stationary level of performance, consistent ability in executing a few limited skills is your goal, then engaging only in your sport will keep you there. However, if you want the utmost efficiency, consistent improvement, and balanced abilities sportsmen and women must participate in year round conditioning programs.

The bottom line in sports conditioning and fitness training is stress, not mental stress, but adaptive body stress. Sportsmen and women must put their bodies under a certain amount of stress (overload) to increase physical capabilities.

Physical fitness is used in two close meanings: **general fitness** (a state of health and well-being) and **specific fitness** (a task-oriented definition based on the ability to perform specific aspects of sports or occupations).

The Components of Fitness

Health is a state of complete mental, physical and social well being where as fitness is the ability to meet the demands of a physical task.

Basic fitness can be classified in four main components: strength, speed, stamina and flexibility. However, exercise scientists have identified nine components that comprise the definition of fitness:

- **Strength** - the extent to which muscles can exert force by contracting against resistance (e.g. holding or restraining an object or person)
- **Power** - the ability to exert maximum muscular contraction instantly in an explosive burst of movements. The two components of power are strength and speed. (e.g. jumping or a sprint start)
- **Agility** - the ability to perform a series of explosive power movements in rapid succession in opposing directions (e.g. Zigzag running or cutting movements)
- **Balance** - the ability to control the body's position, either stationary (e.g. a handstand) or while moving (e.g. a gymnastics stunt)
- **Flexibility** - the ability to achieve an extended range of motion without being impeded by excess tissue, i.e. fat or muscle (e.g. executing a leg split)

- **Local Muscle Endurance** - a single muscle's ability to perform sustained work (e.g. rowing or cycling)
- **Cardiovascular Endurance** - the heart's ability to deliver blood to working muscles and their ability to use it (e.g. running long distances)
- **Strength Endurance** - a muscle's ability to perform a maximum contraction time after time (e.g. continuous explosive rebounding through an entire basketball game)
- **Co-ordination**- the ability to integrate the above listed components so that effective movements are achieved.

Of all the nine elements of fitness cardiac respiratory qualities are the most important to develop as they enhance all the other components of the conditioning equation.

Physical Fitness

Physical fitness refers to the capacity of an athlete to meet the varied physical demands of their sport without reducing the athlete to a fatigued state. The components of physical fitness are:

- Strength
- Endurance and Stamina
- Speed
- Flexibility
- Body Composition

Motor Fitness

Motor Fitness refers to the ability of an athlete to perform successfully at their sport. The components of motor fitness are:

- Agility
- Balance
- Co-ordination
- Power
- Reaction Time and Reflexes

Many sources also cite mental and emotional health as an important part of overall fitness. This is often presented in textbooks as a triangle made up of three sub-sections, which represent physical, emotional, and mental fitness. Hence, one may be physically fit but may still suffer from a mental illness or have emotional problems. The "ideal triangle" is balanced in all areas. Physical fitness can also prevent or treat many chronic health conditions brought on by unhealthy lifestyle or aging, among other implications. Working out can also help to sleep better. To stay healthy it's important to participate in physical activity.

Specific Fitness

Specific or task-oriented fitness is a person's ability to perform in a specific activity with a reasonable efficiency, for example, sports or military service. Specific training prepares athletes to perform well in their sports. Examples are:

- 400 m sprint - in a sprint the athlete must be trained to work anaerobically throughout the race.
- Marathon - in this case the athlete must be trained to work aerobically and their endurance must be built-up to a maximum.

Athletes must undergo regular Fitness testing to determine if they are capable of the physically demanding tasks required for the sport.

Improving Your Condition

One should identify the most important fitness components for success in the chosen sport or event and then design sport/event specific conditioning and training programs that will enhance these fitness components and energy systems.

♦♦♦♦♦♦♦♦

Part II

PERFORMANCE EVALUATION

Physical fitness tests are tests designed to measure physical strength, agility, and endurance. Throughout the 20th century, scientific evidence emerged demonstrating the usefulness of strength training and aerobic exercise in maintaining overall health, and more agencies began to incorporate standardized fitness testing. In the United States, the President's Council on Youth Fitness was established in 1956 as a way to encourage and monitor fitness in schoolchildren and in 1982, FITNESSGRAM was developed and is mandated by a number of states.

By undertaking a sport test, one can measure the performance in a number of ways. Sports tests as a part of program assessment ensure one get a better idea of how well his/her training is going to help with on court or field performance.

In the multiple performance tests that actually exist, the choice of the most representative evaluation of the physical activity is crucial. For the general or field practitioner who wants to give his or her athlete the most useful information for the follow-up, this choice may be very difficult. Nevertheless, the results of those tests, once a correct interpretation have been done, will give opportunity to built an efficient training's program, whatever the type of sports or the athlete's level.

♦♦♦♦♦♦♦♦

1

PERFORMANCE EVALUATION TO MONITOR ATHLETIC DEVELOPMENT

Performance is an assessment of how well a task is executed and the success of a training program is largely dependent upon satisfying the performance aims associated with it.

How can performance be monitored?

Testing and measurement are the means of collecting information upon which subsequent performance evaluations and decisions are made.

What is the evaluation process?

The whole measurement/evaluation process is a six stage, cyclic affair, involving:

- The selection of characteristics to be measured
- The selection of a suitable method of measuring
- The collection of that data
- The analysis of the collected data
- The making of decisions
- The implementation of those decisions

All of the above stages should be completed with the athlete - especially the analysis of the collected data and making decision of appropriate way forward.

What are the requirements of a test?

In constructing tests it is important to make sure that they really measure the factors required to be tested, and are thus objective rather than subjective. In doing so all tests should therefore be specific (designed to assess an athlete's fitness for the activity in question), valid (test what they propose to test), reliable (capable of consistent repetition) and objective (produce a consistent result irrespective of the tester).

In conducting tests the following points should be considered:

- Each test should measure ONE factor only
- The test should not require any technical competence on the part of the athlete (unless it is being used to assess technique)
- Care should be taken to make sure that the athlete understands exactly what is required of him/her, what is being measured and why
- The test procedure should be strictly standardized in terms of administration, organization and environmental conditions

What are the benefits of testing?

The results from tests can be used to:

- motivate the athlete
- place the athlete in appropriate training group
- measure improvement
- indicate weaknesses
- predict future performance
- enable the coach to assess the success of his training program

Tests additionally break up, and add variety to, the training program. They can be used to satisfy the athlete's competitive urge out of season. Since they demand maximum effort of the athlete, they are useful at times as a training unit in their own right.

What factors may influence test results?

The following factors may have an impact on the results of a test (test reliability):

- The ambient temperature, noise level and humidity.
- The time of day.
- The time since the athlete's last meal.
- The athlete's caffeine intake.
- The amount of sleep the athlete had prior to testing.
- The athlete's emotional state.
- Medication the athlete may be taking.
- The test environment - surface (track, grass, road, gym).
- The athlete's prior test knowledge/experience.
- Accuracy of measurements (times, distances etc.).
- Is the athlete actually applying maximum effort in maximal tests?
- Inappropriate warm up.
- People present.
- The personality, knowledge and skill of the tester.

Why record information?

For the coach and athlete it is important to monitor the program of work, to maintain progression in terms of the volume of work and its intensity. Both coach and athlete must keep their own training records. A training diary can give an enormous amount of information about what has happened in the past and how training has gone in the past. When planning future training cycles, information of this kind is invaluable.

What should be recorded?

The information to be recorded falls into two broad categories: -

The day-to-day information from training:

- o State of the athlete (health, composure).

- o Physiological data (body weight, resting heart rate, etc.).
- o The training unit (speed, speed endurance, strength, technique).
- o The training load (the number of miles, the number of sets and repetitions, the number of attempts).
- o The training intensity (kilograms, percentage of maximum, percentage of VO_2).
- o The prevailing conditions (wet, windy, hot etc.).
- o The response to training (the assignments completed, the resultant heart rate recovery, felt tired, etc.).

Information that measures status: This can take the form of a test. If the test is repeated throughout the program, it can then be used as a measure of progress within the training discipline. Examples of such tests are:

- o Time trials - speed, speed endurance, endurance.
- o Muscular endurance - chins, push ups, dips.
- o Strength maximum - single repetitions, maximum repetitions.
- o Explosive strength - power bounding, vertical jump, overhead shot put.
- o Mobility - objective measurements of the range of movement.
- o Event specific.

Competition Evaluation

Following competition, it is important that the coach and athlete get together as soon as possible in order to evaluate the athlete's performance. Elements to be considered are pre race preparations, focus and performance plans and achievement of these plans. An evaluation form is useful to help the athlete and coach conduct this review.

Performance Evaluation Categories

Performance evaluation can be grouped under different categories:

- Aerobic Endurance - VO_2 max
- Heart Rate Tests
- Anaerobic Endurance
- Agility
- Balance
- Event Time Predictors
- Fitness (General)
- Flexibility
- Psychology
- Reaction Time
- Strength (Core)
- Strength (Elastic)
- Strength (General)
- Speed and Power

- Talent Evaluation
- Body Composition

For performance evaluation, tests can be divided into two categories: maximal and submaximal.

Maximal Tests

Maximal means the athlete works at maximum effort or tested to exhaustion. Examples of maximal anaerobic tests are the 30 meter acceleration test and the Wingate Anaerobic 30 cycle test. Examples of maximal aerobic tests are the Multistage Fitness Test or Bleep test and the Cooper VO_2max test

Disadvantages of maximal tests are:

- Difficulty in ensuring the subject is exerting maximum effort.
- Possible dangers of over exertion and injury.
- Dependent on the athlete's level of arousal.

Submaximal Tests

Submaximal means the athlete works below maximum effort. In sub maximal tests, extrapolation is used to estimate maximum capacity. Examples of submaximal aerobic test are the PWC-170 test and the Queens College Step Test.

Disadvantages of submaximal tests are:

- Depend on extrapolation being made to unknown maximum.
- Small measurement inaccuracies can result in large discrepancies as a result of the extrapolation.

♦♦♦♦♦♦♦

2

AEROBIC FITNESS

Aerobic fitness is a synonymous with endurance or stamina. It describes the ability, part inherited and part trained, to persevere or persist in prolonged endeavors. Those who pursue fitness earn far more than enhanced health and performance.

Aerobic fitness, defined as the maximal capacity to take in, transport and use oxygen, is best measured by test called the maximum oxygen intake or VO_2max test. The VO_2max test signifies the maximum volume (V) of oxygen (O_2) used.

VO_2max, Aerobic Power and Maximal Oxygen Uptake

Wilmore and Costill (2005) defined VO_2max as: **"The highest rate of oxygen consumption attainable during maximal or exhaustive exercise"**. As exercise intensity increases so does oxygen consumption. However, a point is reached where exercise intensity can continue to increase without the associated rise in oxygen consumption. To understand this in more practical terms, take a look at the diagram below:

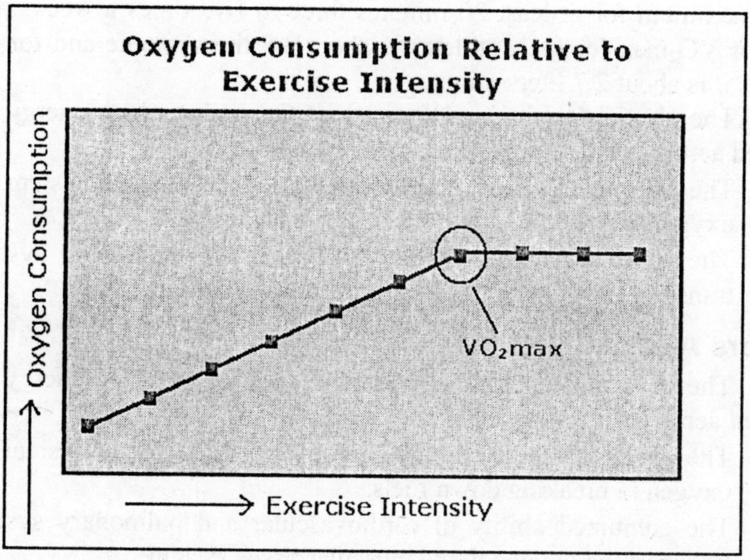

The point at which oxygen consumption plateaus defines the VO_2max or an individual's maximal aerobic capacity. It is generally considered the best indicator of cardiorespiratory endurance and aerobic fitness. However, as we'll discuss in a moment, it is more useful as an indicator of a person's aerobic potential or upper limit than as a predictor of success in endurance events.

Aerobic power, aerobic capacity and maximal oxygen uptake are all terms used interchangeably with VO_2max. VO_2max is usually expressed relative to bodyweight because oxygen and energy needs differ relative to size. It can also be expressed relative to body surface area and this may be a more accurate when comparing children and oxygen uptake between sexes.

The correct way to write VO_2max is: **VO_2max**

It is usually measured in milliliters of oxygen per kilogram of body weight per minute: **$ml.kg^{-1}.min^{-1}$**

The rate of ventilation has to be measured.

Fitness can be measured by the volume of oxygen you can consume while exercising at your maximum capacity. VO_2max is the maximum amount of oxygen in millilitres, one can use in one minute per kilogram of body weight. Those who are fit have higher VO_2max values and can exercise more intensely than those who are not as well conditioned. In previously sedentary people, training at 75 % of aerobic power, for 30 minutes, 3 times a week over 6 months increases VO_2max an average of 15-20 %. However, this is an average and there are large individual variations with increases as wide ranging as 4 % to 93 % reported *(Pollock,1973).*

Numerous studies show that you can increase your VO_2max by working out at an intensity that raises your heart rate to between 65 and 85 % of its maximum for at least 20 minutes three to five times a week. A mean value of VO_2max for male athletes is about 3.5 liters/minute and for female athletes it is about 2.7 liters/minute.

The physical limitations that restrict the rate at which energy can be released aerobically are dependent upon:

- The chemical ability of the muscular cellular tissue system to use oxygen in breaking down fuels.
- The combined ability of cardiovascular and pulmonary systems to transport the oxygen to the muscular tissue system

Factors Affecting VO_2max

The physical limitations that restrict the rate at which energy can be released aerobically are dependent upon:

- The chemical ability of the muscular cellular tissue system to use oxygen in breaking down fuels.
- The combined ability of cardiovascular and pulmonary systems to transport the oxygen to the muscular tissue system.

There are various physiological factors that combine to determine VO_2max for which there are two theories: Utilization Theory and Presentation Theory.

Utilization Theory maintains that VO_2max is determined by the body's ability to utilize the available oxygen whereas **Presentation Theory**

maintains it is the ability of the body's cardiovascular system to deliver oxygen to active tissues.

VO_2max and Genetics

Genetics plays a major role in a person's VO_2max *(Bouchard et al.,1992)* and heredity can account for up to 25-50 % of the variance seen between individuals. Untrained girls and women typically have a maximal oxygen uptake 20-25 % lower than untrained men. However, when comparing elite athletes, the gap tends to close to about 10 % *(Wilmore and Costill ,2005)* . *Cureton and Collins (1980)* suggest that sex-specific essential fat stores account for the majority of metabolic differences in running between men and women.

VO_2max and Age

As one gets older VO_2max decreases. The decline is due to a number of factors including a reduction in maximum heart rate and maximum stroke volume.

VO_2max and Altitude

VO_2max decreases as altitude increases above 1600m (5249 ft). For every 1000 m (3281 ft) above that, maximal oxygen uptake decreases further by approximately 8-11% *(Wilmore and Costill, 2005).* The decrease is mainly due to a decrease in maximal cardiac output which is the product of heart rate and stroke volume. Stoke volume is known to decreases due to an immediate decrease in blood plasma volume. Maximal heart rate may also decrease and the net effect is that less oxygen is "pushed" from the blood into the muscles *(McArdle et al.,2000).*

VO_2max and Body Fat

Fitness is calculated per unit of body weight, so if fat increases, aerobic fitness declines. About half of the decline in fitness with age can be attributed to an increase in body fat.

The extent by which VO_2max can change with training also depends on the starting point. The fitter an individual is to begin with, the less potential there is for an increase and most elite athletes hit this peak early in their career. There also seems to be a genetic upper limit beyond which, further increases in either intensity or volume have no effect on aerobic power *(Costill,1986).* This upper limit is thought to be reached within 8 to 18 months.

Crucially, once a plateau in VO_2max has been reached further improvements in performance can be seen with training. This is because the athlete is able to perform at a higher percentage of their VO_2max for prolonged *periods (McArdle et al. ,2000).* Considerable training is required to reach the upper limit for VO_2max. However, much less is required to maintain it. In fact peak aerobic power can be maintained even when training is decreased by two thirds *(Hickson et al.,1985)*. Runners and swimmers have reduced training volume by 60 % for a period of 15-21 days prior to competition (a technique known as tapering) with no loss in VO_2max *(Costill etal.,1985;Houmard et al.,1990 and Houmard et al., 1994)*.

VO_2max for Various Groups

The tables below present detail normative data for VO_2max (ml/kg/min) in various population groups.

Normative Data for VO_2max for Athletes

Sport	VO_2max (ml/kg/min)		
	Age (yrs)	Males	Females
Baseball	18-32	48-56	52-57
Basketball	18-30	40-60	43-60
Cycling	18-26	62-74	47-57
Canoeing	22-28	55-67	48-52
Football	20-36	42-60	-
Gymnastics	18-22	52-58	35-50
Ice Hockey	10-30	50-63	-
Mountaineering	20-60	47-53	46-60
Rowing	20-35	60-72	58-65
Skiing alpine	18-30	57-68	50-55
Skiing Nordic	20-28	65-94	60-75
Soccer	22-28	54-64	50-60
Speed skating	18-24	56-73	44-55
Swimming	10-25	50-70	40-60
Track & Field - Discus	22-30	42-55	-
Track & Field - Running	18-39	60-85	50-75
Track & Field - Running	40-75	40-60	35-60
Track & Field - Shot	22-30	40-46	-
Volleyball	18-22	-	40-56
Weight Lifting	20-30	38-52	-
Wrestling	20-30	52-65	-

Source: Wilmore and Costill (2005)

Normative Data for VO_2max for Non Athletes

Age (yrs)	VO_2max (ml/kg/min)	
	Males	Females
10-19	47-56	38-46
20-29	43-52	33-42
30-39	39-48	30-38
40-49	36-44	26-35
50-59	34-41	24-33
60-69	31-38	22-30
70-79	28-35	20-27

Source: Wilmore and Costill (2005)

VO_2max Assessment

The VO_2max assessment is based on the Cooper VO_2max tables and comprises of the following grades: Very Poor, Poor, Fair, Good, Excellent and Superior.

Normative Data for VO_2max

Females (values in ml/kg/min)

Age (yrs)	Very Poor	Poor	Fair	Good	Excellent	Superior
13-19	<25.0	25.0 - 30.9	31.0 - 34.9	35.0 - 38.9	39.0 - 41.9	>41.9
20-29	<23.6	23.6 - 28.9	29.0 - 32.9	33.0 - 36.9	37.0 - 41.0	>41.0
30-39	<22.8	22.8 - 26.9	27.0 - 31.4	31.5 - 35.6	35.7 - 40.0	>40.0
40-49	<21.0	21.0 - 24.4	24.5 - 28.9	29.0 - 32.8	32.9 - 36.9	>36.9
50-59	<20.2	20.2 - 22.7	22.8 - 26.9	27.0 - 31.4	31.5 - 35.7	>35.7
60+	<17.5	17.5 - 20.1	20.2 - 24.4	24.5 - 30.2	30.3 - 31.4	>31.4

Males (values in ml/kg/min)

Age (yrs)	Very Poor	Poor	Fair	Good	Excellent	Superior
13-19	<35.0	35.0 - 38.3	38.4 - 45.1	45.2 - 50.9	51.0 - 55.9	>55.9
20-29	<33.0	33.0 - 36.4	36.5 - 42.4	42.5 - 46.4	46.5 - 52.4	>52.4
30-39	<31.5	31.5 - 35.4	35.5 - 40.9	41.0 - 44.9	45.0 - 49.4	>49.4
40-49	<30.2	30.2 - 33.5	33.6 - 38.9	39.0 - 43.7	43.8 - 48.0	>48.0
50-59	<26.1	26.1 - 30.9	31.0 - 35.7	35.8 - 40.9	41.0 - 45.3	>45.3
60+	<20.5	20.5 - 26.0	26.1 - 32.2	32.3 - 36.4	36.5 - 44.2	>44.2

Source: The Physical Fitness Specialist Certification Manual, The Cooper Institute for Aerobics Research, Dallas TX, revised 1997 printed in Advance Fitness Assessment & Exercise Prescription, 3rd Edition, Vivian H. Heyward, 1998.page 48.

The aerobic fitness score (VO_2max) is viewed as the best measure of fitness and is believed to be correlated to health and related to performance in work and sport.

% MHR (Maximum Heart Rate) and % VO_2max

For many athletes it is not possible for them to determine their VO_2max. This can be due to limited access to appropriate testing facilities and/or the associated costs of testing. For those athletes who cannot determine their VO_2max and prefer to set their training based on a percentage of their VO_2max then there is a way, provided they know their Maximum Heart Rate (MHR). The relationship has been shown to hold true across sex, age and activity.

David Swain (1994) and his US based research team using statistical procedures examined the relationship between % MHR and % VO_2max. Their results led to the following regression equation:

- % MHR = (0.64 X % VO_2max) + 37

Example: 70 % VO_2max is equivalent to 81.8 % MHR.

Maximum Heart Rate for % VO_2max to % MHR and % MHR to % VO_2max Conversion Table

% VO_2max to % MHR		% MHR to % VO_2max	
10	43.4	40.0	4.7
15	46.6	45.0	12.5
20	49.8	50.0	20.3
25	53.0	55.0	28.1
30	56.2	60.0	35.9
35	59.4	65.0	43.8
40	62.6	70.0	51.6
45	65.8	75.0	59.4
50	69.0	80.0	67.2
55	72.2	85.0	75.0
60	75.4	90.0	82.8
65	78.6	95.0	90.6
70	81.8	100.0	98.4
75	85.0		
80	88.2		
85	91.4		
90	94.6		
95	97.8		
100	101.0		

Finding Your Maximum Heart Rate

Maximum Heart Rate (also called STD, or HR_{max}) is the highest number of times your heart can contract in one minute, or the heart rate that a person could achieve during maximal physical exertion. It is not the maximum one should obtain often during exercise. MHR is used as a base number to calculate target heart rate for exercise. The average adult heart beats about 60 to 80 times a minute at rest. The resting heart rate usually rises with age, and it's generally lower in physically fit people. Resting heart rate is used to determine one's training target heart rate. Athletes sometimes measure their resting heart rate as one way to find out if they're over trained. The heart rate adapts to changes in the body's need for oxygen, such as during exercise or sleep.

The first step to knowing the proper zone to exercise or train in is to know your exercise Maximum heart rate (MHR). Your maximum heart rate is the highest possible heart rate you can achieve or the highest number of times your heart can contract in one minute. Once you know your max heart rate figuring out you heart rate training zones is easy. The most accurate way to measure your max heart rate is to take a max stress test. It is always wise to undergo a physical exam before taking a max stress test is you are over the age of 35.

The factors which can influence MHR are genetics and age. Genetics is something we are born with. MHR can vary in individuals as much as 15 beats per minute depending on the person. This means that a 45 year old could have a max heart rate of 160 - 190. With age heart rate does not change very much. On average about one beat per minute per year. However, if you train consistently over the years your max heart rate may not change all that much.

Without the presence of a max stress test finding your maximum heart rate can be difficult, however, a formula used by *Sally Edwards*, an expert and author in heart rate training, uses the following method -

Males:

210 - 1/2 your age - 1% of your total body weight + 4 = Predicted Maximum Heart Rate

Females:

210 - 1/2 your age - 1% of your total body weight + 0 = Predicted Maximum Heart Rate

This means a male of 45 years with a weight of 190 would have an estimated max heart rate of: - 210 - 22.5 - 1.9 + 4 = 189 beats per minute.

In general this formula is fine for most people and is likely to be the most accurate formula within plus or minus 10 beats of the actual maximum heart rate.

Heart Rate Reserve (HRR) is a term used to describe the difference between a person's measured or predicted maximum heart rate and resting heart rate. Some methods of measurement of exercise intensity measure percentage of heart rate reserve. Additionally, as a person increases their cardiovascular fitness, their HR_{rest} will drop, thus the heart rate reserve will increase. Percentage of HRR is equivalent to percentage of VO_2 reserve.

$HRR = HR_{max} - HR_{rest}$

A very effective method of calculating your zones is by the **Karvonen Formula.** This formula takes into account your resting heart rate (RHR). Knowing your resting heart rate helps you to determine your Heart Rate Reserve (HRR) or working Heart Rate. Heart Rate Reserve (HRR) or working Heart Rate is the difference between the Maximum Heart Rate (MHR) and Resting Heart Rate (RHR). The greater the difference of your MHR and your RHR the greater your HHR or WHR. This is important because this tells you how great your heart rate intensities can be.

The best way to measure your resting heart rate (RHR) is when you first wake up in the morning and before you get out of bed. Simply count your pulse for 15 seconds beginning on the zero count and multiply by 4. You can do this for 5 days and then average the results. This is your resting heart rate. Keep in mind that lack of proper rest, stress and lack of proper nutrition, and medication can influence your RHR. One sign of over-training is an elevated RHR. By becoming aware of your RHR you can more closely become in-tuned with how your body is reacting to different stimulus.

Guidelines for MHR

% MHR	bpm
50 %	90 bpm
60 %	108 bpm
70 %	126 bpm
80 %	144 bpm
90 %	162 bpm

Measuring HR_{max}

Karvonen Method

This method factors in Resting Heart Rate (RHR or HR_{rest}) to calculate % MHR or Target Heart Rate (THR):

% MHR/THR = ((MHR/HR_{max} − RHR/HR_{rest}) × %Intensity) + RHR/HR_{rest}

Example for someone with a HR_{max} of 180 and a HR_{rest} of 70:

50 % intensity: ((180 − 70) × 0.50) + 70 = 125 bpm

85 % intensity: ((180 − 70) × 0.85) + 70 = 163 bpm

Variations in % MHR According to Intensity

180 - 60 =	120 x 50% = 60 + 60 (RHR) =	120 bpm (50 %)
180 - 60 =	120 x 60% = 72 + 60 (RHR) =	132 bpm (60 %)
180 - 60 =	120 x 70% = 84 + 60 (RHR) =	144 bpm (70 %)
180 - 60 =	120 x 80% = 96 + 60 (RHR) =	156 bpm (80 %)
180 - 60 =	120 x 90% = 108 + 60 (RHR) =	168 bpm (90 %)

Zoladz Method

An alternative to the Karvonen method is the Zoladz method, which derives exercise zones by subtracting values from HR_{max} (Maximum Heart Rate)

THR (Target Heart Rate) = HR_{max} − Adjuster ± 5 bpm
Zone 1 Adjuster = 50 bpm
Zone 2 Adjuster = 40 bpm
Zone 3 Adjuster = 30 bpm
Zone 4 Adjuster = 20 bpm
Zone 5 Adjuster = 10 bpm

Example for someone with a HR_{max} of 180:

Zone 1 (easy exercise) : 220 − age = 0; X 65 → 125
Zone 2 (tough exercise): 220 − age = 0; X 85 → 155

Fox and Haskell Formula

The most accurate way of measuring HR_{max} for an individual is via a cardiac stress test. During the test, the intensity of exercise is periodically increased (if a treadmill is being used, through increase in speed or slope of the treadmill), or until certain changes in heart function are detected at which point the subject is directed to stop. Typical durations of such a test range from 10 to 20 minutes.

The most common formula encountered is: $HR_{max} = 220 - age$

Other often cited formulas are:

$HR_{max} = 205.8 - (0.685 \times age)$

$HR_{max} = 206.3 - (0.711 \times age)$

(Often attributed to "**Londeree and Moeschberger** ")

$HR_{max} = 217 - (0.85 \times age)$

(Often attributed to "**Miller et al**")

These figures are still dependent on physiology and fitness; for example an endurance runner's rates will typically be lower due to the increased size of the heart required to support the exercise, while a sprinter's rates will be higher due to the improved response time and short duration.

Once you know your percentages of max heart rate then you can exercise according to your goals and fitness capacity in the following heart rate zones.

Zone 1 (50 – 60 % of MHR) - The lowest level you can exercise in and still increase fitness levels. For beginners or people who have not exercised for a long period of time. This zone can be for just improving your overall health. It can also be a good recovery zone for people who are over-training and need to take a break. This mode is also good for people who want to lose weight as the main source of fuel used by the body is fat stores.

Zone 2 (60 – 70 % of MHR) - This is the zone where the heart begins to benefit. Training in this zone will begin improve your hearts ability to pump blood and improve the muscle cells ability to utilize oxygen. In this zone stored body fat is the primary source of energy utilized hence this zone is referred to as the weight management zone. This is a good zone for long slow distance exercise as the body becomes more efficient at feeding the working muscles more efficiently especially with fat as the main fuel source.

Zone 3 (70 – 80 % of MHR) - This zone is the most effective for overall cardiovascular fitness and is often called the "aerobic zone" or "target heart rate zone". This is the optimal zone to workout in to increase your cardio-respiratory capacity or the body's ability to transport oxygenated blood to the muscle cells and carbon dioxide away from the cells. After a while you will be able to cover more distance during workouts in less time. Your body will burn less glucose and more stored fat as fuel thereby working more efficiently. This zone is also effective for increasing overall muscle strength.

Zone 4 (80 – 90 % of MHR) (85 – 90 % = Anaerobic Threshold) - This level is where you cross over from aerobic training to anaerobic training which is called the anaerobic threshold or AT. This is the point where the body cannot effectively remove lactic Acid from the working muscles quickly enough. Lactic Acid is a by product of glycogen consumption by the working muscles. This zone is primarily for people who want to increase their performance levels. You would characterize this zone as hard. During this zone your muscles are tired, your breathing is heavy and you're fatigued. The benefit of training in this zone is you can increase your body's ability to tolerate and deal with lactic acid for a longer period of time as the enzymes in your muscles responsible for anaerobic metabolism are increased. For competitors it is good to know your anaerobic threshold as many fit athletes can compete at or about their anaerobic threshold.

Zone 5 (90 - 100% of MHR) (VO_2max) - You will only be able to train in this zone for short periods of time. You should not train at this level unless you are very fit. In this zone lactic acid develops very quickly as you are operating with oxygen debt to the muscles. The value of training in this zone is you can increase your fast twitch muscle fibers which increase speed. You will not be able to stay at this level very long and should be used in intervals or sprinting works at the track.

♦♦♦♦♦♦♦

Part III

PERFORMANCE EVALUATION TESTS

Performance evaluation tests can be grouped under various heads.

Aerobic Endurance-VO_2max Evaluation Tests

Run/Jog Tests
Treadmill Tests
Step Tests
Cycle Test
Run and Treadmill Test
Swim Test
Multistage Fitness Test

Heart Rate Tests

Orthostatic Heart Rate Test
Resting Heart Rate

Anaerobic Endurance Evaluation Tests

Cunningham and Faulkner Test
Running-based Anaerobic Sprint Test (RAST)

Agility Evaluation Tests

Run/Change of Direction Tests
Obstacle Test
Quick Feet Test

Balance Evaluation Tests

Standing Stork Tests – Static and Blind
Balance Test – Motion

Event Time Predictors

Run Tests

Fitness (General) Evaluation Tests

Physical Fitness Tests - General

Flexibility Evaluation Tests

Flexion Tests – Hip and Trunk
Sit and Reach Tests
Static Flexibility Tests

Reaction Time Evaluation Tests

Reaction Time and Quickness Assessment Tests

Strength (Core) Evaluation Tests

Core Muscle Strength and Stability Test

Strength (Elastic) Evaluation Tests

Jump Tests
Leg Strength (Elastic) Tests

Strength (General) Evaluation Tests

Upper Body/Abdominal Strength Tests
Lower Body/Leg Strength Tests
Hand/Arm/Shoulder Strength Tests
Burpee Test

Speed and Power Evaluation Tests

Run Tests
Cycle Tests
Power and Run Test
Rowing Test

Psychology Evaluation Tests

Anxiety, Task and Ego Orientation Tests

Talent Evaluation Tests

Evaluation of Male and Female Physical Talent

Testing and evaluation should be viewed as an essential feedback mechanism in developing the power and team sport athletes. Testing should establish a baseline, to measure progress from each training period and cycle. Testing is an invaluable tool in athletic development and coaching. It is the tool for quality control of coaching and the training process.

A testing programme indicates athlete's strengths and weaknesses in relation to his/her sport. Furthermore, the testing provides a baseline data for individualized training programme. As team sports involve several physiological components, a well designed testing programme can isolate these components to be assessed objectively. As a result performance profile of athlete can be designed. This profile can be used to prescribe an optimal training programme especially concentrating on identified areas of weakness. Athlete's test results can be compared to his/her previous tests, which provides a basis for evaluation of training programme or period. Valid tests can confirm the effectiveness of training programme on each fitness component.

Physical performance testing is always an educational process. Athletes learn to better understand the functions of the body in relation to training and demands of the sport. With through interpretation of the test results athletes can gain understanding on physiological factors of the sport as well as the body awareness i.e. "listens to his/her body". Athletes gain understanding on how training affect their body and improve the physical performance ability which in turn can increase their motivation and commitment to the sport.

♦♦♦♦♦♦♦

3

AEROBIC ENDURANCE (VO_2max) EVALUATION TESTS

An estimate of your VO_2max can be determined using any of the following tests:

- **Run/Jog Tests**
  - o 2.4 kilometer Run Test
  - o Balke VO_2max Test
  - o Cooper VO_2max Test
  - o VO_2max from a One mile Jog
- **Walk Test**
  - o Rockport Fitness Walking Test
- **Treadmill Tests**
  - o Astrand Treadmill Test
  - o Balke Treadmill Test
  - o Bruce Treadmill Test
  - o Treadmill VO_2max Test
- **Step Tests**
  - o Home Step Test
  - o Harvard Step Test
  - o Queens College Step Test
  - o Tecumseh Step Test
- **Cycle Test**
  - o Astrand 6 minute Cycle Test
- **Run and Treadmill Test**
  - o Conconi Test
- **Swim Test**
  - o Critical Swim Speed
- **Shuttle Run Test**
  - o Multistage Fitness Test

Testing and measurement are the means of collecting information upon which subsequent performance evaluations and decisions are made but in the analysis one needs to bear in mind the factors that may influence the results.

RUN TESTS

2.4 km RUN TEST

A great way to assess aerobic fitness is to perform a 2.4 km run test. This is the standard assessment that is used by the US Navy personnel every six months as a way to help determine whether participants are in the required shape they need to be in. The 2.4 km run test is also often performed by many schools in physical education classes so that the students can be monitored with regards to their current fitness level as well as improvements.

Objective

The objective of this test is to monitor the development of the athlete's aerobic endurance.

Required Resources

To undertake this test you will require:

- 400 meter track
- Stop watch
- An assistant

How to Conduct the Test?

- Athlete to complete a 10 minute warm up.
- Athlete to complete the 2.4 km (6 laps of a 400 m track).
- Assistant to keep athlete informed of the number of laps remaining to complete the test.
- Assistant to record the time taken for the athlete to run 2.4 km

Analysis

Analysis of the result is by comparing it with the results of previous tests. It is expected that, with appropriate training between each test, the analysis would indicate an improvement. Scores will vary between males, females and age levels with regards to categories of excellence however in general a good time to aim for to score excellent would be between 7 and 8 minutes, a good time for average would be 11-12 minutes and below average would be classified as taking 15 minutes or longer.

Predicted Times

To obtain a predicted 1.5 km, 5 km and 10 km times, use the time for 2.4 km and then calculate.

2.4 km time	minutes	seconds
Predicted 1.5 km time	minutes	seconds
Predicted 5 km time	minutes	seconds
Predicted 10 km time	minutes	seconds

BALKE VO_2max TEST

Objective

The objective of the Balke test is to monitor the development of the athlete's VO_2max

Required Resources

To undertake this test you will require:

- 400m track
- Stop watch
- Assistant

How to Conduct the Test?

The Balke Test is conducted as follows:

- Choose a windless day and run around a track for 15 minutes.
- The assistant notes the total distance run to the nearest 25 meters.

Performance Assessment

The formula used to calculate VO_2max ("Obsession for Running" by Frank Horwill) is:

$$(((\text{Total distance covered} \div 15) - 133) \times 0.172) + 33.3$$

For an analysis of VO_2max score, refer VO_2max normative data tables (page 12-13).

COOPER VO_2max TEST

The Cooper test is a test of physical fitness. It was designed by Kenneth H. Cooper in 1968 for US military use. In the original form, the point of the test is to run as far as possible within 12 minutes. The test is meant to measure the condition of the person taking it and therefore it is supposed to be run at a steady pace instead of sprints. The outcome is based on the distance the test person ran, their age and gender. The results can be correlated with VO_2max. It is an easy test to perform on larger groups, but difficult for the runners, as the length of the run is considered to be that of a long distance run, since everything above 3 km is rated "long distance" - which means the runner will have more use and focus on his red muscle-cells. The 5000 meters world record of Kenenisa Bekele is 12.37,35. In 12 minutes, he would reach a distance of around 4750 meters.

Objective

To monitor the development of the athlete's aerobic endurance and to obtain an estimate of their VO_2max

Required Resources

To undertake this test you will require:

- 400 meter track - marked every 100 meters
- Stop watch
- Assistant

How to Conduct the Test?

- The athlete conducts a 10 to 15 minute warm up.
- Using the track the athlete runs/walks as far as possible in 12 minutes.
- The assistant records the total distance covered to the nearest 100 meters.
- The athlete conducts a cool down.

Analysis

Analysis of the result is by comparing it with the results of previous tests. It is expected that, with appropriate training between each test, the analysis would indicate an improvement.

Normative Data for the Cooper Test

For Athletes and Juniors

Age (yrs)	Distance (meter)				
	Excellent	Above Average	Average	Below Average	Poor
Male 13-14	>2700	2400-2700	2200-2399	2100-2199	<2100
Females 13-14	>2000	1900-2000	1600-1899	1500-1599	<1500
Males 15-16	>2800	2500-2800	2300-2499	2200-2299	<2200
Females 15-16	>2100	2000-2100	1700-1999	1600-1699	<1600
Males 17-19	>3000	2700-3000	2500-2699	2300-2499	<2300
Females 17-20	>2300	2100-2300	1800-2099	1700-1799	<1700
Male 20-29	>2800	2400-2800	2200-2399	1600-2199	<1600
Females 20-29	>2700	2200-2700	1800-2199	1500-1799	<1500
Males 30-39	>2700	2300-2700	1900-2299	1500-1999	<1500
Females 30-39	>2500	2000-2500	1700-1999	1400-1699	<1400
Males 40-49	>2500	2100-2500	1700-2099	1400-1699	<1400
Females 40-49	>2300	1900-2300	1500-1899	1200-1499	<1200
Males >50	>2400	2000-2400	1600-1999	1300-1599	<1300
Females >50	>2200	1700-2200	1400-1699	1100-1399	<1100

For Experienced Athletes

Gender	Distance (meter)				
	Excellent	Above Average	Average	Below Average	Poor
Male	>3700	3400-3700	3100-3399	2800-3099	<2800
Females	>3000	2700-3000	2400-2999	2100-2399	>2100

VO_2max

An estimate of your VO_2max can be calculated as follows:

(Distance covered in meters - 504.9) ÷ 44.73

For an analysis of VO_2max score, refer VO_2max normative data tables (page 12-13).

VO_2max FROM A ONE MILE JOG

Testing and measurement are the means of collecting information upon which subsequent performance evaluations and decisions are made but in the analysis we need to bear in mind the factors that may influence the results.

Using statistical techniques, Brigham Young University scientists used the heart rates, body weights, and one mile jog times from 54 students to create a fairly simple mathematical equation for VO_2max. They then checked the predictive power of the equation by using it to forecast the VO_2max of another 52 runners involved in the study. When these predicted VO_2max were compared with the runners' VO_2max determined in the exercise physiology laboratory, the equation was determined to be remarkably accurate.

Objective

To monitor the development of the athlete's VO_2max

Required Resources

To undertake this test you will require:

- 400 meter track
- Stop watch
- Heart Rate Monitor

How to Conduct the Test?

- Warm up by jogging for a couple of minutes.
- Jog one mile at an easy, steady pace, making sure that you take longer (yes longer) than eight minutes (males), or more than nine minutes (females).
- Record how long it actually takes you to jog one mile.
- Record your heart rate immediately on completing the mile.

Analysis

The algorithms to calculate VO_2max are:

- Male Athlete's $VO_2max = 108.844 - 0.1636W - 1.438T - 0.1928H$
- Female Athlete's $VO_2max = 100.5 - 0.1636W - 1.438T - 0.1928H$

Where W = Weight in kg, T = Time for the one mile run and H = Heart Rate at the end of the run

For an analysis of VO_2max, refer VO_2max normative data tables (page 12-13).

WALK TEST

ROCKPORT FITNESS WALKING TEST

Objective

The objective of this test is to monitor the development of the athlete's VO_2max (Kilne, et al., 1987).

Required Resources

To undertake this test you will require:

- 400 meter track
- A stop watch
- An assistant

How to Conduct the Test?

The Rockport Fitness Walking Test is conducted as follows:

- Choose a windless day to conduct the test.
- Record your weight.
- Walk one mile (1609 meters) as fast as possible.
- Record the time to complete the one mile walk.
- Immediately on finishing the walk record your heart rate (beats per minute).
- Determine your VO_2max.

Analysis

The formula used to calculate VO_2 max is:

$$132.853 - (0.0769 \times \text{Weight}) - (0.3877 \times \text{Age}) + (6.315 \times \text{Gender}) - (3.2649 \times \text{Time}) - (0.1565 \times \text{Heart rate})$$

Where:

Weight is in pounds (lbs) & Age is in years & Heart rate is in beats/minute

Gender Male = 1 and Female = 0

Time is expressed in minutes and 100ths of minutes

For an analysis of VO_2max score, refer VO_2max normative data tables (page 12-13).

TREADMILL TESTS

ASTRAND TREADMILL TEST

Objective

To monitor the development of the athlete's general endurance (VO_2 max)

Required Resources

To undertake this test you will require:

- Treadmill where the speed can be set at 5 mph (8.05 km/hr) and grade of slope can be adjusted.
- Stopwatch.
- An assistant

How to Conduct the Test?

The treadmill is set up at the start with a speed of 8.05 km/hr (5 mph) and a grade of slope of 0 %. The athlete commences the test. After 3 minutes, the grade is set to 2.5 % (1.4°) and then every 2 minutes the grade is increased by 2.5 % (1.4°).

The assistant starts the stopwatch at the start of the test and stops it when the athlete is unable to continue.

Analysis of the Test Result

Analysis of the result is by comparing it with the results of previous tests. It is expected that, with appropriate training between each test, the analysis would indicate an improvement.

From the total running time an estimate of the athlete's VO_2max can be calculated as follows:

- $VO_2max = (Time \times 1.444) + 14.99$

"Time" is the total time of the test expressed in minutes and fractions of a minute.

Example

The athlete stopped the test after 15 minutes 30 seconds of running (15.50 minutes).

- $VO_2max = (15.50 \times 1.444) + 14.99$
- $VO_2max = 37.083$ ml/kg/min

For an analysis of VO_2max score, refer VO_2max normative data tables (page 12-13).

For example, if the above case is male (age 25 yrs), then as per the norms his VO_2max is rated as fair.

BALKE TREADMILL TEST

Objective

To monitor the development of the athlete's general endurance (VO_2max)

Required Resources

To undertake this test you will require:

- Treadmill where speed and grade of slope can be adjusted

- Stop watch
- Assistant

How to Conduct the Test?

The athlete walks on a treadmill to exhaustion. At timed stages during the test the grade of slope (%) of the treadmill is increased as follows:

- **Active and Sedentary Men**
  - o Treadmill speed set at 3.3 mph.
  - o Start - Grade is 0 %.
  - o After 1 minute - Grade set at 2 %.
  - o After 2 minutes and each minute thereafter the grade is increased by 1%.
- **Active and Sedentary Women**
  - o Treadmill speed set at 3.0 mph.
  - o Start - Grade is 0 %.
  - o After 3 minutes and every 3 minutes thereafter the grade is increased by 2.5 % (1.4°).

The assistant starts the stopwatch at the start of the test and stops it when the athlete is unable to continue - this ideally should be between 9 and 15 minutes.

Active and Sedentary Men -

From the total time an estimate of the athlete's VO_2max can be calculated as follows:

- $VO_2max = 1.444 \times T + 14.99$

"T" is the total time of the test expressed in minutes and fractions of a minute e.g. 13 minutes 15 seconds = 13.25 minutes

Active and Sedentary Women -

From the total time an estimate of the athlete's VO2 max can be calculated as follows:

- $VO_2max = 1.38 \times T + 5.22$

"T" is the total time of the test expressed in minutes and fractions of a minute e.g. 13 minutes 15 seconds = 13.25 minutes.

For an analysis of VO_2max score, refer VO_2max normative data tables (page 12-13).

BRUCE TREADMILL TEST

The Bruce treadmill test has now become a standardized procedure used to evaluate the cardiovascular fitness of athletes... or anyone else for that matter.

The original Bruce protocol was developed by Dr. Robert. A. Bruce in 1963.

This protocol for a multilevel treadmill test was developed as a means to detect chest pain and discomfort in patients as well as any evidence of possible heart attacks or ischaemic heart disease.

The test is now used:

- For athletes or coaches, to check the development of a sportsperson's general endurance or, what is known as VO_2max. VO_2max is simply the most amount of oxygen that a person can consume and utilize and is measured by the volume of oxygen per minute per kg body weight per time (mL/kg/min).
- For patients with suspected coronary heart disease. The Bruce treadmill test can be used by doctors as a non-invasive test procedure to determine whether there are any abnormalities in the electrical "firing patterns" of the myocardium (heart muscle).

When it's used in a medical context a treadmill test like this is often referred to an Exercise Tolerance Test or Exercise Stress Test.

Objective

To monitor the development of the athlete's general endurance (VO_2 max)

Required Resources

To undertake this test you will require:

- Treadmill where speed and grade of slope can be adjusted.
- Stop watch.
- Assistant

How to Conduct the Test?

The athlete runs on a treadmill to exhaustion. At timed stages during the test the speed (km/hr) and grade of slope (%) of the treadmill are increased as detailed in the table below.

- The treadmill is set up with the Stage 1 speed (2.74 km/hr) and grade of slope (10 %) and the athlete commences the test.
- At the appropriate times during the test, the speed and slope of the treadmill are adjusted.
- Therefore, after 3 minutes into the test the speed is adjusted to 4.02 km/hr and the slope to 12 %, after 6 minutes into the test the speed is adjusted to 5.47 km/hr and the slope to 14 %, and so on.
- The assistant starts the stopwatch at the start of the test and stops it when the athlete is unable to continue - this ideally should be between 9 and 15 minutes.

Men -

From the total walk/run time an estimate of the athlete's VO_2max can be calculated as follows:

- $VO_2max = 14.8 - (1.379 \times T) + (0.451 \times T^2) - (0.012 \times T^3)$

Women -

From the total walk/run time an estimate of the athlete's VO_2max can be calculated as follows:

- $VO_2max = 4.38 \times T - 3.9$

For both males and females, "T" is the total time of the test expressed in minutes and fractions of a minute e.g. 13 minutes 15 seconds =13.25 minutes.

For an analysis of VO2max score, refer VO_2max normative data tables (page 12-13).

Guidelines for Bruce Treadmill Test

Stage	Time (min)	km/hr	Slope (%)
1	0	2.74	10
2	3	4.02	12
3	6	5.47	14
4	9	6.76	16
5	12	8.05	18
6	15	8.85	20
7	18	9.65	22
8	21	10.46	24
9	24	11.26	26
10	27	12.07	28

TREADMILL VO2 max TEST

Objective

To monitor the development of the athlete's general endurance (VO_2 max)

Required Resources

To undertake this test you will require:

- Treadmill where speed and grade of slope can be adjusted.
- Stop watch.
- An assistant

How to Conduct the Test?

- The athlete runs on a treadmill to exhaustion. At timed stages during the run the slope of the treadmill is increased as detailed in the table below.
- The treadmill is set up with a speed of 11.3 km/hour (7.02 miles/hr) and a slope of 0° and the athlete commences the test. At minute intervals during the test the slope of the treadmill is adjusted.
- The assistant starts the stopwatch at the start of the test and stops it when the athlete is unable to continue - this ideally should be between 9 and 15 minutes.

Guidelines for Treadmill VO_2max Test

Time (minutes)	km/hour	Slope	Time (minutes)	km/hour	Slope
0	11.3	0°	8	11.3	13°
1	11.3	2°	9	11.3	14°
2	11.3	4°	10	11.3	15°
3	11.3	6°	11	11.3	16°
4	11.3	8°	12	11.3	17°
5	11.3	10°	13	11.3	18°
6	11.3	11°	14	11.3	19°
7	11.3	12°	15	11.3	20°

Analysis

Analysis of the result is by comparing it with the results of previous tests. It is expected that, with appropriate training between each test, the analysis would indicate an improvement. From the total running time, an estimate of the athlete's VO_2max can be calculated as follows:

- $VO_2max = 42 + (Time \times 2)$

"Time" is the total time of the test expressed in minutes and fractions of a minute.

Example: The athlete stopped the test after 13 minutes 15 seconds of running (13.25 minutes).

- $VO_2max = 42 + (13.25 \times 2) = 68.5$ mL/kg/min

For an analysis of VO_2max score, refer VO_2max normative data tables (page 12-13).

STEP TESTS

HOME STEP TEST

Objective

The objective of this test is to monitor the development of the athlete's cardiovascular system.

Required Resources

To undertake this test you will require:

- A 12 inch high bench or step
- A stop watch
- Metronome or cadence tape

- Heart rate monitor (optional)
- An assistant

How to Conduct the Test?

The Home Step Test is conducted as follows:

- Step up and down, one foot at a time, onto the step or bench for 3 minutes.
- Try to maintain a steady four beat cycle (approximately 22 to 24 steps/minute).
- Use a metronome or have someone to help you keep to the required pace.
- On finishing the test count the number of heart beats for 15 seconds.
- Multiply the number of beats in 15 seconds by 4.
- Use this final value to assess your performance using the table below.

Normative Data for Home Step Test (Male Athletes)

Age	18-25	26-35	36-45	46-55	56-65	65+
Excellent	<79	<81	<83	<87	<86	<88
Good	79-89	81-89	83-96	87-97	86-97	88-96
Above Average	90-99	90-99	97-103	98-105	98-103	97-103
Average	100-105	100-107	104-112	106-116	104-112	104-113
Below Average	106-116	108-117	113-119	117-122	113-120	114-120
Poor	117-128	118-128	120-130	123-132	121-129	121-130
Very Poor	>128	>128	>130	>132	>129	>130

Source: Canadian Public Health Association

Normative Data for Home Step Test (Female Athletes)

Age	18-25	26-35	36-45	46-55	56-65	65+
Excellent	<85	<88	<90	<94	<95	<90
Good	85-98	88-99	90-102	94-104	95-104	90-102
Above Average	99-108	100-111	103-110	105-115	105-112	103-115
Average	109-117	112-119	111-118	116-120	113-118	116-122
Below Average	118-126	120-126	119-128	121-129	119-128	123-128
Poor	127-140	127-138	129-140	130-135	129-139	129-134
Very Poor	>140	>138	>140	>135	>139	>134

Source: Canadian Public Health Association

HARVARD STEP TEST

The Harvard Step Test is a type of cardiac stress test. It also is a good measurement of fitness, and your ability to recover after a strenuous exercise.

The more quickly your heart rate returns to resting, the better shape you are in.

Objective

The objective of this test is to monitor the development of the athlete's cardiovascular system.

Required Resources

To undertake this test you will require:

- Gym bench (45 cm high)
- Stop watch
- Assistant

How to Conduct the Test?

The Harvard Step Test is conducted as follows:

- Step up on to a standard gym bench once every two seconds for five minutes (150 steps).
- Have someone to help you keep to the required pace.
- One minute after finishing the test take your pulse rate (bpm) - Pulse 1.
- Two minutes after finishing the test take your pulse rate (bpm) - Pulse 2.
- Three minutes after finishing the test take your pulse rate (bpm) - Pulse 3.

Analysis

Analysis of the result is by comparing it with the results of previous tests. It is expected that, with appropriate training between each test, the analysis would indicate an improvement.

Using the three pulse rates your level of fitness can be determined as follows:

- Result = 30000 ÷ (pulse1 + pulse 2 + pulse 3)

Normative Data for Harvard Step Test

For 16 Year Old Athletes

Gender	Excellent	Above Average	Average	Below Average	Poor
Male	>90	80-90	65-79	55-64	<55
Female	>86	76-86	61-75	50-60	<50

Source: McArdle et al, 2000

QUEENS COLLEGE STEP TEST

Objective

The objective of this test is to monitor the development of the athlete's cardiovascular system.

Required Resources

To undertake this test you will require:

- A step 16.25 inches or 41.3 cm high
- A stop watch
- Metronome or cadence tape
- Heart rate monitor (optional)
- An assistant

How to Conduct the Test?

The Queens College Step Test is conducted as follows:

- Step up and down on the step for 3 minutes at the following rate:
  - Male - 24 steps per minute
  - Female - 22 steps per minute
- Use a metronome or have someone to help you keep to the required pace.
- 5 seconds after finishing the test - count the heartbeats for fifteen seconds.

Normative Data for Queen's College Step Up Test

The following are national norms for 16 to 19 year olds.

Gender	Excellent	Above Average	Average	Below Average	Poor
Male	<121	148 - 121	156 - 149	162 - 157	>162
Female	<129	158 - 129	166 - 159	170 - 167	>170

Source: Davis et al. (2000)

For an analysis of VO_2max score, refer VO_2max normative data tables (page 12-13).

TECUMSEH STEP TEST

Objective

The objective of this test is to monitor the development of the athlete's cardio respiratory fitness.

Required Resources

To undertake this test you will require:

- A gym bench or step (8 inches/20.3 cm high)
- A stop watch
- An Assistant

How to Conduct the Test?

The Tecumseh Step Test is conducted as follows:

- Perform a step cycle of four-step cadence (right foot up, left foot up, right foot down and left foot down) completing 24 cycles in one minute. This is 2 cycles in a 5 second period.
- Have someone to help you keep to the required pace or you could use a metronome set at 96 beats/minute.
- Perform the test for 3 minutes.
- 30 seconds after finishing the test count the number of pulse beats for 30 seconds.
- The number of beats counted in 30 seconds is then used in the table below to determine the athlete's grade.

Normative Data for Tecumseh Step Test (Males over 19 yrs)

Classification	20-29	30-39	40-49	49+
Outstanding	34-36	35-38	37-39	37-40
Very Good	37-40	39-41	40-42	41-43
Good	41-42	42-43	43-44	44-45
Fair	43-47	44-47	45-49	46-49
Low	48-51	48-51	50-53	50-53
Poor	52-59	52-59	54-60	54-62

Source: McArdle et al., 2000

Normative Data for Tecumseh Step Test (Females over 19 yrs)

Classification	20-29	30-39	40-49	49+
Outstanding	39-42	39-42	41-43	41-44
Very Good	43-44	43-45	44-45	45-47
Good	45-46	46-47	46-47	48-49
Fair	47-52	48-53	48-54	50-55
Low	53-56	54-56	55-57	56-58
Poor	57-66	57-66	58-67	59-66

Source: McArdle et al., 2000

CYCLE TEST

ASTRAND 6 MINUTE CYCLE TEST

Objective

The objective of this test is to monitor the athlete's VO_2max.

Required Resources

To undertake this test you will require:

- Cycle ergometer
- Heart rate monitor
- Stop watch
- An assistant

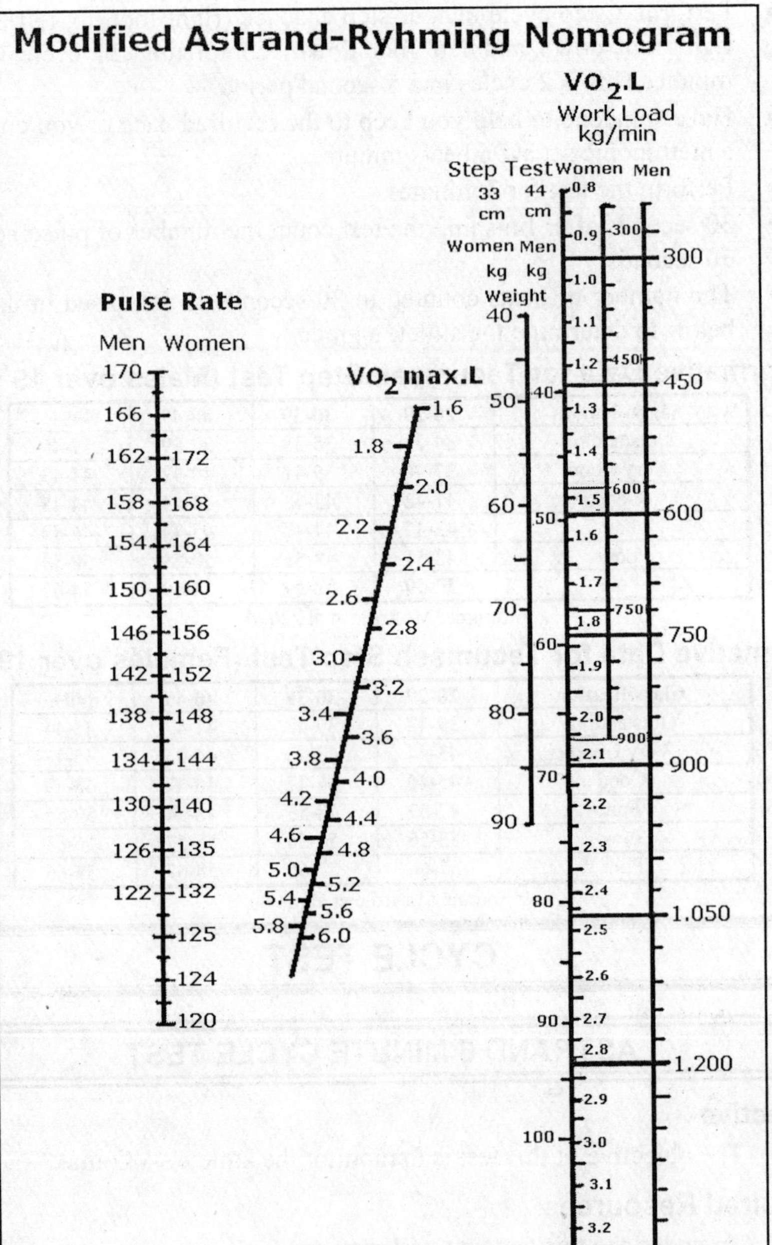

Reference: ACSM Guidelines for Exercise Testing and Prescription, 5th edition

How to Conduct the Test?

- Set up the cycle ergometer with correct handlebar and seat adjustments.
- Select a load to begin the test - see the Astrand Test Loading Wattages table below. Whether you use the lower or upper wattages will depend upon your weight and fitness level. The selected load should raise your pulse rate to steady state between 130-160 bpm (beats per minute).

Guidelines for Astrand Cycle Test

Astrand Test Loading Wattages		
Age (years)	**Males**	**Females**
Under 35	100-150	100-125
35-55	100-125	75-100
Over 55	75-100	50-75

- Pedal at 60 rpm (rotations per minute) for 6 minutes at your chosen loading, taking pulse every minute. Your pulse rate should be steady state between 130-160 bpm.
- If your pulse rate is not in the target range after 2 minutes then adjust your loading accordingly by 25 watts for the remainder of the test.
- At the end of minute 6 record your pulse rate and the loading wattage.
- Use the Astrand-Ryhming Nomogram to determine your VO_2max
- Multiply your VO_2max value by 1000 and divide by your weight (kg) to determine your VO_2max.

For an analysis of VO_2max score, refer VO_2max normative data tables (page 12-13).

RUN AND TREADMILL TEST

CONCONI TEST

Objective

The Conconi test (Conconi et al, 1982) is a simple method for measuring the approximate values of an individual's maximum, anaerobic and aerobic threshold rates.

Required Resources

To perform the test you require

- A Heart Rate Monitor (HRM)
- A 400 meter track or Treadmill
- Stop watch

- Assistant to record 200 meter times and heart rate

Before you start the test you need to determine your starting speed and how much you increment your speed by every 200 meters.

Conducting the Conconi Test on a 400m Track

In the Conconi test, the athlete increases their speed gradually every 200 meters and the heart rate and time, at each 200 meter point, are recorded. This gradual increase in speed every 200 meters is maintained until the athlete is unable to maintain the pace. The total distance covered by the test should be between 2.5 km and 4 km to ensure sufficient information is available for subsequent calculations. Speed versus heart rate is then plotted on a graph from which the athlete's anaerobic threshold can be determined.

- Perform a five to ten minute warm up program.
- Set the HRM to use a 5 second recording interval.
- Start the HRM watch at the starting point.
- Every 200 meters record the time and heart rate.
- Every 200 meters increase your speed.
- End the test when you can no longer maintain the pace.
- Stop the HRM recording.
- Perform a 10 minute cool down program.

Conducting the Conconi Test on a Treadmill

- Perform a five to ten minute warm up program.
- Set the HRM to use a 5 second recording interval.
- Start the treadmill speed at the required start speed.
- Start the HRM stop watch.
- Record the time and heart rate every 200 meters.
- Increase the treadmill speed every 200 meters by 0.5km/hr.
- End the test when you have reached your maximum heart rate or you can continue no longer.
- Stop the HRM recording.
- Perform a 10 minute cool down program.

Calculation of Anaerobic Threshold

Determine the speed for each 200 meters and then for each 200 meters plot speed versus heart rate on a graph. You will find the graph gradually rises to start with and then flattens before rising again. This flattening in the graph indicates the athlete's anaerobic threshold. In the example Conconi graph below this flattening appears to be around 182 bpm.

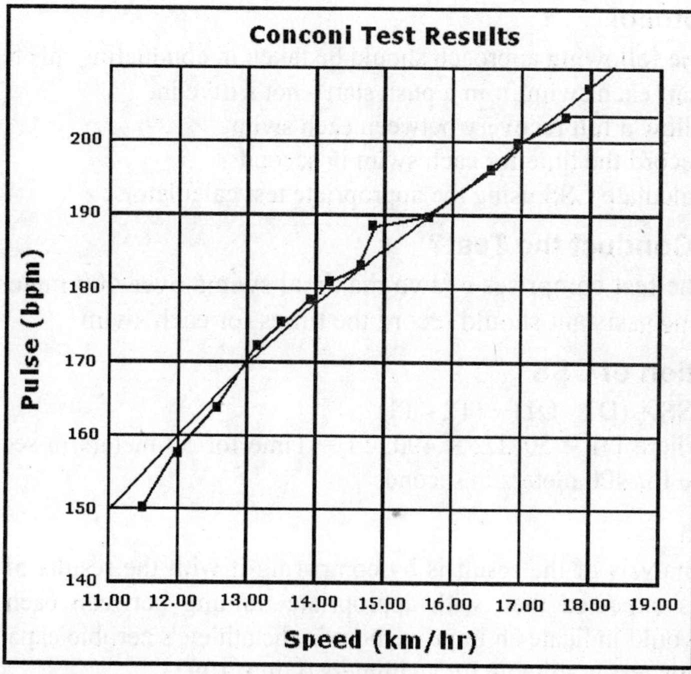

Calculation of Aerobic Threshold

A good estimate for aerobic threshold has proved to be the anaerobic threshold minus 20 bpm.

Analysis

Analysis of the result is by comparing it with the results of previous tests. It is expected that, with appropriate training between each test, the analysis would indicate an improvement.

SWIM TEST

CRITICAL SWIM SPEED

Objective

The objective of the Critical Swim Speed (CSS) test is to monitor the athlete's aerobic capacity.

Required Resources

To undertake this test you will require:

- Swimming pool
- Stop watch
- An assistant

Test Protocol

The following approach should be taken in conducting this test:

- Start each swim from a push start - not a dive in.
- Allow a full recovery between each swim.
- Record the time for each swim in seconds.
- Calculate CSS using the appropriate test calculator.

How to Conduct the Test?

The test comprises of two maximal swims over 400 meters and 50 meters. The assistant should record the times for each swim.

Calculation of CSS

$CSS = (D2 - D1) \div (T2 - T1)$

Where $D1 = 50$, $D2 = 400$, $T1$ = Time for 50 meters in seconds and $T2$ = Time for 400 meters in seconds

Analysis

Analysis of the result is by comparing it with the results of previous tests. It is expected that, with appropriate training between each test, the analysis would indicate an improvement in the athlete's aerobic capacity.

This test is suitable for swimmers (Ginn, 1993).

SHUTTLE RUN TEST

MULTI-STAGE FITNESS TEST (MFST)

This is a maximal test which means it is performed until exhaustion. The test is excellent for multi-sprint sports such as soccer and rugby and it allows testing for an entire team simultaneously.

The test involves running 20 meter shuttles. The test is split into a series of 1-minute levels. Each level consists of a number of bleeps that dictates the pace at which each 20 meter shuttle must be run. As the levels progress the bleeps become quicker and more frequent so a greater number of shuttles has to be completed inside 1 minute. The starting speed (level 1) is 8.5 km/hr and increases by 0.5 km/hr for each level.

The test ends when the athlete(s) can no longer maintain the pace of the bleeps.

The test, also known as the "Bleep Test", "Beep Test", "Pacer Test" "Shuttle Run Test" and "Yo-Yo Test", was developed by Leger, L.A. & Lambert, J. (1982). It is used by sports coaches and trainers to estimate an athlete's VO_2max (maximum oxygen uptake). The test is especially useful for players of sports like Cross Country, football, hockey, rugby, cricket or tennis and is employed by many international sporting teams as an accurate test of cardiovascular fitness, one of the all-important "Components of Fitness".

Objective

The objective of the Multi-Stage Fitness Test (MSFT) is to monitor the development of the athlete's maximum oxygen uptake (VO_2max).

This test is very good for games players as it is specific to the nature of the sport but, due to the short turns, is perhaps not suitable for rowers, runners or cyclists.

Required Resources

To undertake this test you will require:

- A flat, non slippery surface at least 20 meters in length
- 30 meter tape measure
- Marking cones
- The Multi-Stage Fitness Test audio tape or CD**
- Tape recorder or CD Player
- Recording sheets
- Assistant

** The Multi-Stage Fitness Test audio tape or CD can be purchased.

How to Conduct the Test?

The test is made up of 23 levels where each level lasts approximately one minute. Each level comprises of a series of 20 m shuttles where the starting speed is 8.5 km/hr and increases by 0.5 km/hr at each level. On the tape/CD a single beep indicates the end of a shuttle and 3 beeps indicates the start of the next level. The test is conducted as follows:

- Measure out a 20 meters section and mark each end with a marker cone
- The athlete carries out a warm up program of jogging and dynamic stretching exercises.
- The test is conducted ------

o The athlete must place one foot on or beyond the 20 m marker at the end of each shuttle.

o If the athlete arrives at the end of a shuttle before the beep, the athlete must wait for the beep and then resume running.

o The athlete keeps running for as long as possible until he/she can longer keep up with the speed set by the tape/CD at which point they should voluntarily withdraw.

o If the athlete fails to reach the end of the shuttle before the beep they should be allowed 2 or 3 further shuttles to attempt to regain the required pace before being withdrawn.

o Record the level and number of shuttles completed at that level by the athlete.

o At the end of the test the athletes conduct a cool down program, including static stretching exercises.

Performance Assessment

The athlete's maximum oxygen uptake (VO_2max) can be determined from the MSF Table using the Level and Shuttle achieved.

The calculator from the CD will provide you with an estimate of your VO2max. Note that, when compared to the MSF Table values, the calculator result can be in error by up to ± 0.3 mls/kg/min.

Enter the Level and Shuttle you achieved in the MSF test and then calculate.

Level	1	Shuttle	1
		VO_2 max	mls/kg/min (± 0.3 mls/kg/min)

For an analysis of VO_2max score, refer VO_2max normative data tables (page 12-13).

Normative Data for MSFT

The following are National team scores for the MSFT

Sport	Male	Female
Basketball	L11 - S5	L9 - S6
Hockey	L13 - S9	L12 - S7
Rugby League	L13 - S1	-
Netball	-	L9 - S7
Squash	L13 - S13	-

Source: Beashel et al., 1997

MSFT Guidelines

Level	Shuttles	Speed (km/h)	Seconds per shuttle	Total level time (s)	Distance (m)	Cumulative Distance (m)	Cumulative Time (min and seconds)
1	7	8.0	9.0	63	140	140	1:03
2	8	8.5	8.47	67.8	160	300	2:11
3	8	9.0	8.0	64.00	160	460	3:15
4	8	9.5	7.58	60.64	160	620	4:15
5	9	10.0	7.20	64.80	180	800	5:20
6	9	10.5	6.86	61.74	180	980	6:22
7	10	11.0	6.55	65.50	200	1180	7:27
8	10	11.5	6.26	62.60	200	1380	8:30
9	11	12.0	6.0	66.00	220	1600	9:36
10	11	12.5	5.76	63.36	220	1820	10:39
11	11	13.0	5.54	60.94	220	2040	11:40
12	12	13.5	5.33	63.96	240	2280	12:44
13	12	14.0	5.14	61.68	240	2520	13:46
14	13	14.5	4.97	64.61	260	2780	14:51
15	13	15.0	4.80	62.40	260	3040	15:53
16	13	15.5	4.65	60.45	260	3300	16:53
17	14	16.0	4.50	63.00	280	3580	17:56
18	14	16.5	4.36	61.04	280	3860	18:57
19	15	17.0	4.24	63.60	300	4160	20:00
20	15	17.5	4.11	61.65	300	4460	21:02
21	16	18.0	4.00	64.00	320	4780	22:06
Total=	4780 meters						
Total Time=	22:06 minutes and seconds						

Source:"Multi-Stage Fitness Test". BrainMac, Sports Coach – retrieved from http://www.brianmac.co.uk/eval.

Notes

A degree of caution is required in administering the test, in that you have to push yourself relatively hard to the point where you can no longer maintain the pace dictated by the tape/CD. If you are suffering from any injury or illness, or if you have any reason to think you may not be in a good general state of health, you should consult a doctor before doing this test.

The original beep test was first only available on audio tape format. A problem with the tape was that it could stretch over time, or the tape player did not play at a consistent speed, therefore making the timing between beeps inaccurate. On most versions of the tape there was a one minute recorded interval for calibrating the tape and tape player. The compact disc or MP3 format is now used predominantly, and does not have the above problems with calibration. Downloadable software is also used because it has no timing errors, no calibration errors, and is accurate to $1/100^{th}$ of a second.

As the audio tapes may stretch over time, the tapes need to be calibrated which involves timing a one-minute interval and making adjustment to the distance between markers. The recording is also available on compact disc, which does not require calibration.

Knowing that the starting speed is 8.5 km/hr and increases by 0.5 km/hr at each level then the time for each 20 meter section, at each level, can be estimated from the following equation:

- 20 m Time = 72 ÷ (((Level - 1) × 0.5) + 8.5)

Example- the time for 20 m at level 11 is 5.33 seconds.

Knowing that the starting speed is 8.5 km/hr and increases by 0.5 km/hr at each level and the duration of each level is approximately one minute then the number of shuttles at each level, can be estimated from the following equation:

- Shuttles = (((Level - 1) × 0.5) + 8.5) × 0.838

The result is rounded up to the nearest whole number e.g. the number of shuttles at level 17 is 13.82 which is rounded up to 14 shuttles.

For an analysis of VO_2max score, refer VO_2max normative data tables (page 12-13).

♦♦♦♦♦♦♦♦

4

HEART RATE TESTS

Doing heart rate tests is an excellent way to track the progress you've made. Various heart rates tests include taking the beats per minute while exercising, shortly after exercising, ten or more minutes after exercising (to determine recovery ability) and first thing in the morning (to determine overtraining status).

ORTHOSTATIC HEART RATE TEST

Overtraining is a very serious condition that some high level athletes really need to be paying attention too. If they are not monitoring their current exercise output along with how much rest they are getting they can really set themselves up for injuries and a lack of recovery. If this condition is left to progress long enough, the individual may be required to take a number of weeks to months off in order to fully allow the body to heal itself. This test lets you know how close you are to pushing your body too hard. The point of the Orthostatic Heart Rate test is to find out if you are pushing yourself too hard on your training regime.

What do you need?

- The knowledge-how to take your pulse
- A clock or stopwatch

How do you do the test?

Lie down and rest for a period of fifteen minutes or so. This will allow your body to bring its heart rate back down to a calm level if you have been up and moving around in the past few minutes.

- Record your pulse rate, as determined by beats per minute.
- Stand up and then calculate your pulse rate once again in the standing position.
- After you have arrived at these two numbers, calculate the difference between both heart rates and that is your score.

What Results you will get?

If the difference you have is greater than fifteen to twenty beats per minute then this is a very strong signal that your body is not recovery effectively from your workouts and is currently under a great deal of stress. If this is the case, you should be looking at reducing both your intensity and volume of your workouts immediately or even possibly taking a full week off, allowing only for simple exercise such as walking.

What is being measured again?

These tests measure your body's ability to recover from your workouts. Your ability to recover from your workouts will help you to know if you are pushing yourself too hard.

RESTING HEART RATE

What is the significance of a resting heart rate (RHR)? Often a good determination as to how fit you are, to calculate your heart rate at rest check our charts and use as a way of indicating your fitness levels, whether you are over training or even whether you are unwell (unexplained increases in your resting heart rate numbers).

The best way to take your resting heart rate is over a 3 or 4 day period in order to get an average result. This makes sure any oddities are allowed for. If you are using a heart rate monitor, please check first (before you panic!) whether you have a good connection between the chest strap and your chest. Also check whether you have a good connection between the unit and your body - body perspiration is perfect for this.

The key to getting accurate resting heart rate figures is to take this test first thing in the morning immediately after you wake. As soon as you get up walking around will cause your heart rate to rise as well as smoking or caffeine, they all cause an increase making the test unreliable or useless.

By using multiple days, day one shows 80 bpm (beats per minute), day two 76 bpm; day three 74 bpm etc. you can then average out your bpm. Record based on a full minute to make the test as accurate as possible.

If you undertake aerobic exercise or other cardio work, you will become fitter - therefore your heart is more efficient at pumping blood around the body and therefore you should see a lower result for beat per minute. The evaluation of resting heart rate for men and women is shown in following table:

Evaluation of RHR for MEN (M) and WOMEN (F)

Age Groups (Yrs)	Gender	Athletic	Excellent	Good	Above Average	Average	Below Average	Poor
18-25	M	49-55	56-61	62-65	66-69	70-73	74-81	82+
	F	54-60	61-65	66-69	70-73	74-78	79-84	85+
26-35	M	49-54	55-61	62-65	66-70	71-74	75-81	82+
	F	54-59	60-64	65-68	69-72	73-76	77-82	83+
36-45	M	50-56	57-62	63-66	67-70	71-75	76-82	83+
	F	54-59	60-64	65-69	70-73	74-78	79-84	85+
46-55	M	50-57	58-63	64-67	68-71	72-76	77-83	84+
	F	54-60	61-65	66-69	70-73	74-77	78-83	84+
56-65	M	51-56	57-61	62-67	68-71	72-75	76-81	82+
	F	54-59	60-64	65-68	69-73	74-77	78-83	84+
65+	M	50-55	56-61	62-65	66-69	70-73	74-79	80+
	F	54-59	60-64	65-68	69-72	73-76	77-84	84+

♦♦♦♦♦♦♦

5

ANAEROBIC ENDURANCE EVALUATION TESTS

Anaerobic means "without oxygen". During anaerobic work, involving maximum effort, the body is working so hard that the demands for oxygen and fuel exceed the rate of supply and the muscles have to rely on the stored reserves of fuel. In this case waste products accumulate, the chief one being lactic acid.

The muscles, being starved of oxygen, take the body into a state known as oxygen debt. The body's stored fuel soon runs out and activity ceases - painfully. This point is often measured as the lactic threshold or anaerobic threshold or onset of blood lactate accumulation (OBLA). Activity cannot be resumed until the lactic acid is removed and the oxygen debt repaid.

Fortunately the body can resume limited activity after even only a small proportion of the oxygen debt has been repaid. Since lactic acid is produced, the correct term for this pathway is lactic anaerobic energy pathway. The lactic anaerobic pathway is the one in which the body is working anaerobically but without the production of lactic acid. This pathway can exist only so long as the fuel actually stored in the muscle lasts, approximately 4 seconds at maximum effort.

Anaerobic endurance can be sub-divided as follows:

- **Short anaerobic** - less than 25 seconds (mainly lactic)
- **Medium anaerobic** - 25 seconds to 60 seconds (mainly lactic)
- **Long anaerobic** - 60 seconds to 120 seconds (lactic + aerobic)

Anaerobic endurance can be developed by using repetition methods of relatively high intensity work with limited recovery.

The anaerobic threshold, the point at which lactic acid starts to accumulates in the muscles, is considered to be somewhere between 85 % and 90 % of your maximum heart rate. This is approximately 40 beats higher than the aerobic threshold. Your anaerobic threshold can be determined with anaerobic threshold testing.

Following are two very common tests to assess anaerobic endurance:

- Cunningham and Faulkner Test
- Running Based Anaerobic Sprint Test (RAST)

CUNNINGHAM AND FAULKNER TEST

The ability to work in oxygen debt is crucial for many athletes. The Cunningham and Faulkner anaerobic capacity test is an excellent way to measure this. Athletes have to be able to work even when their oxygen supplies have been depleted - this is called anaerobic work.

The Cunningham and Faulkner anaerobic capacity test was designed to assess this, allowing athletes to measure their capacity and make adjustments to their training.

Objective

The objective of this test is to monitor the development of the athlete's anaerobic capacity.

Required Resources

To undertake this test you will require:

- Treadmill capable of 20 % gradient
- Stop watch
- An assistant

How to Conduct the Test?

- The athlete undertakes a warm-up on the treadmill.
- A few short practice starts getting onto the treadmill at the test speed should also be performed.
- The treadmill is set at 8.0 miles/hr (12.9 km/hr) speed and incline of 20 %.
- The assistant starts the stopwatch when the athlete starts running unsupported.
- The test continues until exhaustion, meaning the athlete cannot maintain the speed required.
- The assistant records the time to the nearest 0.5 seconds.

Analysis

Analysis of the result is by comparing it with the results of previous tests. It is expected that, with appropriate training between each test, the analysis would indicate an improvement.

Regularly performing this test will allow you to assess the effectiveness of your training program - the time to exhaustion should increase if your training is effective.

This test allows you to track the development of anaerobic capacity.

RUNNING BASED ANAEROBIC SPRINT TEST (RAST)

Objective

RAST was developed at the University of Wolver Hampton (United Kingdom) to test an athlete's anaerobic performance. RAST is similar to the Wingate Anaerobic 30 cycle Test (WANT) in that it provides coaches with measurements of power and fatigue index. The Wingate test is more specific for cyclists whereas the RAST provides a test that can be used with athletes where running forms the basis of the movement.

Required Resources

To undertake this test you will require:

- 400 meter track - with a 35 meter marked section on the straight
- Two cones to mark the 35 meter section
- Stop watch
- An assistant

How to Conduct the Test?

The athlete:

- Is weighed prior to the test.
- Undertakes a 10 minute warm session.
- Has a 5 minute recovery.
- Completes six 35 meter runs at maximum pace (10 seconds allowed between each sprint for turnaround).
- The assistant records the time taken for each 35 meter sprint to the nearest hundredth of a second.
- Makes appropriate calculations.

Calculations

Power output for each sprint is found using the following equations:

- Velocity = Distance ÷ Time
- Acceleration = Velocity ÷ Time
- Force = Weight × Acceleration
- Power = Force × Velocity
- <u>OR</u> Power = Weight × Distance ^{2} ÷ Time ^{3}

From the six times calculate the power for each run and then determine:

- Maximum power - the highest value
- Minimum power - the lowest value
- Average power - sum of all six values ÷ 6
- Fatigue Index - (Maximum power - Minimum power) ÷ Total time for the 6 sprints

<u>Example</u>: Athlete's weight = 76 kilograms

Sprint	Time (secs)	Power (watts)	Sprint	Time (secs)	Power (watts)
1	4.52	1008	4	5.21	658
2	4.75	869	5	5.46	572
3	4.92	782	6	5.62	525

Maximum Power = 1008 watts; Minimum Power = 525 watts; Average Power = 736 watts; Fatigue Index = 483 ÷ 30.48 = 15.8 watts/sec.

Interpretation of the Results

Maximum Power

Is a measure of the highest power output and provides information about strength and maximal sprint speed. Research range is 1054 watts to 676 watts.

Minimum Power

Is the lowest power output achieved and is used to calculate the Fatigue Index. Research range is 674 watts to 319 watts.

Average Power

It gives an indication of an athlete's ability to maintain power over time. The higher the score the better the athlete's ability to maintain anaerobic performance.

Fatigue Index

It indicates the rate at which power declines for the athlete. The lower the value the higher the ability for the athlete to maintain anaerobic performance. With a high fatigue index value (>10) the athlete may need to focus on improving their lactate tolerance.

How to use?

The test is conducted on a regular basis throughout the training program. Results should be compared with the athlete's previous results to determine if the training program is achieving the desired results. Results can then be used to appropriately adjust the athlete's training program.

When to use?

RAST can be used on a regular basis (3 to 6 weeks) throughout the season. The period between tests will be determined by the training phase and the amount of training being conducted.

Target Group

This test is suitable for sprint and endurance athletes and players of endurance sports (e.g. football, rugby).

Reliability

Reliability would depend upon, how strict the test is conducted and the individual's level of motivation to perform the test.

♦♦♦♦♦♦♦

6

AGILITY EVALUATION TESTS

- **Run/Direction Change Tests**
  - 505 Agility Test
  - Illinois Agility Run Test
  - Lateral Change of Direction Test
  - Shuttle Run Test
  - "T" Drill Test
  - Zig-Zag Test
- **Obstacle Test**
  - Hexagonal Obstacle Agility Test
- **Quick Feet Test**

Agility is the ability to change position and direction rapidly, with precision and without loss of balance. It depends on strength, speed, balance and coordination. Agility is undeniably important in the world of sport. Because agility is associated with specific skills, no one test predicts agility of all situations. You can improve agility with practice and experience. Excess weight hinders agility, for obvious reasons. Extreme strength is not a prerequisite, nor is aerobic fitness. But because agility deteriorates with fatigue, aerobic and muscular endurance can help maintain agility for extended periods.

RUN AND DIRECTION CHANGE TEST

505 AGILITY TEST

Objective

The objective of this test is to monitor the development of the athlete's speed and agility.

Required Resources

To undertake this test you will require:

- 6 cones

- Non slip surface
- Stopwatch
- An assistant

How to Conduct the Test?

- Mark out the course as per the diagram below. The distance from A to B is 10 meters and the distance from B to C is 5 meters.
- The athlete runs from the start line (A) towards the 10 meter line (B) (run in distance to build up speed).
- The assistant starts the stopwatch as the athlete passes through the 10 meter line (B).
- The athlete runs on to the 15 meter line (C), turns and runs back towards the start line.
- The assistant stops the stopwatch when the athlete passes through the 10 meter line (B) on their return to the start line.
- The best of two trails is recorded.

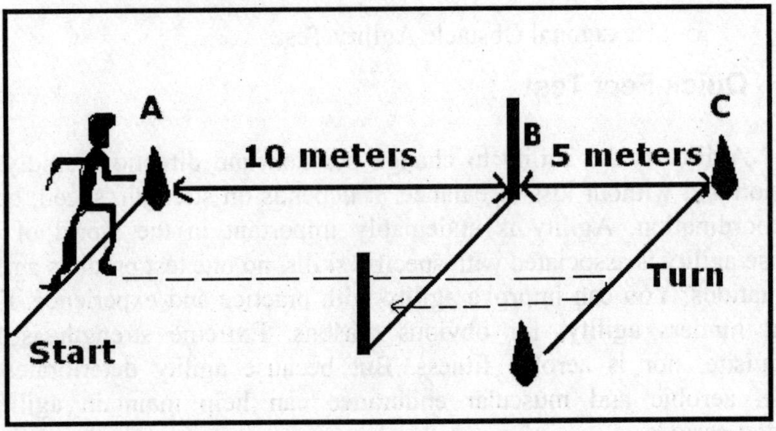

ILLINOIS AGILITY RUN TEST

This test measures your ability to change direction quickly, or an athlete's agility.

Objective

The objective of the Illinois Agility Run Test is to monitor the development of the athlete's agility.

Required Resources

To undertake this test you will require:

- Flat surface - a 400 meter track
- 8 cones

- Stop watch
- Assistant

The Illinois Course

The length of the course is 10 meters and the width (distance between the start and finish points) is 5 meters. On an athletics track, you could use 5 lanes.

Four cones can be used to mark the start, finish and the two turning points. Each cone in the centre is spaced 3.3 meters apart.

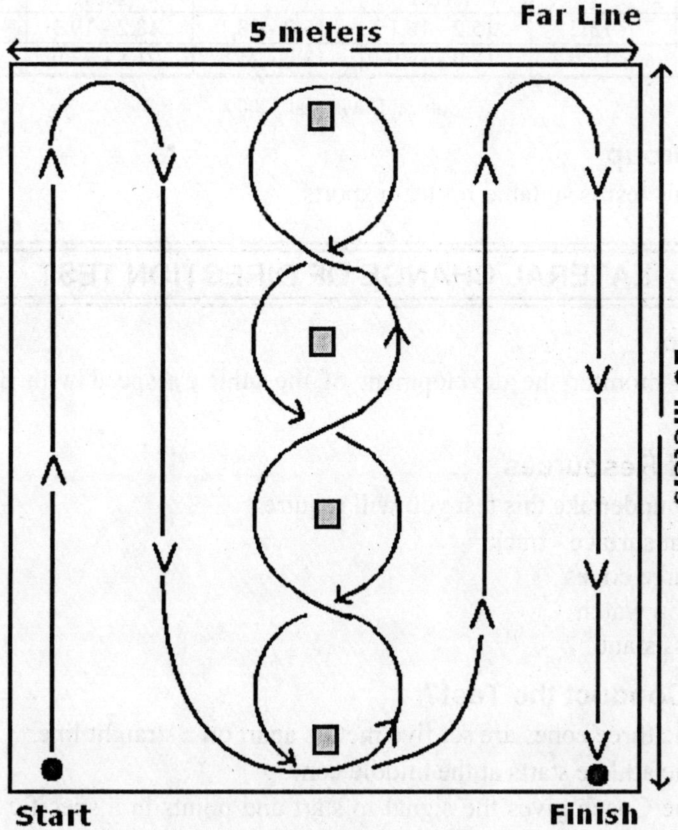

How to Conduct the Test?

The Illinois Agility Run Test is conducted as follows:

- The athlete lies face down on the floor at the start point.
- On the assistant's command the athlete jumps to his/her feet and negotiates the course around the cones to the finish.
- The assistant records the total time taken from their command to the athlete completing the course.

Analysis

Analysis of the result is by comparing it with the results of previous tests. It is expected that, with appropriate training between each test, the analysis would indicate an improvement.

Normative Data for the Illinois Agility Run Test

The following are National norms for 16 to 19 year olds.

Gender	Excellent (secs)	Above Average (secs)	Average (secs)	Below Average (secs)	Poor (secs)
Male	<15.2	15.2 - 16.1	16.2 - 18.1	18.2 - 19.3	>19.3
Female	<17.0	17.0 - 17.9	18.0 - 21.7	21.8 - 23.0	>23.0

Source: Davis et al., 2000

Target Group

This test is suitable for team sports.

LATERAL CHANGE OF DIRECTION TEST

Objective

To monitor the development of the athlete's speed with directional change

Required Resources

To undertake this test you will require

- Flat surface - track
- Three cones
- Stop watch
- Assistant

How to Conduct the Test?

The three cones are set five meters apart on a straight line.

- The athlete starts at the middle cone.
- The Coach gives the signal to start and points in a specific direction, right or left.
- The athlete moves to and touches the first cone, returns past the middle cone (start) to the far cone and touches that one and then returns to the middle cone, touching that one.
- The coach starts the stopwatch on giving the 'Go' command and stops the watch when the athlete touches the middle cone. The better of the two trails in each starting direction, right and left, are recorded and the best score in each direction is used for scoring.

Normative Data for the Lateral Change of Direction Test

% Rank	Females	Males
91-100	3.22 - 3.37 secs	2.90 - 3.05 secs
81 - 90	3.38 - 3.53 secs	3.06 - 3.21 secs
71 - 80	3.54 - 3.69 secs	3.22 - 3.37 secs
61 - 70	3.70 - 3.85 secs	3.38 - 3.53 secs
51 - 60	3.86 - 4.01 secs	3.54 - 3.69 secs
41 - 50	4.02 - 4.17 secs	3.70 - 3.85 secs
31 - 40	4.18 - 4.33 secs	3.86 - 4.01 secs
21 - 30	4.34 - 4.49 secs	4.02 - 4.17 secs
11 - 20	4.50 - 4.65 secs	4.18 - 4.33 secs
1 - 10	4.66 - 4.81 secs	4.34 - 4.49 secs

Source: Chu, 1996

SHUTTLE RUN TEST

Objective

The objective of this test is to assess the athlete's ability to accelerate between marked lines and to rapidly change direction

Required Resources

To undertake this test you will require:

- Two marked parallel lines 9.14m (30 feet) apart
- Two wooden blocks 5 cm x 5 cm x 10 cm
- Stopwatch
- Assistant

How to Conduct the Test?

- The athlete is required to sprint from the starting line to pick up a block and then place it on the ground behind the starting line. The athlete then sprints to pick up the second block and turns to sprint over the starting line.
- The stopwatch is started on the command "Go" and stopped when the athlete's chest crosses the line.
- An attempt is not counted if the block is dropped rather than placed on the floor. Also the block must be placed behind and not on the line.
- Repeat the test 3 times.
- Record the best time.

Analysis

Analysis of the result is by comparing it with the results of previous tests. It is expected that, with appropriate training between each test, the analysis would indicate an improvement.

'T' DRILL TEST

The T-test is the standard test used to measure agility.

Objective

To monitor the development of the athlete's speed with directional change

Required Resources

To undertake this test you will require:

- Flat surface
- Four cones
- A stop watch
- An assistant

How to Conduct the Test?

Three cones are set five meters apart on a straight line. A fourth cone is placed 10 meters from the middle cone so that the cones form a 'T'.

- The athlete starts at the cone at the base of the 'T'.
- The coach gives the signal to 'Go' and starts the stop watch.
- Set out 4 cones according to the diagram below.
- Starting on cone A sprint to cone B touching the base.
- Turn left and shuffle to cone C also touching its base. Face forwards when shuffling (i.e. so the left foot leads) and do not cross your feet over one another.
- Shuffle right to cone D facing the same way (i.e. leading with right foot) and touch the base.
- Shuffle back to cone B (still facing the same way) and touch the base.
- Finally, run backwards to cone A and stop the clock.

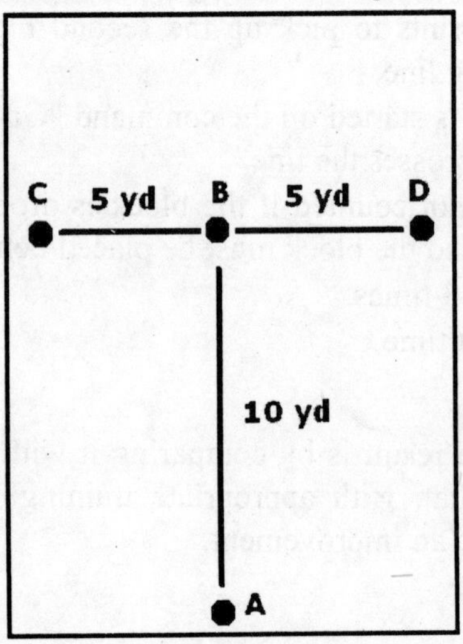

Take the best time of two trials to the nearest 0.1 seconds. Compare your results to the chart below:

T Scores

T Test Scores	
Sport/Position	**Seconds**
College Basketball Players (Men)	8.9
College Basketball Players (Women)	9.9
College Basball Players (Men)	9.2
College Tennis Players (Men)	9.4
College Tennis Players (Women)	11.1
Recrational College Athletes (Men)	10.5
Recrational College Athletes (Women)	12.5
Sedentary College Students (Men)	11.1
Sedentary College Students (Women)	13.5

ZIG-ZAG TEST

Objective

The objective of this test is to monitor the development of the athlete's speed and agility.

Required Resources

To undertake this test you will require:

- 5 cones
- Non slip surface
- Stop watch
- An assistant

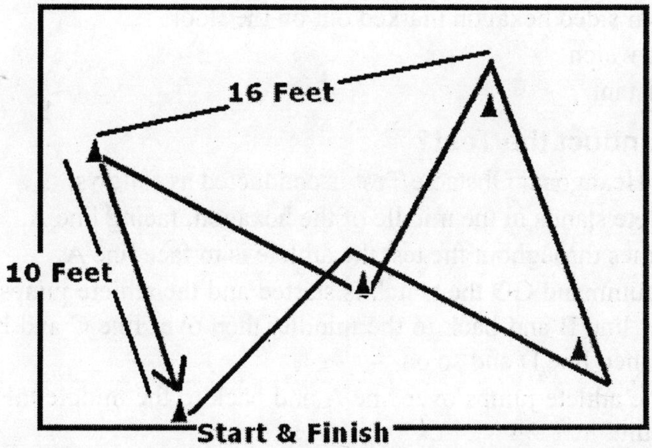

How to Conduct the Test?

- Mark out the course with four cones placed on the corners of a rectangle 10 by 16 feet, with one more cone placed in the centre.
- The athlete follows the grey route identified on the diagram.
- The athlete completes one circuit of the course starting and finishing at the Start & Finish cone (see diagram).
- The assistant records the time to the nearest 0.5 seconds.

Analysis

Analysis of the result is by comparing it with the results of previous tests. It is expected that, with appropriate training between each test, the analysis would indicate an improvement.

OBSTACLE AGILITY TEST

HEXAGONAL OBSTACLE AGILITY TEST

This test is also known as Hexagon Drill Quickness Test. This drill was developed by the US Tennis Association as part of their player assessment program. It is useful for all kinds of athletes to measure their agility, quickness and co-ordination.

Objective

The objective of the Hexagonal Obstacle test is to monitor the athlete's agility.

Required Resources

To undertake this test you will require:

- 66 cm sided hexagon marked out on the floor
- Stop watch
- Assistant

How to Conduct the Test?

The Hexagonal Obstacle Test is conducted as follows:

- The athlete stands in the middle of the hexagon, facing line A.
- At all times throughout the test the athlete is to face line A.
- On the command GO the watch is started and the athlete jumps with both feet over line B and back to the middle, then over line C and back to the middle, then line D and so on.
- When the athlete jumps over line A and back to the middle this counts as one circuit.
- The athlete is to complete three circuits.

- On completion of three circuits the watch is stopped and the time recorded.
- The athlete rests and then repeats the test.
- On completion of the second test determine the average of the two recorded times.
- If you jump the wrong line or land on a line then the test is to be restarted.

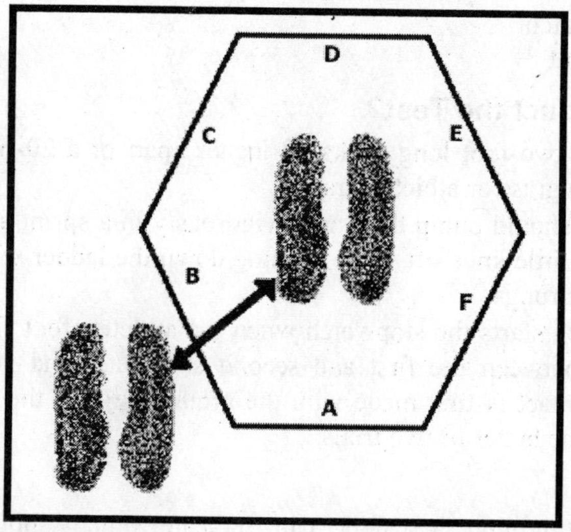

Analysis

Analysis of the result is by comparing it with the results of previous tests. It is expected that, with appropriate training between each test, the analysis would indicate an improvement in the athlete's agility.

Normative Data for the Hexagonal Obstacle Test

The following are national norms for 16 to 19 year olds.

Gender	Excellent (secs)	Above Average (secs)	Average (secs)	Below Average (secs)	Poor (secs)
Male	<11.2	11.2 - 13.3	13.4 - 15.5	15.6 - 17.8	>17.8
Female	<12.2	12.2 - 15.3	15.4 - 18.5	18.6 - 21.8	>21.8

Source: Arnot and Gaines, 1984

QUICK FEET TEST

Objective

The quick feet test provides information on the presence of fast-twitch muscle fibre in the muscles involved in sprinting and indicates your potential to execute quick movements. Hereditary factors such as limb length, muscle attachments, and proportion of fast-twitch fibres do place a limit on one's maximum potential, but we can improve our speed and quickness with proper training.

Required Resources

To undertake this test you will require

- Flat surface
- 20 two-foot long sticks or a 20-rung rope ladder
- Stop watch
- Assistant

How to Conduct the Test?

- Place 20 two-foot long sticks 18 inches apart or a 20-rung stride rope ladder on grass or athletics track.
- Athletes should pump their arms vigorously in a sprint-arm motion and use very little knee lift while running down the ladder without touching the sticks/rungs.
- The coach starts the stopwatch when the athlete's foot first touches the ground between the first and second stick/rung and stops the watch when contact is first made with the ground beyond the last stick/rung. Record the better of two trials.

Analysis

Speed through a ladder can indicate much about an athlete's quickness. A time of less than 2.8 seconds for males and 3.4 seconds for females for running the length of a 20 rung ladder, one foot in each rung at a time, is considered as excellent for college athletes.

Normative Data for Quick Feet Test

Males	Time
Junior High School	< 3.8 seconds
Senior High School	< 3.3 seconds
College	< 2.8 seconds

Females	Time
Junior High School	< 4.2 seconds
Senior High School	< 3.8 seconds
College	< 3.4 seconds

♦♦♦♦♦♦♦♦

7

BALANCE EVALUATION TESTS

- **Standing Stork Tests (Static and Blind)**
  - Standing Stork Test
  - Standing Stork Test – Blind
  - Flamingo Balance Test
- **Balance Test (Motion)**
  - Balance Beam Test

Balance can be static or dynamic. Static balance, as measured by a test such as the stork stand (standing on one foot with hands on hips and eyes closed), measures the ability to maintain balance while stationary.

Balance is important in activities like diving, gymnastics and mountain climbing. You can improve balance with specific training, and balance may be decline with age or inactivity during off season. Dynamic balance is the ability to maintain equilibrium while in motion. Balance depends on the ability to integrate visual input with information from the semicircular canals in the inner ear and from muscle-joint receptors. Although measuring and predicting its role is difficult, dynamic balance certainly contributes to sport performance.

STANDING STORK TESTS (STATIC AND BLIND)

STANDING STORK TEST

Objective

To monitor the development of the athlete's ability to maintain a state of equilibrium (balance) in a static position

Required Resources

To undertake this test you will require:

- Warm dry location - gym
- Stop watch
- An assistant

How to Conduct the Test?

- Stand comfortable on both feet.
- Hands on your hip.
- Lift one leg and place the toes of that foot against the knee of the other leg.

On command from the coach:

- Raise the heel and stand on your toes.
- Coach starts the stop watch.
- Balance for as long as possible without letting either the heel touch the ground or the other foot move away from the knee.
- Coach records the time you were able to maintain the balance.
- Repeat the test for the other leg.

Normative Data for the Stork Test

The following are National norms for 16 to 19 year olds.

Gender	Excellent (sec)	Above Average (sec)	Average (sec)	Below Average (sec)	Poor (sec)
Male	>50	50 - 41	40 - 31	30 - 20	<20
Female	>30	30 - 23	22 - 16	15 - 10	<10

Source: Arnot and Gaines, 1984

STANDING STORK TEST – BLIND

Objective

To monitor the development of the athlete's ability to maintain a state of equilibrium (balance) in a static position

Required Resources

To undertake this test you will require:

- Warm dry location - gym
- Stop watch
- An assistant

How to Conduct the Test?

- Stand comfortable on both feet
- Hands on your hip
- Stand on your preferred leg with the foot flat on the ground, lift the other leg and place the toes of that foot against the knee of the preferred leg

On command from the assistant:

- Close your eyes
- Assistant starts the stop watch
- Balance for as long as possible

- The watch is stopped when you open your eyes or move your hands or take your foot off your knee or move your standing foot
- Assistant records the time you were able to maintain the balance. Repeat the test three times.

Normative Data for Standing Stork Test

Best Time (secs)	60	55	50	45	40	35	30	25	20	15	10	5
Points Males	20	18	16	14	12	10	8	6	4	3	2	1
Points Females	-	-	-	-	-	20	17	14	11	8	4	2

Source: Arnot and Gaines, 1984

FLAMINGO BALANCE TEST

This total body balance test forms part of the Eurofit Testing Battery.

Purpose:

To assess the ability to balance successfully on a single leg

Equipment Required:

- Stopwatch
- Metal beam 50 cm long 5 cm high and 3 cm wide (the beam is stabilized by two supports at each end, and should have a non-slip surface)

Description /Procedure:

Stand on the beam with shoes removed. Keep balance by holding the instructor's hand. While balancing on the preferred leg, the free leg is flexed at the knee and the foot of this leg held close to the buttocks. Start the watch as the instructor lets go. Stop the stopwatch each time the person loses balance (either by falling off the beam or letting goes of the foot being held). Start over, again timing until they lose balance. Count the number of falls in 60 seconds of balancing. If there are more than 15 falls in the first 30 seconds, the test is terminated and a score of zero is given.

Scoring:

The total number of falls or loss of balance in 60 seconds is recorded. Scoring tables are available in the Eurofit Manual.

BALANCE TEST (MOTION)

BALANCE BEAM TEST

Purpose:

To assess active balance, through the ability to maintain balance while walking along an elevated beam.

Equipment Required:

- Gymnastics balance beam
- Stopwatch

Description / Procedure:

The aim of this test is to walk the entire length of a standard balance beam steadily, without falling off, and within a six second time span. The participant will start at one end, step up onto the beam, and walk the length to the other end. The test is repeated three times.

Scoring:

Participants are to be given three trials to complete the beam walk. The table below lists scores based on subjective observations of the beam walker. For more accuracy, use a team of three or more judges to observe a given individual perform. The score for each trial is the average of all the judge's scores. The overall score for the individual is the average of the three trial scores.

Scoring Data for Balance Beam Test

Scores	Description
5	Walks the balance beam flawlessly. Does not need to check balance, does not pause. Completes the walk within six seconds.
4	Walks the beam, but is somewhat unsteady. Completes the walk within six seconds.
3	Walks the beam, but is somewhat unsteady. May pause one or more times. Takes more than six seconds to complete the walk.
2	Walks the beam, but is very unsteady, almost falling off, may pause one or more times, and/or takes more than six seconds.
1	Falls off the beam before completing the walk.
0	Falls off the beam immediately.

Reliability:

Three judges are used to improve reliability of assessors (Inter-rater reliability), and three trials per individual are allowed to improve reliability over time (Test-retest reliability).

Comments:

This test can be used as a screening test for female gymnasts, as walking the beam is a basic skill for gymnastics.

♦♦♦♦♦♦♦♦

8

EVENT TIME PREDICTORS

Event Time Predictor Tests

- **Run Tests**
  - 400 meter Predictor Test
  - 1500 meter Predictor Test
  - 5 kilometer Predictor Test
  - Kosmin Test

Athletes do better by practice. Running tests can predict best times of athletes. One can achieve this by predicting times for the events.

RUN TESTS

400 METER PREDICTOR TEST

Objective

Frank Horwill's 40 yard (36. 6 meters) test is used to predict an athlete's potential 400 meter time.

Required Resources

To undertake this test you will require:

- 400 meter track
- Stop watch
- An assistant

How to Conduct the Test?

- The athlete is required to run 40 yards (36.6 meters) from a crouch start.
- The assistance records the time.
- Repeat the test 2 or 3 times and note the best time.
- The athlete's potential 400 m time, in seconds, can be calculated as follows:
  - Male athletes = (Time for 40 yards × 10) + 2
  - Female athletes = (Time for 40 yards × 10) + 4

When to Use?

To predict performance and monitor progress this test can be used at the:

- Beginning of the winter training to establish a baseline (September/ October).
- Just prior to indoor racing (December/January).
- Just prior to the outdoor season (March/April).

Analysis

Analysis of the result is by comparing it with the results of previous tests. It is expected that, with appropriate training between each test, the analysis would indicate an improvement.

1500 METER PREDICTOR TEST

Objective

The 1500 meter predictor test is used to predict an athlete's 1500 meter time.

Required Resources

To undertake this test you will require:

- 400 meter track
- Stop watch
- An assistant

How to Conduct the Test?

The athlete is required to run 2 sets of

- 400 meters
- 45 seconds Recovery
- 800 meters
- 90 seconds Recovery
- 300 meters
- 3 minutes Recovery

The time for each run is recorded and the accumulated time for each set is recorded. The average time of these two accumulated times is the predicted 1500 meters time for the athlete.

Example

__Set 1__

- o 400 meters in 63 seconds
- o 800 meters in 129 seconds
- o 300 meters in 48 seconds

- Accumulated time for set 1 is 240 seconds (4 minutes).

Set 2

- o 400 meters in 67 seconds
- o 800 meters in 164 seconds
- o 300 meters in 52 seconds
- Accumulated time for set 2 is 283 seconds (4 minutes 43 seconds).

Average time of the two accumulated times is (240 + 283) ÷ 2 = 261.5 seconds.

Predicted time for the 1500 meters is 4 minutes 21.5 seconds.

When to Use

To predict performance and monitor progress this test can be used at the:

- Beginning of the winter training to establish a baseline (September/October).
- Just prior to indoor racing (December/January).
- Just prior to the outdoor season (March/April)

Analysis

Analysis of the result is by comparing it with the results of previous tests. It is expected that, with appropriate training between each test, the analysis would indicate an improvement.

5 KILOMETER PREDICTOR TEST

Objective

The 5 km Predictor Test is used to predict an athlete's 5 kilometer time

Required Resources

To undertake this test you will require:

- 400 meter track
- Stop watch
- An assistant

How to Conduct the Test?

The athlete is required to run 4 × 1600 meters with 90 seconds recovery between each run and the time for each 1600 meters is recorded.

Calculate the average of the 4 recorded times and multiply the result by 3.125. The result is the predicted 5 km time for the athlete.

The 3.125 comes from the fact the average time is for 1600 meters and we require a time for 5000 meters hence we need to divide the time by 1600 and multiply the result by 5000 (5000 ÷ 1600 = 3.125).

Example

The recorded times for each 1600 meters are:

- 4 minutes 5 seconds
- 4 minutes 10 seconds
- 4 minutes 18 seconds
- 4 minutes 32 seconds

Average time of the four runs is 4 minutes 16.25 seconds (256.25 seconds).

Multiply the result by 3.125 = 13 minutes 20.8 seconds.

Predicted time for the 5 km is 13 minutes 20.8 seconds.

When to Use

To predict performance and monitor progress this test can be used at the:

- Beginning of the winter training to establish a baseline (September/October).
- Just prior to indoor racing (December/January).
- Just prior to the outdoor season (March/April).

Analysis

Analysis of the result is by comparing it with the results of previous tests. It is expected that, with appropriate training between each test, the analysis would indicate an improvement.

KOSMIN TEST

Objectives

The Kosmin Test was devised in the USSR to predict an athlete's 800 meter or 1500 meter time.

Required Resources

To undertake this test you will require:

- 400 meter track
- Stop watch
- An assistant

How to Conduct the Test?

800 meters:

The athlete is required to run two controlled maximal efforts of 60 seconds with a recovery of 3 minutes. The athlete commences their second run from the point where the first run was completed. The total distance covered by the two runs is recorded

1500 meters:

The athlete is required to run four controlled maximal efforts of 60 seconds with a diminishing recovery of 3 minutes, 2 minutes and 1 minute.

The athlete commences their next run from the point where the previous run was completed. The total distance covered by the four runs is recorded

Kosmin Tables

Due to their size, the Kosmin tables have not been included here. However, the athlete's potential 800 meter or 1500 meter time can be predicted by using the total distance covered in the following appropriate equation.

Guidelines for Kosmin Test

Gender	Distance	Equation
Males	800 meters	Time = 217.77778 - (Total Distance X 0.119556)
Females	800 meters	Time = 1451.46 - (198.54 X Log (Total Distance))
Males	1500 meters	Time = 500.52609 - (Total Distance X 0.162174)
Females	1500 meters	Time = (500.52609 - (Total Distance X 0.162174)) + 10

Limitations

The equations can be used for male and female athletes but they do tend to over predict for female athletes. The on line calculators here have taken adjustments for female athletes into consideration.

When to Use

To predict performance and monitor progress the Kosmin tests can be used at the:

- Beginning of the winter training to establish a baseline (September/October).
- Just prior to indoor racing (December/January).
- Just prior to the outdoor season (March/April).

♦♦♦♦♦♦♦♦

9

FITNESS (GENERAL) EVALUATION TESTS

- **Physical Fitness Tests (General)**
  - Medicine Ball Javelin Quadrathlon
  - McCloy Physical Fitness Test
  - Quadrathlon
  - Wilf Paish Rugby Football Tests

General fitness training works towards broad goals of overall health and well-being, rather than narrow goals of sport competition, larger muscles or concerns over appearance. A regular moderate workout regimen and healthy diet can improve general appearance markers of good health such as muscle tone. Diet itself helps to increase calorie burning by boosting metabolism, a process further enhanced while gaining more lean muscle. An aerobic exercise program can burn fat and increase the metabolic rate. **Physical fitness** is used in two close meanings: *general fitness* (a state of health and well-being) and *specific fitness* (a task-oriented definition based on the ability to perform specific aspects of sports or occupations).

Physical fitness is the functioning of the heart, blood vessels, lungs, and muscles to function at optimum efficiency. In previous years, fitness was defined as the capacity to carry out the day's activities without undue fatigue. Optimum efficiency is the key. Physical fitness is now defined as the body's ability to function efficiently and effectively in work and leisure activities, to be healthy, to resist hypokinetic diseases, and to meet emergency situations.

PHYSICAL FITNESS TESTS (GENERAL)

MEDICINE BALL JAVELIN QUADRATHLON

Objective

To monitor the development of the athlete's fitness and upper body strength

Required Resources

To undertake this test you will require:

- 1.5 kg, 2 kg and a 3 kg medicine balls.

- 30 meter tape measure.
- An assistant

How to Conduct the Test?

The test comprises of four medicine ball throws:

- Standing throw one (Men 2 kg - Ladies 1.5 kg).
- Standing throw two (Men 3 kg - Ladies 2 kg).
- 3 Step throw one (Men 2 kg - Ladies 1.5 kg).
- 3 Step throw two (Men 3 kg - Ladies 2 kg).

The athlete performs each throw and the assistance records the distance achieved. Points are then calculated for each throw from the tables below. Add the 4 sets of points together to give a total score.

Explanation of the Throws

Standing Throw

- Face forward with the medicine ball held overhead in two hands.
- Feet should be parallel and toeing the measuring line.
- Throw the ball for distance.
- A follow through step is allowed.
- Distance is measured from the front foot (on release) to where the ball lands.

Three Step Throw

- Start with both feet together in a stationary position.
- Take three steps forward with the medicine ball held overhead in two hands.
- Throw the ball for distance.
- A follow through step is allowed.
- Distance is measured from the front foot (on release) to where the ball lands.

Points for Medicine Ball Javelin Quadrathlon

Points	Standing Throw One Distance (meters)	Standing Throw Two Distance (meters)	3 Step Throw One Distance (meters)	3 Step Throw Two Distance (meters)
1	3.00	2.00	4.50	2.75
2	4.50	3.25	6.00	4.00
3	6.00	4.50	7.50	5.25
4	7.50	5.75	9.00	6.50
5	9.00	7.00	10.50	7.75
6	10.50	8.25	12.00	9.00
7	12.00	9.50	13.50	10.25
8	13.50	10.75	15.00	11.50
9	15.00	12.00	16.50	12.75
10	16.00	13.00	17.50	14.00
11	17.00	14.00	18.50	15.25
12	18.00	15.00	19.50	16.50
13	19.00	16.00	20.50	17.75
14	20.00	16.75	21.50	18.50
15	21.00	17.50	22.50	19.25
16	22.00	18.25	23.50	20.00
17	23.00	19.00	24.50	20.75
18	24.00	19.75	25.50	21.50
19	25.00	20.50	26.75	22.25
20	26.00	21.25	28.00	23.00
21	27.00	22.00	28.75	23.75
22	28.00	22.75	29.50	24.50
23	29.00	23.50	30.25	25.25
24	30.00	24.25	31.00	26.00
25	31.00	25.00	31.75	26.75

The world best score for this test is 76 points and the UK best score is 66 points.

Analysis

Analysis of the result is by comparing it with the results of previous tests. It is expected that, with appropriate training between each test, the analysis would indicate an improvement in the athlete's fitness and strength.

Target Group

This test is suitable for throwers (e.g. javelin, discus).

MCCLOY PHYSICAL FITNESS TEST

Objective

To monitor the development of the athlete's strength

Required Resources

To undertake this test you will require:

- Gym with mats and a bar on which to do pull ups
- Stop watch
- Assistant

How to Conduct the Test?

The athlete undertakes a series of exercises with the coach recording the number of repetitions completed for each exercise. The coach should allow a three minute recovery between each exercise. The test comprises of the following exercises:

- Chins (Pull Ups) to maximum
- Press Ups to maximum
- Squat Thrusts for 1 minute
- Squat Jumps for 1 minute
- Sit Ups for 2 minutes

Analysis

Analysis of the result is by comparing it with the results of previous tests. It is expected that, with appropriate training between each test, the analysis would indicate an improvement.

The Physical Fitness Index (P.F.I.) is calculated by adding together the repetitions completed for each exercise and then dividing the total by five.

QUADRATHLON

The Quadrathlon was devised in 1982 to test for explosive power improvement of the Great Britain National Throws Squad. The Quadrathlon is easy to carry out and is an excellent way to test an athlete's fitness and progress during the winter months. The Quadrathlon comprises of 4 activities:

- Standing long jump.
- Three jumps.
- 30 meter sprint.
- Overhead shot throw.

Practical Uses

The Quadrathlon can be used to gauge whether an athlete is becoming more powerful. The benefits are threefold:

- If the athlete's scores increase, then their power has increased.
- Weakness can be identified if the athlete underscores and these areas can be worked on.
- Motivational help during the long winter months.

How to Conduct the Test?

Standing Long Jump

Athlete to place their feet over the edge of the sandpit, crouch and lean forward, swing the arms backwards, swing the arms forward and jump horizontally as far as possible, jumping with both feet into the sandpit. Measure the distance from the edge of the sandpit to the nearest point of contact. The start of the jump must be from a static position.

Three Jumps

Start with the feet comfortably apart with the toes just behind the take off mark. The athlete takes three continuous two footed bounds. Measure the distance covered. The start must be from a static position and the feet must be parallel on each jump phase. Spikes allowed.

30 Meter Sprint

The athlete sprints from a stationary position (standing or from blocks) as fast as possible to the 30 meter finish line. The timekeeper stands at the finish line and times the run from the moment that the runner contacts the ground on the first stride to the moment when the runner's torso crosses the line. Spikes allowed.

Overhead Shot Throw

The athlete stands on the shot stop board, facing away from the landing area, with their feet a comfortable distance apart. The shot is held cupped in both hands. The athlete crouches, lowering the shot between the legs, then drives upwards to cast the shot back over the head. There is no penalty for following through, but the athlete must land feet first and remain upright. Measurement is taken from the inside of the stop board to the nearest point of contact. Shot weight as per the BAF age group. Please watch the safety aspect.

Quadrathlon Tables

Points are allocated from the Quadrathlon tables depending on the distance or time achieved for each activity. Scores should be compared with the athlete's previous activity scores to determine the level of improvement. Competition can be based on the improvement from the previous test for each activity. The number of points for each event can be calculated using the following equations:

Event Points for Quadrathlon

Event	Points Equation
Standing Long Jump	Points = -36.14048 + (D × 37.268536) + (D × D × -0.128057)
Three Jumps	Points = -36.36996 + (D × 12.478922) + (D × D × -0.007423)
30 Meter Sprint	Points = 209.70039 + (T × -36.94427) + (T × T × 0.165766)
Overhead Shot	Points = -22.32216 + (D × 5.8318756) + (D × D × -0.000334)

Where, D is the distance in meters and T is the time in seconds

THE WILF PAISH RUGBY FOOTBALL TESTS

Wilf Paish was a senior coach with the British Athletic Association. He is well known for his coaching of many International Track and Field athletes but he also assisted athletes of many other sports. In his work with rugby football players, he devised the following series of rugby football tests.

The Wilf Paish Rugby Football Tests

Test 1	The Cooper 12 minutes run test or multistage fitness test.
Test 2	30 meter sprint time, best of three attempts
Test 3	Count the number of Squat thrusts that can be completed in one minute
Test 4	Count the number of Sit-ups that can be completed in one minute
Test 5	Count the number of Press-ups that can be completed in one minute
Test 6	Stamina bound over 22 meters, shuttle system, immediate turnabouts, in the following sequence: • Hop right leg; • Giant strides • Hop left leg • Giant strides • Double foot bounds • Sprint Record the total time taken for the shuttle sequence

Test 7

Zigzag Run

Record the time taken to run from A to B, pick up a ball and run to C, zigzag between cones to D, and then zigzag back to C. Sprint to E, put the ball down and sprint to F.

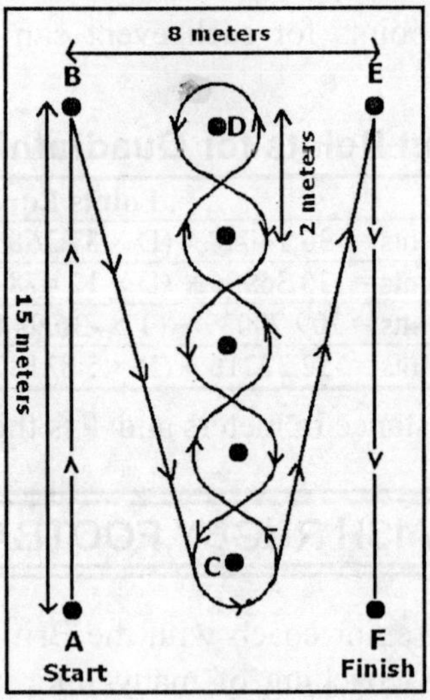

Test 8

Star Run

Balls are placed at A and E. The player starts at A with the ball and runs to E, changes the balls over, sprints around the cone at B and back to E to change the balls over. He then runs round cones C and D in turn, changing the ball over at E each time before returning to A. The distance from A to B is 8 meters and from A to D is 15 meters. Record the Total time taken to complete the agility run.

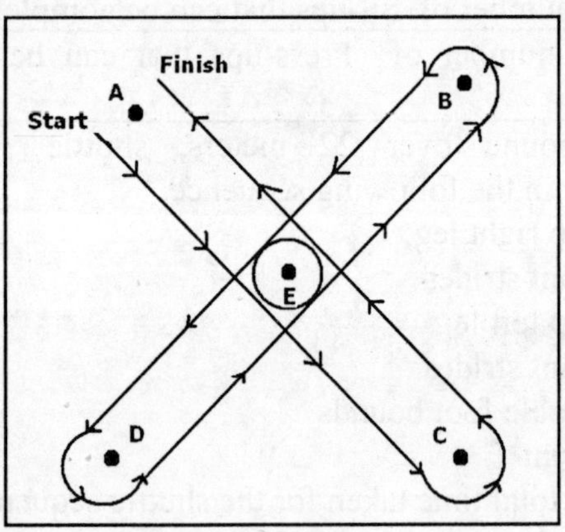

Test 9

Diagonal Pitch Run

Record the time taken to sprint from A to B, to C to D, and finish back at A.

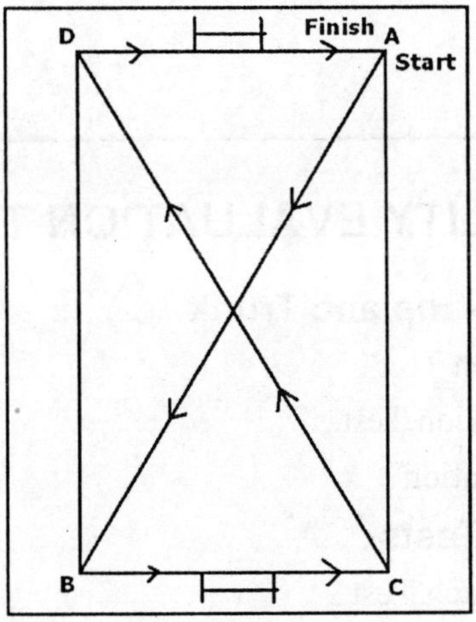

How Many Points Did You Score?

Enter the results of each test in the appropriate Test box and then calculate.

Scoring for the Wilf Paish Rugby Football Tests

Test		Points
Test 1	meters	
Test 2	seconds	
Test 3	squat thrusts	
Test 4	sit ups	
Test 5	press ups	
Test 6	seconds	
Test 7	seconds	
Test 8	seconds	
Test 9	seconds	
	Total	
	Assessment	

Forward & Back Differential

In certain circumstances, the coach might need to compare the test results of a heavy forward with a much lighter back. When making this comparison a total of 50 points should be added to those achieved by the forward.

Injury Return

In rugby football, a coach is frequently faced with a situation of deciding when a key player is ready to return to squad training and playing. When the injured player is able to score the same total from the tests as was scored prior to the injury then he/she is probably ready for squad training and competition.

♦♦♦♦♦♦♦♦

10

FLEXIBILITY EVALUATION TESTS

- **Flexion Tests – Hip and Trunk**
  - Hip Flexion Test
  - Trunk Flexion Test
  - Trunk Rotation
- **Sit and Reach Tests**
  - Sit and Reach Test
  - Modified Sit and Reach Test
- **Static Flexibility Tests**
  - Static Flexibility Test – Ankle
  - Static Flexibility Test – Hip and Trunk
  - Static Flexibility Test – Shoulder and Wrist
  - Static Flexibility Test – Trunk and Neck
  - Static Flexibility Test – Shoulder
  - Groin Flexibility Test

Flexibility is a range of motion through which the limbs are able to move. Skin, connective tissue and conditions within joints restrict range of motion, as does excessive body fat. Injury can occur when limb is forced beyond its normal range. Improved flexibility reduces this potential. Range of motion increases when joint and muscles are warm. Stretching exercises are most successful after some warm-up but before vigorous effort. Stretching after exercise, during the cool-down period, may reduce delayed onset muscle soreness and improve flexibility for the next workout.

Flexibility exercises are important when you are training for strength or endurance. They help you maintain the range of motion that might otherwise decrease. The need for stretching increases with age.

Using a flexibility test enables you to measure range of hip and trunk movement. Flexibility testing is used by gyms sometimes in your induction to get an overall picture of the state of your body. Flexibility tests also include reach or flexion tests and are a great idea if you are regularly participating in physical activity. Be sure when you use a flexibility test that you use them for all areas of the body like hip and trunk and not just the hamstrings.

FLEXION / ROTATION TESTS

HIP FLEXION TEST

The iliopsoas muscle can often become quite stiff; therefore performing a regular hip flexion test is a good way to determine what your current condition is like.

The test measures the degree of flexibility in your hip sockets.

Objective

The objective of this test is to monitor the development of the athlete's hip flexors (the muscles that lift your knees).

Required Resources

To undertake this test you will require:

- Non slip surface

How to Conduct the Test?

- The athlete lies on their back.
- The athlete lifts the left knee and using their hands pulls the left knee to their chest.
- Normal flexibility is indicated when their right leg remains flat on the floor.
- Hip flexors are considered tight if, as they attempt to lift their left knee toward their chest, their right leg leaves the floor.
- Repeat with your other leg.

Analysis

Analysis of the result is by comparing it with the results of previous tests. It is expected that, with appropriate training between each test, the analysis would indicate an improvement.

If while doing this you experience a great amount of pain and a general sense of weakness, you are likely having some problems and need to put in some good stretching time. Obviously if the person doing this is considerably stronger than you, you might feel weak since their strength outperforms yours, however if the iliopsoas is inflamed or tight, the weakness will be felt with even a small amount of pressure being applied. These test measures the flexibility and strength of the iliopsoas muscle, which governs the movement in the hip joint.

TRUNK FLEXION TEST

Good flexibility is vital for athletes, and the trunk flexion test is an excellent way to measure flexibility in two key areas - your lower back and hamstrings.

Objective

The objective of this test is to monitor the development of the athlete's lower back and hamstrings flexibility.

Required Resources

To undertake this test you will require:

- Non slip surface
- Yardstick
- Assistant

How to Conduct the Test?

- Athlete to remove their shoes and sit with their knees straight and feet 12 inches apart.
- Place a yardstick between their legs with the 15 inch mark level with their feet - the zero inch mark should be closer to their knees.
- Athlete places one of their hands on top of the other with the tips of their fingers aligned.
- Athlete exhales and slowly leans forward by dropping their head toward their arms, sliding their fingers along the yardstick as far as possible.
- The assistant records the best of three measurements.

TRUNK ROTATION TEST

This flexibility test measures trunk and shoulder flexibility. The only equipment required is a wall and a piece of chalk or pencil.

- Mark a vertical line on the wall. Stand with your back to the wall directly in front of the line. You should be about arms length away from the wall with your feet shoulder width apart.
- Extend your arms out directly in front of you so they are parallel to the floor. Twist your trunk to your right and the touch the wall behind you with your fingertips. Your arms should stay extended and parallel to the floor. You can turn your shoulders, hips and knees as long as your feet don't move.
- Mark the position where your fingertips touched the wall. Measure the distance from the line. A point before the line is a negative score and a point after the line is a positive score.

- Repeat for the left side and take the average of the 2 scores and compare with the table below:

Scores for Trunk Rotation Test

Trunk Rotation Test				
Poor	**Fair**	**Good**	**Very Good**	**Excellent**
0 cm	5 cm	10 cm	15 cm	20 cm

SIT AND REACH TESTS

SIT AND REACH TEST

Objective

The objective of this test is to monitor the development of the athlete's lower back and hamstring flexibility.

Required Resources

To undertake this test you will require:

- A 'sit & reach table' or a bench with a ruler.
- An assistant.

How to Conduct the Test?

The Sit and Reach Test is conducted as follows:

- The starting position is sitting on the floor with shoes removed, feet flat against the table, and legs straight.
- Reach forward and push the fingers along the table as far as possible.
- The distance from the finger tips to the edge of the table represents the score for that person.
- As the 'sit and reach' table has an overhang of 15 cm, a person who reaches 10 cm past their toes scores 25 cm.
- It is important to have several warm-up attempts first, and to record the best score.

Normative Data for Sit and Reach Test

The following are national norms for 16 to 19 year olds

Gender	Excellent	Above average	Average	Below average	Poor
Male	>14	11 - 14	7 - 10	4 - 6	<4
Female	>15	12 - 15	7 - 11	4 - 6	<4

Source: Davis et al, 2000

The following table is for adults

Gender	Excellent	Above average	Average	Below average	Poor
Male	>17	6 to 16	0 to 5	-8 to -1	<-20
Female	>21	11 to 20	1 to 10	-7 to 0	<-15

Source: Davis et al, 2000

MODIFIED SIT AND REACH TEST

The sit and reach test is the most common flexibility test.

Objective

The objective of this test is to monitor the development of the athlete's hip and trunk flexibility.

Required Resources

To undertake this test you will require:

- A 'sit & reach table' about 30 cm (12 inches) high
- Yard stick
- An assistant

How to Conduct the Test?

Starting Position:

- Sit on the floor with the back and head against a wall, legs fully extended with the bottom of the feet against the sit-and-reach box.
- Place the hands on top of each other, stretching the arms forward while keeping the head and back against the wall.
- Measure the distance from the fingertips to the box edge with a ruler. This becomes zero or starting point.

Movement:

- Slowly bend and reach forward as far as possible sliding the fingers along the ruler.
- Hold the final position for two seconds.
- Record the distance reached to the nearest 1/10 of an inch.
- Repeat the test 3 times and note the best distance.

Normative Data for Modified Sit and Reach Test

The following are national norms for 16 to 19 year olds

Gender	Excellent (cm)	Above Average (cm)	Average (cm)	Below Average (cm)	Poor (cm)
Males	>14	11 – 14	7 – 10	4 – 6	<4
Females	>15	12 – 15	7 – 11	4 – 6	<4

Source: Davis et al., 2000

The following table is for adults

Gender	Excellent (cm)	Above Average (cm)	Average (cm)	Below Average (cm)	Poor (cm)
Males	>17	6 – 16	0 – 5	-8 to -1	<-20
Females	>21	11 – 20	1 – 10	-7 to 0	<-15

Source: Davis et al., 2000

Sit and Reach Test Scores

Percentile Rank	Men				Women			
	20-29 yrs		30-39 yrs		20-29 yrs		30-39 yrs	
	Inches	cm	Inches	cm	Inches	cm	Inches	cm
99	>23.0	>58.0	>22.0	>56.0	>24.0	>61.0	>24.0	>61.0
90	21.75	55.0	21.0	53.0	23.75	60.0	22.5	57.0
80	20.5	52	19.5	50.0	22.5	57.0	21.5	55.0
70	19.5	50.0	18.5	47.0	21.5	55.0	20.5	52.0
60	18.5	47.0	17.5	44.0	20.5	52.0	20.0	51.0
50	17.5	44.0	16.5	42.0	20.0	51.0	19.0	48.0
40	16.5	42.0	15.5	39.0	19.25	49.0	18.25	46.0
30	15.5	39.0	14.5	37.0	18.25	46.0	17.25	44.0
20	14.5	37.0	13.0	33.0	17.0	43.0	16.5	42.0
10	12.25	31.0	11.0	28.0	15.5	39.0	14.5	37.0
01	<10.5	<27.0	<9.25	<23.0	<14.0	<36.0	<12.0	<30.0

American College of Sports Medicine (1995)

STATIC FLEXIBILITY TESTS

STATIC FLEXIBILITY TEST – ANKLE

Objective

The objective of this test is to monitor the development of the athlete's Ankle flexibility.

How to Conduct the Test?

Starting Position

- Stand facing a wall.
- Feet flat on the ground toes touching the wall.
- Lean into the wall.

Movement

- Slowly slide the feet back from the wall as far as possible.
- Keep the feet flat on the ground, body and knees fully extended and the chest in contact with the wall.

- Measure the distance between the toe line and the wall - to the nearest 1/4 of an inch.
- Repeat the test 3 times and record the best distance.

Normative Data for Ankle Flexibility Test

Measurements are in inches

Rating	Men	Women
Excellent	>35.00	>32.00
Good	35.00 - 32.51	32.00 - 30.51
Average	32.50 - 29.51	30.50 - 26.51
Fair	29.50 - 26.50	26.50 - 24.25
Poor	<26.50	<24.25

Source: Johnson & Nelson, 1986

STATIC FLEXIBILITY TEST - HIP AND TRUNK

Objective

The objective of this test is to monitor the development of the athlete's hip and trunk flexibility.

How to Conduct the Test?

Starting Position

- Sit on the floor with the back and head against a wall, legs fully extended with the bottom of the feet against the sit-and-reach box.
- Place the hands on top of each other, stretching the arms forward while keeping the head and back against the wall.
- Measure the distance from the fingertips to the box edge with a ruler. This becomes zero or starting point.

Movement

- Slowly bend and reach forward as far as possible sliding the fingers along the ruler.
- Hold the final position for two seconds.
- Record the distance reached to the nearest 1/10 of an inch.
- Repeat the test 3 times and note the best distance.

Normative Data for Hip and Trunk Flexibility Test

(Age <36 years)

Rating	Men	Women
Excellent	>17.9	>17.9
Good	17.0 - 17.9	16.7 - 17.9
Average	15.8 - 16.9	16.2 - 16.6
Fair	15.0 - 15.7	15.8 - 16.1
Poor	<15.0	<15.8

Source: Johnson & Nelson, 1986

Normative Data for Hip and Trunk Flexibility Test

(Age 36 to 49 years)

Rating	Men	Women
Excellent	>16.1	>17.4
Good	14.6 - 16.1	16.2 - 17.4
Average	13.9 - 14.5	15.2 - 16.1
Fair	13.4 - 13.8	14.5 - 15.1
Poor	<13.4	<14.5

Source: Johnson & Nelson, 1986

STATIC FLEXIBILITY TEST - SHOULDER & WRIST

Objective

The objective of this test is to monitor the development of the athlete's shoulder and wrist flexibility.

How to Conduct the Test?

Starting position

- Lay prone on the floor with the arms fully extended holding a stick.

Movement

- Raise the stick as high as possible, keeping the nose on the ground.
- Measure the vertical distance the stick rises from the floor to the nearest 1/2 inch.
- Repeat the test 3 times and record the best distance.
- Measure the arm length from the acromial extremity to the tip of the longest finger.
- Subtract the best score from the arm length.

Normative Data for Shoulder and Wrist Flexibility Test

Rating	Men (inches)	Women (inches)
Excellent	>12.50	>11.75
Good	12.50 - 11.50	11.75 - 10.75
Average	11.49 - 8.25	10.74 - 7.50
Fair	8.24 - 6.00	7.49 - 5.50
Poor	<6.0	<5.50

Source: Johnson & Nelson, 1986

STATIC FLEXIBILITY TEST - TRUNK AND NECK

Objective

The objective of this test is to monitor the development of the athlete's trunk and neck flexibility.

How to Conduct the Test?

Starting Position

- Lay prone on the floor with hands clasped at the side of the head.

Movement

- Raise the trunk as high as possible whilst keeping the hips in contact with the ground.
- An assistant can hold the feet down.
- Record the vertical distance, to the nearest 1/4 of an inch, from the tip of the nose to the ground.
- Repeat the test 3 times and record the best distance.

Normative Data for Trunk and Neck Flexibility Test

Rating	Men (inches)	Women (inches)
Excellent	>10.00	>9.75
Good	10.00 - 8.00	9.75 - 7.75
Average	7.99 - 6.00	7.74 - 5.75
Fair	5.99 - 3.00	5.74 - 2.00
Poor	<3.00	<2.00

Source: Johnson & Nelson, 1986

STATIC FLEXIBILITY TEST – SHOULDER

Objective

The objective of this test is to monitor the development of the athlete's shoulder flexibility.

How to Conduct the Test?

Starting Position

- Grasp one end of the rope with the left hand.
- Four inches away grasp the rope with the right hand.

Movement

- Extend both arms in front of the chest and rotate the arms overhead and behind the neck until the rope touches the back.
- As resistance occurs allow the right hand to slide along the rope.
- Measure the distance between the two thumbs - to the nearest 1/4 of an inch.
- Measure shoulder width from deltoid to deltoid - to the nearest 1/4 of an inch.
- Subtract the shoulder width distance from the thumb distance.
- Repeat the test 3 times and record the best distance.

Normative Data for Shoulder Flexibility Test

Rating	Men	Women
Excellent	<7.00	<5.00
Good	11.50 - 7.00	9.75 - 5.00
Average	14.50 - 11.49	13.00 - 9.74
Fair	19.75 - 14.49	17.75 - 12.99
Poor	>19.75	>17.75

Source: Johnson & Nelson, 1986

GROIN FLEXIBILITY TEST

This flexibility test measures flexibility in the adductors. The only piece of equipment you require is a ruler or tape measure:

- Sit on the floor with your knees bent, feet flat on the floor and legs together.
- Let your knees drop sideways as far as possible keeping your feet together. The soles of your feet should be together.
- Clasp your feet with both hands and pull you ankles as close to your body as possible. Measure the distance from your heels to your groin.
- Compare the results with the table below...

Normative Data for Groin Flexibility Test

Groin Flexibility Test				
Poor	**Fair**	**Good**	**Very Good**	**Excellent**
25 cm	20 cm	15 cm	10 cm	5 cm

♦♦♦♦♦♦♦

.11

REACTION TIME EVALUATION TESTS

- **Reaction Time and Quickness Tests**
  - Ruler Drop Test
  - Make Your Own Reaction Timer Test
  - Reaction Light Board Test
  - Batak Reaction Tests

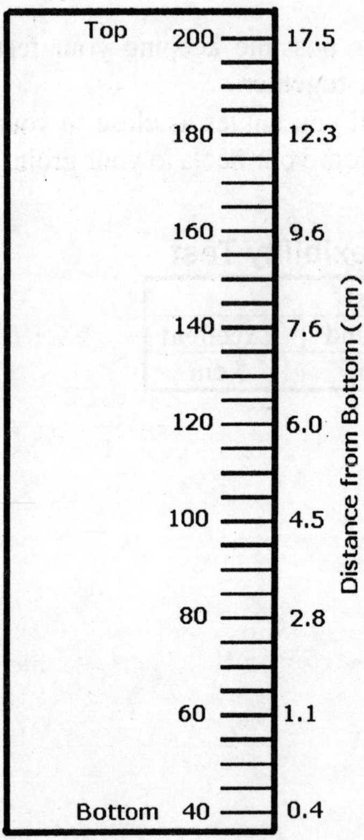

Reaction time is the ability to respond quickly to a stimulus. It is important in many sports and day-to-day activities, though it is not often measured. Simple reaction time is the time taken between a stimulus and movement e.g., sprint start. Such simple reaction time depends on nerve connections and signal pathways, is 'hard wired' in your body composition and cannot be improved. Another type of reaction time, choice reaction time, is the time taken between stimulus and action which requires a choice.

Choice reaction time can be improved by practice and training.

Performers receive stimuli from the eyes (position of other players, the ball etc), the ears (calling from players, the referee, even spectators), and kinesthetic sense (the performer's position, their options etc). Skilled players reduce reaction time by selecting the most important information, and by anticipating other player's actions and the path of the ball quickly. As with all sports fitness testing, specificity is very important, and if you were to seriously want to measure an athlete's reaction time in a certain sport, you would want a test that is more specific to the visual cues and muscle reactions that are encountered during that sport.

What is it Measuring?

For example, in the click reaction time test, when you see the screen color change, the signal for the change in color travels from your eye along the optic nerve to be registered in your brain, from which a message is sent to another part of your brain that controls your muscles. Your brain must then send a signal along the nerves to your muscles, telling them to depress the mouse button. Signals travel fast along each of the nerve pathways required, however the majority of the reaction time is taken up at the junction points in between the different nerves involved, and between the nerves and the muscles at your fingers.

However, if you compare your results of the click reaction time to the 'make your own' test, you may notice that you get quite different scores, even though the tests are measuring similar abilities. The slight differences between the tests and the computer software may explain the different results you will get. On the site www.topendsports.com/testing/reactime.htm *you can find several* tests of reaction time.

REACTION TIME AND QUICKNESS ASSESSMENT TESTS

RULER DROP TEST

Objective

The objective of this test is to monitor the athlete's reaction time.

Required Resources

To undertake this test you will require:

- A one 1 meter ruler
- An assistant

How to Conduct the Test?

The ruler is held by the assistant between the outstretched index finger and thumb of the athlete's dominant hand, so that the top of the athlete's thumb is level with the zero centimeter line on the ruler. The assistant instructs the athlete to catch the ruler as soon as possible after it has been released.

The assistant is to record distance between the bottom of the ruler and the top of the athlete's thumb where the ruler has been caught.

Analysis

The algorithm to calculate the reaction speed is $d = vt + \frac{1}{2}at^2$ where

- d = distance in meters
- v = initial velocity = 0
- a = acceleration due to gravity = $9.81 m/s^2$

- t = time in seconds

We need to manipulate $d = vt + ½at^2$ to give us an algorithm for t

As v = 0 then vt = 0; therefore, the algorithm is t = Sqrt (2d/a)

Example

- d = 9 cm
- t = sqrt (2 × 0.09 ÷ 9.81)
- t = sqrt (0.01835)
- t = 0.135 seconds

Analysis of the result is by comparing it with the results of previous tests. It is expected that, with appropriate training between each test, the analysis would indicate an improvement.

Normative Data for Ruler Drop Test

The following are national norms for 16 to 19 year olds

Excellent	Above Average	Average	Below Average	Poor
<7.5 cm	7.5 - 15.9 cm	15.9 - 20.4 cm	20.4 – 28 cm	>28 cm

Source: Davis et al, 2000

MAKE YOUR OWN REACTION TIMER TEST

Here is a simple method of making your own reaction timer. It is basic, and probably not the most accurate test, but it is fun anyway.

Equipment Required

- A piece of thick paper or cardboard, approximately 20 cm long and 5 cm wide.
- A ruler.
- A pen or pencil.

Construction Method

- Cut the card to at least 20 cm long and 5 cm wide.
- Mark the piece of paper or cardboard as illustrated.
- The numbers 40 to 200 (time in milliseconds) are to be written on the card at the specified distances (in centimeters) from the bottom of the card.

Test Method

- Have a friend hold the reaction timer at the top.
- Line up your fingers with the bottom edge of the reaction timer.
- Have the friend drop the reaction timer at any time, without warning, and try and grab it between your fingers. Don't chase it, that's cheating!

- Read off your score from the side.

Scoring

Speed (milliseconds)	Rating
40	Pretty good
60	A little below average
80	Slow
100	Very slow
120	Have another go
140	I wouldn't get into a car with you
160	What drugs are you on?
180	Hello?
200	Wake up!

REACTION LIGHT BOARD TEST

The Light Board Test is part of the SPARQ rating system for boxing, and their protocol is listed here.

SPARQ is an acronym for Speed, Power, Agility, Reaction and Quickness. The SPARQ Rating is a scoring system designed to measure sport-specific athleticism. The results from various tests in each of the areas of speed, power, agility, reaction and quickness are combined and weighted using a sport specific formula. The SPARQ Rating tells you in which areas you should concentrate your training and where you can improve. A companion system, SPARQ Training, gives the athletes a variety of drills, programs and information to improve in their sport.

Purpose:

To measure reaction time, hand-eye quickness and coordination

Equipment Required:

- Bosu ball, instrumented light board

Description/Procedure:

The light board is constructed so that when active, the board displays a target light that moves to different cells across the board. The lights are located a different distances on lines radiating out from the center of the board. The athlete stands upon a Bosu ball and facing the light board. The light board is positioned so that the center is directly in front of the face. The athlete tries to press as many active lights as possible.

Scoring:

The score is the number of lights that are pressed during the test, out of a total possible of 90.

Target Population:

Boxing

BATAK REACTION TEST

Purpose:

To measure a person's ability to see, process and react to visual information quickly

Equipment Required:

BATAK light board (roughly illustrated)

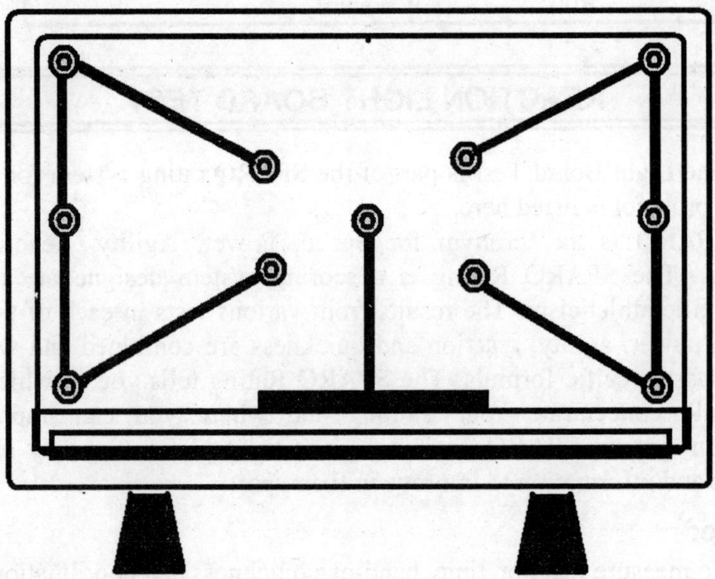

Description/Procedure:

Participants stand comfortably in front of the BATAK board. Light buttons are lit randomly, and the subject must strike out as many as possible in the allocated time (30 or 60 seconds). As soon as one target is struck the next target lights up. Plenty of practice is very important, as performance can increase rapidly in the first few attempts.

Routines:

There are several different routines that can be run on the BATAK system. Here are just a few.

- Accumulator - randomly lit targets over 30 seconds & 60 seconds
- Batakathon - 3 minutes of randomly lit targets. The targets remain on until struck out. The user sets the pace - slow - or - fast - or - speedup. Ideal for warm-up sessions.

- 50 Target Race - the user must strike out 50 targets at random as quickly as possible.
- 50 timed targets - there are 50 timed targets which illuminate at random. The targets remain on for one second. If you strike the wrong target or strike one 'out of time' then the test speeds up!
- 4 corner stretch - the user is shown 100 random corner targets and must strike out the illuminated target within one second to score a point.

Scoring:

In the accumulator routine, the score is the number of lights that are pressed during 30 or 60 seconds.

Comments:

- The word BATAK derives from the two words 'BAT' and 'ATTACK'
- One such Batak system is installed at the play zone of the Millennium Dome in London.
- Batak have a whole range of reaction time boards for different situations, such as the more portable and reasonably priced BATAK Lite.
- The test described here is just one example of a reaction test that can be done with their systems.
- BATAK featured on the ITV series 'BODYHEAT'. At the end of each show the exhausted challengers faced the BATAK wall to test their reaction times, stamina levels and hand eye co-ordination.

♦♦♦♦♦♦♦

12

STRENGTH (CORE) EVALUATION TESTS

Besides muscular endurance and flexibility, strength is one of the most important primary components of muscular fitness.

Strength is defined as the maximal force that can be exerted in a single voluntary contraction. Strength is not an absolute value. It is subject to change. Regular strength training is valuable in sport. Several factors like gender, age, fiber type and training affect the strength. Strength may be grouped under core, elastic or general. You can measure the strength in several ways.

What you ideally want from a strength test is to see a quantifiable measurement! Strength testing on both upper body and lower body at the start of your training and every few months is a smart approach - especially when strength tests can measure a range of areas.

A strength test will allow you to see which muscle groups are progressing the most and which are still lacking. Undoubtedly a key area for many, why not check the strength tests you didn't know about to help you start a new approach.

CORE MUSCLE STRENGTH AND STABILITY TEST

As strong abdominal and back muscles are critical to preventing injuries, core tests should be performed on a regular basis to ensure you are staying on top of your training for this body part. Common core tests to perform are sit-up assessments and the plank position hold.

Objective

The objective of the core muscle strength & stability test is to monitor the development of the athlete's abdominal and lower back muscles.

Required Resources

To undertake this test you will require:

- Flat surface
- Mat
- Watch

How to Conduct the Test?

The Core Muscle Strength & Stability Test is conducted as follows:

- Position the watch on the ground where you can easily see it.

- Assume the basic press up position (elbows on the ground) - as in the picture below.
- Hold this position for 60 seconds.
- Lift your right arm off the ground.
- Hold this position for 15 seconds.
- Return your right arm to the ground and lift the left arm off the ground.
- Hold this position for 15 seconds.
- Return your left arm to the ground and lift the right leg off the ground.
- Hold this position for 15 seconds.
- Return your right leg to the ground and lift the left leg off the ground.
- Hold this position for 15 seconds.
- Lift your left leg and right arm off the ground.
- Hold this position for 15 seconds.
- Return you left leg and right arm to the ground.
- Lift your right leg and left arm off the ground.
- Hold this position for 15 seconds.
- Return to the basic press up position (elbows on the ground) - as in the picture below.
- Hold this position for 30 seconds.

Analysis

Analysis of the result is by comparing it with the results of previous tests. It is expected that, with appropriate training between each test, the analysis would indicate an improvement.

If you were able to complete this test then it indicates you have good core strength. If you are unable to complete the test then repeat the routine 3 or 4 times a week until you can.

If core strength is poor then the torso will move unnecessarily during motion and waste energy. Good core strength indicates that the athlete can move with high efficiency.

♦♦♦♦♦♦♦♦

13

STRENGTH (ELASTIC) EVALUATION TESTS

- **Jump Tests**
  - Jumps Decathlon
  - Standing Long/Broad Jump Test
  - Sergeant Jump Test
- **Leg Strength Tests**
  - Leg Strength Test
  - Sprint Bound Index (SBI) Test

The general conditioning programme is needed to build higher levels of strength. As the athlete matures and becomes more experienced, the exercises become more specific to the sports and are performed against increasing training tools. This enables the greatest development of strength relevant to the sport.

Strength and power are, besides efficient skills, the deciding performance factors in all track and field events, with the exception of distance running where the dominating contribution comes from endurance. The development of strength at top performance levels covers a wide and complex field of information, particularly in the throwing events. Strength development of young athletes should be based on the established principles of basic training, aiming for a many-sided technical and physical development. Specific strength improvement to force the performance level of a particular event is not recommended. The development of strength must fit into the frame of the all-round training procedures and is not to be singled out for preferential attention.

Elastic strength is the source of power. It is the combination of speed of contraction and speed of movement. Elastic strength is most important in explosive events — sprints, jumping and throwing.

JUMP TESTS

JUMPS DECATHLON

The 10 Events: The Jumps Decathlon is easy to carry out and is an excellent way to test an athlete's elastic strength. The Jumps Decathlon comprises of the following 10 events:

• Standing long jump • Standing Triple jump • 2 hops, step and jump • 2 hops, 2 steps and jump • 2 hops, 2 steps and 2 jumps	• 5 spring jumps (Bunny hops) • Standing 4 hops and jump • Running 4 hops and jump • 25 meter hop for time • 5 stride long jump

How to Conduct the Test?

For each event allow two or three successful attempts recording the best distance/time.

Standing Long Jump

- Place feet over the edge of the sandpit. The athlete crouches, leans forward, swings their arms backwards, the jumps horizontally as far as possible, jumping with both feet into the sandpit. Measure from the edge of the sandpit to the nearest point of contact. The start of the jump must be from a static position.

Standing Triple Jump

- Take off foot to remain in flat contact with the ground and free swinging of the non contact leg can be used.

2 Hops, Step and Jump

- As per Standing Triple jump.

2 Hops, 2 Steps and Jump

- As per Standing Triple jump.

2 Hops, 2 Steps and 2 Jumps

- The second jump is a two footed take off.

5 Spring Jumps (Bunny Hops)

- 5 successive two footed bounds (bunny hops) with the feet kept together in a continuous movement.

Standing 4 Hops and A Jump

- As per Standing Triple jump - repeat test for each leg and record the mean distance

Running 4 Hops and Jump

- Length of run unlimited - repeat test for each leg and record the mean distance.

25 Meter Hop

- Start from a standing position - repeat test for each leg and record the mean time.

5 Stride Long Jumps

- Normal long jump rules apply.

Analysis

Analysis of the result is by comparing it with the results of previous tests. It is expected that, with appropriate training between each test, the analysis would indicate an improvement.

Jumps Decathlon Scoring Tables

Points are allocated from the Jumps Decathlon Scoring Tables depending on the distance or time achieved. Scores should be compared with the athlete's previous scores to determine the level of improvement.

STANDING LONG / BROAD JUMP TEST

For sports that value explosive leg strength, such as track and field, basketball, and volleyball, regularly assessing this strength, through tests such as the Standing broad jump, is an excellent way to monitor the effectiveness of your training program.

Objective

To monitor the development of the athlete's elastic leg strength

Required Resources

To undertake this test you will require:

- Long Jump pit
- 30 meter tape measure
- An assistant

How to Conduct the Test?

The athlete places their feet over the edge of the sandpit. The athlete crouches, leans forward, swings their arms backwards, the jumps horizontally as far as possible, jumping with both feet into the sandpit. The coach should measure from the edge of the sandpit to the nearest point of contact. The start of the jump must be from a static position.

Analysis

Analysis of the result is by comparing it with the results of previous tests. It is expected that, with appropriate training between each test, the analysis would indicate an improvement.

The following data has been obtained from the results of tests conducted with world class athletes.

Normative Data for Standing Long Jump Test

% Rank	Distance (Meters)	
	Females	Males
91-100	2.94 - 3.15	3.40 - 3.75
81 - 90	2.80 - 2.93	3.10 - 3.39
71 - 80	2.65 - 2.79	2.95 - 3.09
61 - 70	2.50 - 2.64	2.80 - 2.94
51 - 60	2.35 - 2.49	2.65 - 2.79
41 - 50	2.20 - 2.34	2.50 - 2.64
31 - 40	2.05 - 2.19	2.35 - 2.49
21 - 30	1.90 - 2.04	2.20 - 2.34
11 - 20	1.75 - 1.89	2.05 - 2.19
1 - 10	1.60 - 1.74	1.90 - 2.04

Source: Chu, 1996

The following table is for 15 to 16 year old athletes.

Gender	Grades (Distance in meters)				
	Excellent	Above Average	Average	Below Average	Poor
Male	> 2.01	2.00 - 1.86	1.85 - 1.76	1.75 - 1.65	< 1.65
Female	>1.66	1.65 - 1.56	1.55 - 1.46	1.45 - 1.35	< 1.35

The following table is for adults.

Gender	Grades (Distance in meters)				
	Excellent	Above Average	Average	Below Average	Poor
Male	>3.0	2.7	2.5	2.3	<2.0
Female	>2.8	2.5	2.2	1.9	<1.7

SERGEANT JUMP TEST

For athletes who play sports like basketball, volleyball, or even football, their vertical jump is a crucial skill. The vertical jump test (sergeant jump) is an effective assessment that allows you to chart your progress over the course of a training program.

Objective

To monitor the development of the athlete's elastic leg strength

Required Resources

To undertake this test you will require:

- A wall
- 1 meter tape measure
- Chalk

- An assistant

How to Conduct the Test?

The athlete:

- Chalks the end of his finger tips.
- Stands side onto the wall, keeping both feet remaining on the ground, reaches up as high as possible with one hand and marks the wall with the tips of the fingers (M1).
- From a static position jumps as high as possible and marks the wall with the chalk on his finger tips (M2).
- The coach then measures the distance from M1 to M2. The test can be performed as many times as the athlete wishes.

Figures are presented in Section I.

Normative Data for Sergeant Jump Test

The following normative data has been obtained from the results of tests conducted with world class athletes.

% Rank	Distance (cm)	
	Females	Males
91-100	76.20 - 81.30	86.35 - 91.45
81 - 90	71.11 - 76.19	81.30 - 86.34
71 - 80	66.05 - 71.10	76.20 - 81.29
61 - 70	60.95 - 66.04	71.10 - 76.19
51 - 60	55.90 - 60.94	66.05 - 71.09
41 - 50	50.80 - 55.89	60.95 - 66.04
31 - 40	45.71 - 50.79	55.90 - 60.94
21 - 30	40.65 - 45.70	50.80 - 55.89
11 - 20	35.55 - 40.64	45.70 - 50.79
1 - 10	30.50 - 35.54	40.65 - 45.69

Source: Chu, 1996.

The following are National norms for 16 to 19 year olds

Gender	Distance (cm)				
	Excellent	Above Average	Average	Below Average	Poor
Male	>65	50 – 65	40 – 49	30 – 39	<30
Female	>58	47 – 58	36 – 46	26 – 35	<26

Source: Chu, 1996.

The following table is for adult athletes (20+)

Gender	Distance (cm)				
	Excellent	Above Average	Average	Below Average	Poor
Male	>65	60	55	50	<46
Female	>55	50	45	40	<36

Source: Chu, 1996.

Power Score

Jump height can be converted into a power score as follows:

- $P = W \times (4.9 \times D)^2$

Where: P = power in kg.m/sec
W = body mass in kilograms
D = height jumped in meters

LEG STRENGTH (ELASTICITY) TESTS

LEG STRENGTH TEST

Objective

To monitor the development of the athlete's elastic leg strength

Required Resources

To undertake this test you will require:

- 400 meter track - 25 meter marked section on the straight
- Cones
- Stop Watch
- Assistant

How to Conduct the Test?

Mark out a 25 meter section on the straight section of the track with two cones. The athlete starts 10 to 15 meters behind the starting line. Using a jog run up, the athlete starts hopping on the dominant leg from the first cone. The time taken to hop between the two cones is recorded. The test is then repeated with the other leg.

Normative Data for Leg Strength Test

The following data has been obtained from the results of tests conducted with world class athletes.

% Rank	Time Taken (seconds)	
	Females	Males
91-100	3.13 - 3.75	2.70 - 3.25
81 - 90	3.76 - 4.50	3.36 - 3.90
71 - 80	4.51 - 5.70	3.91 - 5.00
61 - 70	5.71 - 6.90	5.01 - 6.10
51 - 60	6.91 - 8.15	6.11 - 7.20
41 - 50	8.16 - 8.90	7.21 - 7.90
31 - 40	8.91 - 9.45	7.91 - 8.40
21 - 30	9.46 - 10.05	8.41 - 8.95
11 - 20	10.06 - 10.34	8.96 - 9.25
1 - 10	10.35 - 10.70	9.26 - 9.60

Source: Chu, 1996

SPRINT BOUND INDEX (SBI) TEST

Objcctive

To monitor the development of the athlete's elastic leg strength

Required Resources

To undertake this test you will require:

- 400 meter track - 30 meter marked section on the straight
- Cones
- Stop Watch
- Two assistants

How to Conduct the Test?

- Begin with one foot on the start line and place the other foot two to three feet behind you.
- Place both of your helpers at the finish line - one to count the number of foot contacts and the other to time your sprint-bound effort over the 30 meter distance.
- On your own command, sprint-bound down the track for the entire 30 meter distance.
- The timer should start the watch when the foot on the start line breaks contact with the ground and then stop the watch when your torso crosses the finish line
- The time is recorded by rounding up to the nearest tenth of a second.
- Your second helper is responsible for counting the number of bounds it takes you to reach the finish line.
- The number of bounds should be rounded down to the nearest half-bound.
- Perform three trials, with three to five minutes between each trial.
- Record the results of all three trials.

Calculate the 'sprint-bounding index' for each trial using the following formula:

Sprint-Bound Index (SBI) = (No. of Bounds) × (Time for 30 meters)

Example:

You have taken 15.5 bounds to cover the 30 meters, in a time of 4.5 seconds.

SBI = 15.5 × 4.5 = 69.75.

Record your best result from the three trials. Lower the index, better the result.

♦♦♦♦♦♦♦♦

14

STRENGTH (GENERAL) EVALUATION TESTS

- **Upper Body/Abdominal Strength Tests**
  - o NCF Abdominal Curl Conditioning Test
  - o Canadian Crunch Test
  - o Flexed Arm-Hang Test
  - o Sit Ups Test
  - o Curl Up Test
  - o Overhead Press Test
  - o Press Up Test
  - o Bench Press Test
  - o Squats Test
  - o Wall Squat Test
- **Lower Body/Leg Strength Tests**
  - o Dynamic Knee Extension Test
  - o Leg Press Test
  - o Leg Strength Test
- **Hand/Arm/Shoulder Strength Tests**
  - o Biceps Curl Test
  - o Chin Up Test
  - o Grip Strength Test
- **Burpee Test**

General strength circuits are usually bodyweight exercises that involve no external loading. General Strength work will help maintain healthy joint and soft tissue strength, provide some aerobic capacity work, is a good recovery workout, is core strengthening, helps with balance/coordination/ and enhances gross motor performance. General strength circuits are great because they can be used all year round and by any sport.

Strength and conditioning programs have helped many athletes become stronger, faster, and, in some cases, larger. These programs have also succeeded in providing athletes with the ability to enhance their performance. It is a commonly accepted fact that many skills can be enhanced through proper strength training and conditioning. A strength and conditioning program is an important fixture in careers of players. The effectiveness of a well-developed strength and conditioning program that is designed to improve the athlete's physical development and his performance on the field has been documented through scientific research.

Athletes spend a lot of time and effort trying to improve their athletic performance. Strength and conditioning coaches help these athletes achieve a high level of athletic performance through resistance training. This training is used to help improve the athlete's strength, power, flexibility, and speed.

UPPER BODY/ABDOMINAL STRENGTH TESTS

NCF ABDOMINAL CURL CONDITIONING TEST

Objective

The objective of the NCF Abdominal Curl Conditioning Tests is to monitor the condition and tone of the athlete's abdominal muscles. The curl up test measures abdominal strength and endurance, which is important in back support and core stability.

Required Resources

To undertake this test you will require:

- Gym mat
- NCF Abdominal Curl Conditioning Test audio tape or CD
- Tape recorder or CD Player
- Stop watch
- Assistant

The NCF Abdominal Curl Conditioning Test audio tape or CD can be purchased.

How to Conduct the Test?

Follow the instructions on the tape or CD. Athletes are required to perform as many sit ups as possible, keeping in time to the beeps emitted from the tape or CD. The assistant counts the number of sit ups completed correctly and records the time from the start of the test until the athlete can no longer keep in time with the beeps or when the sit ups are not performed correctly.

Analysis

Analysis of the result is by comparing it with the results of previous tests. It is expected that, with appropriate training between each test, the analysis would indicate an improvement.

Normative Scores for NCF Abdominal Curl Conditioning Test

Stage	Number of Sit Ups Cumulative	Standard Male	Standard Female
1	20	Poor	Poor
2	42	Poor	Fair
3	64	Fair	Fair
4	89	Fair	Good
5	116	Good	Good
6	146	Good	Very Good
7	180	Excellent	Excellent
8	217	Excellent	Excellent

Source: www.thefitmap.co.uk/exercise/tests/strength/core/ncf.htm

Notes

A degree of caution is required in administering the test, in that you have to push yourself relatively hard to the point where you can no longer maintain the pace dictated by the tape or CD. If you are suffering from any injury or illness, or if you have any reason to think you may not be in a good general state of health, you should consult a doctor before doing this test.

As the audio tapes may stretch over time, the tapes need to be calibrated which involves timing a one-minute interval and making adjustment to the distance between markers. The recording is also available on compact disc, which does not require calibration.

CANADIAN CRUNCH TEST

Objective

The objective of this test is to monitor the development of the athlete's abdominal strength

Required Resources

To undertake this test you will require:

- Strips of tape
- Tape measure
- Metronome
- Assistant

How to Conduct the Test?

- Set the metronome to 40 beats per minute.
- Athlete to lie on their back with arms extended to your sides.
- Place a strip of tape on the floor at the end of their fingertips.
- Place another piece of tape 3 inches away from the first strip.
- To perform a proper crunch, the athlete curls their rib cage toward their pelvis so their fingers move from one strip of tape to the next.
- Athlete to perform as many crunches as possible to a 40 BPM metronome.
- The test is completed when the athlete cannot execute another crunch in time with metronome.
- Assistant counts the number of correctly completed crunches.

Analysis

. Analysis of the result is by comparing it with the results of previous tests. It is expected that, with appropriate training between each test, the analysis would indicate an improvement.

Performance Assessment

An excellent score for men is 60 and excellent score for women is 50 repetitions.

FLEXED ARM-HANG TEST

Having athletes perform the Flexed Arm-Hang Test gives a good basic measure of upper body strength.

Measuring upper body strength is a good way to know if your training is effective. For athletes who struggle to complete pull-ups, the Flexed Arm-Hang Test is a good alternative for measuring the effectiveness of their training program.

Objective

The objective of this test is to monitor the muscular endurance of the athlete's elbow flexors and shoulder extensors.

Required Resources

To undertake this test you will require:

- Bar above head height
- Stopwatch
- Assistant

How to Conduct the Test?

- Athlete uses a flexed arm hang position using a supinated grip (palm facing the subject) grip. The chin is above the bar, hips and knees are extended.
- Once the athlete is in position the assistant start the stopwatch.
- The athlete attempts to maintain this position for as long as possible (maximum time is 30 seconds).
- The timing is stopped when the chin drops below the top of the bar or 30 seconds elapse.
- The assistant records number of seconds that the flexed arm-hang position can be maintained (maximum of 30 seconds).

Analysis

Analysis of the result is by comparing it with the results of previous tests. It is expected that, with appropriate training between each test, the analysis would indicate an improvement.

SIT UPS TEST

Objective

The objective of the Sit Ups Test is to monitor the development of the athlete's abdominal muscles.

Required Resources

To undertake this test you will require:

- Flat surface
- Mat
- An assistant to hold your feet

How to Conduct the Test?

The Sit Ups Test is conducted as follows:

- Lie on the mat with the knees bent, feet flat on the floor and the arms folded across the chest. Assistant can hold your feet on the ground.
- Start each sit up with back on the floor.
- Raise yourself to the 90 degree position and then return to the floor.
- The feet can be held by a partner.
- Record the number of sits up completed in 30 seconds.

Normative Data for Sit Ups Test

The following are National norms for 16 to 19 year olds.

Gender	Number of Sit Ups				
	Excellent	Above Average	Average	Below Average	Poor
Male	>30	26 - 30	20 - 25	17 - 19	<17
Female	>25	21 - 25	15 - 20	9 - 14	<9

Source: Davis et al., 2000

CURL-UP TEST

Objective

The objective of the Curl up test is to assess the endurance of the athlete's abdominal muscles.

Required Resources

To undertake this test you will require:

- Flat surface
- Mat
- Watch
- A partner

How to Conduct the Test?

The Sit Ups Test is conducted as follows:

- Lie on the mat with the knees bent, feet flat on the floor, the hands resting on the thighs and the back of the head on the partner's hands.
- Curl up slowly using the abdominal muscles and slide the hands up the thighs until the finger tips touch the knee caps.
- Return slowly to the starting position.
- The feet are not to be held.
- A complete curl-up is to take 3 seconds - that is 20 repetitions/minute.
- Repeat as many curls as possible at this rate.
- Record the total number of curls.

Normative Data for Curl-Up Test

The following table is for Male Athletes

Classification	Age (yrs)		
	<35	35 - 44	>45
Excellent	60	50	40
Good	45	40	25
Fair	30	25	15
Poor	15	10	5

Source: McArdle et al, 2000

The following table is for Female Athletes

Classification	Age (yrs)		
	<35	35 - 44	>45
Excellent	50	40	30
Good	40	25	15
Fair	25	15	10
Poor	10	6	4

Source: McArdle et al, 2000

OVERHEAD PRESS TEST

Strength is a key component in many sports, so it is crucial that you can regularly measure and compare results. The overhead press test is a god measure of upper body strength, particularly of the shoulders, crucial in sports such as basketball, rugby and American Football.

Objective

The objective of this test is to monitor the strength of the athletes elbow extensors and superior shoulder girdle muscles.

Required Resources

To undertake this test you will require:

- Universal overhead press station
- A supportive lumbar lifting belt
- Assistant

How to Conduct the Test?

- A supportive lumbar lifting belt is recommended for this exercise during maximal lifts.
- The athlete stands and leans into the apparatus with the back leg straight and the front foot leg bent at the knee at about 150 degrees.
- The hand grips are adjacent to the front of the shoulders.
- The initial resistance should be about 33 % of male body mass and 25 % of female body mass.
- As the weight is lifted, the body should move slightly forward so that the extended arms and trunk and rear leg should form a straight line.
- If the athlete can successfully complete one repetition, repeat the procedure after one minute, adding an additional weight to the previous resistance.
- Continue with this procedure, allowing one minute recovery between attempts until the RM-1 has been determined.
- Record the final resistance.

Analysis

Analysis of the result is by comparing it with the results of previous tests. It is expected that, with appropriate training between each test, the analysis would indicate an improvement.

Kindly refer *Appendix I* for detail procedure of RM-1.

PRESS UP TEST

The primary objective of a press up test is to test the ability of the individual's endurance capacity of the upper body muscles while also testing their strength. Since in order to properly perform this action you need to have some strength development, obviously that will be of first concern. Then once you have achieved this strength, you can work on improving your endurance capacity and improving how you do on the assessment itself.

Objective

The objective of the Press up test is to assess the endurance of the athlete's upper body muscles

Required Resources

To undertake this test you will require:

- Flat surface
- Mat
- An Assistant

How to Conduct the Test?

The Press Up Test is conducted as follows:

- Lie on the mat, hands shoulder width apart & fully extend the arms.
- Lower the body until the elbows reach 90°.
- Return to the starting position with the arms fully extended.
- The feet are not to be held.
- The push up action is to be continuous with no rest.
- Complete as many push ups as possible.
- Record the total number of full body press ups.

Female athletes tend to have less relative strength in the upper body and therefore can use the modified press up position to assess their upper body strength. The test is then performed as follows:

- Lie on the mat, hands shoulder width apart, bent knee position & fully extend the arms.
- Lower the upper body until the elbows reach 90°.
- Return to the starting position with the arms fully extended.
- The feet are not to be held.
- The push up action is to be continuous with no rest.
- Complete as many modified push ups as possible.
- Record the total number of modified press ups.

Normative Data for Press Up Tests (Full Body Press Up)

Age	Full Body Press Up per minute				
	Excellent	Good	Average	Fair	Poor
20 - 29	>54	45 - 54	35 - 44	20 - 34	<20
30 - 39	>44	35 - 44	25 - 34	15 - 24	<15
40 -49	>39	30 - 39	20 - 29	12 - 19	<12
50 - 59	>34	25 - 34	15 - 24	8 - 14	<8
60+	>29	20 - 29	10 - 19	5 - 9	<5

Source: McArdle et al., 2000

Normative Data for Press Up Tests Modified Push Ups

Age	Modified Push Up per minute				
	Excellent	Good	Average	Fair	Poor
20 - 29	>48	34 - 38	17 - 33	6 - 16	<6
30 - 39	>39	25 - 39	12 - 24	4 - 11	<4
40 -49	>34	20 - 34	8 - 19	3 - 7	<3
50 - 59	>29	15 - 29	6 - 14	2 - 5	<2
60+	>19	5 - 19	3 - 4	1 - 2	<1

Source: McArdle et al., 2000

How Much Weight Are You Pressing?

When you perform the full press up, you are lifting approximately 75 % of your body weight and in the modified press up position; you are lifting approximately 60 % of your body weight.

BENCH PRESS TEST

This is a standard measure of upper body strength. Upper body strength is important for many athletes, such as rugby players, sprinters, and many field athletes. The bench press maximum test will measure the strength of your upper body, in particular your pectoral muscles - this is the test most commonly used in sports such as American Football to measure an athlete's strength.

The bench press can be used to evaluate an athlete's upper body strength.

Muscle Groups

The bench press works the following muscle groups:

- Shoulder flexors and adductors
- Elbow extensors

Coach's Technique Checklist

Correct technique is very important when using weights, if you wish to avoid injury.

- Bar loaded evenly, collars in place and secure.
- Spotter knows the command when to assist the athlete.
- Athlete lies on bench, eyes under bar.
- Hands placed evenly on bar.
- Grip firm and slightly wider than shoulder width.
- Thumbs around bar, wrists locked.
- Body and head rest on bench throughout exercise.
- Legs placed on each side of bench.
- Feet flat on floor.
- Spotter in position and ready.

- Bar lifted off the rack in a controlled manner.
- Bar stabilized over upper chest, arms straight, elbows locked, and grip tight
- Momentary stop.
- Bar lowered slowly to chest in controlled manner, close to nipples.
- Athlete inhales while lowering the bar.
- Momentary stop.
- Elbows out and under the bar.
- Bar driven up to starting position.
- Athlete exhales while pushing the bar up.
- Head and hips kept on bench.
- Athlete should not arch, twist body, or move feet.
- Bar returned to rack in controlled manner.

Strength is typically measured as a ratio of strength over body weight. With appropriate training, you should be able to bench at least your own body weight. Anything above 1 and 1/2 times body weight is considered excellent. Performed regularly, this will allow you to measure the progress and effectiveness of your strength training.

Kindly refer *Appendix I* for detail testing procedure of RM-1.

SQUATS TEST

Objective

The objective of this test is to monitor the development of the athlete's leg strength

Required Resources

To undertake this test you will require:

- A chair that makes your knees bend at right angles when you are sitting.
- Assistant

How to Conduct the Test?

- Stand in front of a chair, facing away from it, with your feet shoulders width apart.
- Squat down and lightly touch the chair with your backside before standing back up.
- Keep doing this until you are fatigued.
- Record the number of squats completed.

Following is the normative data for squats test for males and females.

Normative Data for Squats Test for Males

Age	Time (seconds)					
	18-25	26-35	36-45	46-55	56-65	65+
Excellent	>49	>45	>41	>35	>31	>28
Good	44-49	40-45	35-41	29-35	25-31	22-28
Above Average	39-43	35-39	30-34	25-38	21-24	19-21
Average	35-38	31-34	27-29	22-24	17-20	15-18
Below Average	31-34	29-30	23-26	18-21	13-16	11-14
Poor	25-30	22-28	17-22	13-17	9-12	7-10
Very Poor	<25	<22	<17	<9	<9	<7

Source: Arnot and Gaines, 1984

Normative Data for Squats Test for Females

Age	Time (seconds)					
	18-25	26-35	36-45	46-55	56-65	65+
Excellent	>43	>39	>33	>27	>24	>23
Good	37-43	33-39	27-33	22-27	18-24	17-23
Above Average	33-36	29-32	23-26	18-21	13-17	14-16
Average	29-32	25-28	19-22	14-17	10-12	11-13
Below Average	25-28	21-24	15-18	10-13	7-9	5-10
Poor	18-24	13-20	7-14	5-9	3-6	2-4
Very Poor	<18	<20	<7	<5	<3	<2

Source: Arnot and Gaines, 1984

WALL SQUAT TEST

Objective

To monitor the development of the athlete's quadriceps strength endurance

Required Resources

To undertake this test you will require:

- Warm dry location - gym
- Smooth wall
- Stop watch
- An assistant

How to Conduct the Test?

- Stand comfortable on both feet with your back against a smooth wall.
- Slide your back down the wall to assume the position.
- There is to be a 90° angle at the hip and knee.
- When you are ready.
- Lift one foot 5 cm off the ground.
- Assistant starts the stop watch.
- Balance for as long as possible.

- The watch is stopped when you put your foot back on the ground.
- Take a rest and then repeat the test with the other leg.

Normative Data for Wall Squat Test

The following are National norms for 16 to 19 year olds.

Gender	Time (seconds)				
	Excellent	Above Average	Average	Below Average	Poor
Male	>102	102 - 76	75 - 58	57 - 30	<30
Female	>60	60 - 46	45 - 36	35 - 20	<20

Source: Arnot and Gaines, 1984

LOWER BODY/LEG STRENGTH TESTS

DYNAMIC KNEE EXTENSION TEST

Regularly measuring leg strength with the Dynamic Knee Extension Test will ensure that your lower body training is effective.

Athletes need strong legs, and the Dynamic Knee Extension Test is a good way to assess it. Essentially a leg extension exercise, this will measure the strength of your knee extensor muscles, which lie along the front of the thigh. These are vital for most sports, not only providing strength for powerful movements, but also helping to keep the knee aligned, thus helping to reduce the risk of injury.

Objective

The objective of this test is to assess the strength of the athlete's knee extensor muscles

Required Resources

To undertake this test you will require:

- Universal knee flexor/extensor bench
- Assistant

How to Conduct the Test?

- The athlete sits on the end of the bench with the padded edge of the bench against the posterior surface of the knee joint.
- The feet are hooked behind the padded rollers. The hands grasp the sides of the bench just behind their buttocks.
- The correct technique involves a complete extension of the knee, conducted in a smooth and continuous movement.
- The initial resistance should be approximately 33 % of male body mass and 25 % of female body mass.

- If the athlete can successfully complete one repetition, repeat the procedure after one minute, adding an additional weight to the previous resistance.
- Continue with this procedure, allowing one minute recovery between attempts until the RM-1 has been determined.
- Record the final resistance.

Analysis

Analysis of the result is by comparing it with the results of previous tests. It is expected that, with appropriate training between each test, the analysis would indicate an improvement.

Kindly refer *Appendix I* for detail procedure of RM-1.

LEG PRESS TEST

The leg press can be used to evaluate an athletc's lower body strength. To assess the strength of your quadriceps muscle, perform a leg press test on a regular basis.

The quadricep muscles are some of the biggest, most powerful muscles in the body, and it's important for athletes to keep them in good shape.

The leg press test is one of the most beneficial types of lower body fitness measures you can do because it will solely focus in on this muscle. When you do other lower body assessments you may also be able to recruit other muscles into action, particularly if it is more aerobic in nature (sprint assessments for example).

With the leg press test however, the rest of your body will stay stationary while only the quads are contracting against the weight that you have loaded onto the machine.

Objective

The objective of the Leg Press Machine test is to evaluate the strength of the muscles of your thighs.

Muscle Groups

The leg press works the following muscle groups:

- Knee extensors
- Hip extensors

Coach's Technique Checklist

Correct technique is very important when using weights, if you wish to avoid injury.

- Hands grasping the seat's handle.
- Back straight.

- Legs parallel.
- Feet on machine rests.
- Toes pointed slightly outward.
- Pressure on balls and heel of feet.
- Knee angle reaches 90-60 degrees.
- Legs extend fully.
- Knees partially locked.
- Athlete stops momentarily.
- Weight lowered slowly back to the start position.
- Weight not bounced at the bottom.
- Athlete should not arch or twist body.
- Athlete inhales at the start or while the weight is being lowered and exhales as the legs are extended.

RM -1 (1-RM) Assessment

The 1-RM leg press assesses the maximum muscular strength of the major muscles of the lower body. Kindly refer *Appendix I* for detail testing procedure of RM-1.

LEG STRENGTH TEST

For runners and speed athletes, the Leg Strength Test is an excellent way to evaluate the effectiveness of your training program. While many tests measure pure strength, the Leg Strength Test is one of the few that evaluates how that strength translates into power and speed. As this is critical for most athletes, this is a highly effective way to know if your training is actively improving these critical skills.

This is an excellent way to evaluate ballistic leg strength.

What do you Need?

- 400 meter track
- Cones
- Stop Watch
- Assistant

How you do the Test?

- Use two cones to mark out a 25 meter straight section of track.
- Start 10 to 15 meters behind the starting line.
- Jog to the start, and then hop the 25 meters from cone to cone.
- Do this first on the dominant leg, then rest and repeat on the other leg.
- The assistant records your time to complete the 25 meters.

What Results you will Get?

As with all tests, the value comes from comparing your results over time.

Normative Data for Leg Strength Test

The following data has been obtained from the results of tests conducted with world class athletes

% Rank	Time (seconds)	
	Females	Males
91-100	3.13 - 3.75	2.70 - 3.25
81 - 90	3.76 - 4.50	3.36 - 3.90
71 - 80	4.51 - 5.70	3.91 - 5.00
61 - 70	5.71 - 6.90	5.01 - 6.10
51 - 60	6.91 - 8.15	6.11 - 7.20
41 - 50	8.16 - 8.90	7.21 - 7.90
31 - 40	8.91 - 9.45	7.91 - 8.40
21 - 30	9.46 - 10.05	8.41 - 8.95
11 - 20	10.06 - 10.34	8.96 - 9.25
1 - 10	10.35 - 10.70	9.26 - 9.60

Source:www.sport-fitness-advisor.com/fitnesstests.html

HAND/ARM/SHOULDER STRENGTH TESTS

BICEPS CURL TEST

Using the Biceps Curl Test is a great way to test your arm strength. More specifically, the Biceps Curl Test measures the strength of your elbow flexors.

Objective

The objective of this test is to assess the strength of the athlete's elbow flexors

Required Resources

To undertake this test you will require:

- A set of dumbbells ranging from 1.4 kg (3 lbs) to at least 22.7 kg (50 lb). The smaller the dumbbell increments the better the resolution for determining 1RM.
- Seat with back rest adjusted to an angle of 30 degrees to the vertical.
- Assistant

How to Conduct the Test?

- Check that the inclined back rest is at 30 degrees to the vertical.
- The initial dumbbell weight should be selected according to the estimated strength of the athlete. For untrained subjects this ranges from 6 kg to 12 kg for males and 3 kg to 6 kg for females.
- The correct technique requires that the subject stands behind the inclined surface with the arm and supinated (palm up) forearm resting on the inclined surface.
- The assistant hands the athlete the dumbbell which also rests against the inclined surface.
- Avoiding any jerking motions, the athlete attempts to flex the elbow to a vertical forearm position. When this position is attained, the dumbbell is taken by the tester.
- If the athlete can successfully complete one repetition, repeat the procedure after one minute, adding an additional weight to the previous resistance.
- Continue with this procedure, allowing one minute recovery between attempts until the 1RM has been determined.
- Record the final resistance

Results are comparative for this test - that is, you can measure progress by comparing against your previous assessments. With appropriate training, you should improve from one assessment to the next. This is a good way to measure the strength of the arms - specifically the elbow flexors.

CHIN UP TEST

Objective

The objective of the Chins Test is to monitor the development of the athlete's arm and shoulder muscular endurance.

Required Resources

To undertake this test you will require:

- Chinning bar
- Assistant

How to conduct the test?

The Chins Test is conducted as follows:

- Hang from the bar with your palms facing your body.
- Pull up until your chin is level with the bar.
- Lower so as to straighten your arms.
- Repeat as many chins as possible.
- Record the number of chins.

Normative Data for Chins Test

The following are national norms for ages 16 to 19.

Gender	Number of Chins				
	Excellent	Above Average	Average	Below Average	Poor
Male	>13	9 - 13	6 - 8	3 - 5	<3
Female	>6	5 - 6	3 - 4	1 - 2	0

Source: Davis et al., 2000

GRIP STRENGTH TEST

Objective

To monitor the development of the athlete's grip strength

Required Resources

To undertake this test you will require a Dynamometer

How to Conduct the Test?

The athlete:

- Use a hand grip dynamometer to measure grip strength.
- Record the maximum reading (kg) from three attempts using the dominant hand.

Normative Data for Grip Strength Test

The following are national norms for 16 to 19 year olds.

Gender	Excellent	Good	Average	Fair	Poor
Male	>56	51-56	45-50	39-44	<39
Female	>36	31-36	25-30	19-24	<19

Source: Davis et al., 2000

BURPEE TEST

Objective

The objective of this test is to monitor the development of the athlete's agility and balance.

Required Resources

To undertake this test you will require:

- Non slip surface
- Stop watch
- An assistant

How to Conduct the Test?

- The athlete practices the technique which involves:
  - Standing erect, arms by the side.
  - Placing the hands on the floor in front of the feet (squat position).
  - Thrusting the legs back to assume a push up position with a straight line from the shoulders to the heels.
  - Returning to the squat position.
  - Returning to the starting position
- The athlete performs as many repetitions as possible in 15 seconds.
- A point is given for every successfully completed repetition.
- Half a point is deducted for each repetition in which poor technique is demonstrated, such as:
  - Not resuming the erect position.
  - Kicking the feet back prior to hand placement.
  - Not assuming a straight push up body position.

Analysis

Analysis of the result is by comparing it with the results of previous tests. It is expected that, with appropriate training between each test, the analysis would indicate an improvement.

♦♦♦♦♦♦♦♦

15

SPEED & POWER EVALUATION TESTS

- **Run Tests**
  - Ten Stride Test
  - 30 meter Acceleration Test
  - 30 meter Sprint Fatigue-Power Maintenance Test
  - 35 meter Sprint Speed Test
  - 40 meter Multiple Sprint Test
  - 40 yard Sprint Speed Test
  - 60 meter Speed Test
  - 150 meter Endurance Test
  - 250 meter Endurance Test
  - 300 yard Shuttle Test
  - 400 meter Drop off Test
  - 400 meter Control Test
  - Flying 30 meter Speed Test
  - Lactic Acid versus Speed (LAS) Test

- **Cycle Tests**
  - PWC-170 Cycle Test
  - Wingate Anaerobic 30 Cycle Test

- **Power and Run Test**
  - Margaria Kalamen Power Test

- **Rowing Test**
  - Concept 2 Rowing Step Test

Speed may be the most exciting ingredient in sport. It requires rapid acceleration, which involves the contraction of fast twitch muscle fibers. Speed of movement includes reaction time and movement time.

Reaction time (the time from the stimulus, such as a starting gun, until the beginning of the movement) is a function of nervous system. We can not change the speed of nerve impulse transmission along a neuron. Thus, the only way to achieve significant improvement in reaction time is by increasing awareness of important stimuli and by repeating appropriate responses, which reduces central nervous system processing time.

Speed of Movement = Reaction Time + Movement Time

Movement time, the interval from the beginning to the end of the movement, may improve (decrease) with appropriate strength and power training. The key of success lies in the principle of specificity: the movement must be specific to the sport. Specificity applies to the rate of movement and the resistance employed, which means that training should stimulate the action as closely as possible.

Power is a combination of strength (force) and velocity or speed. Power is important in every sport that requires speed and acceleration. Even cycling and cross-country skiing require power. Power is defined as work divided by time, or the rate of doing work.

Power = Force X Distance ÷ Time

Power combines strength (force) and velocity or speed (distance divided by time). A person who is able to do more work than someone else in the same unit of time has more power.

RUN TESTS

TEN STRIDE TEST

Objective

The objective of this test is to monitor the athlete's ability to efficiently accelerate from a standing start.

Required Resources

To undertake this test you will require:

- 400 meter track - with a 20 meter marked section on the straight
- 30 meter tape measure
- Stop watch
- An assistant

How to Conduct the Test?

The test comprises of 6 x 20 meter runs from a standing start and with a full recovery between each run. The assistant should record the:

- Time to complete 10 strides - start the watch on the first foot strike.
- The distance covered by the 10 strides.

Analysis

Analysis of the result is by comparing it with the results of previous tests. It is expected that, with appropriate training between each test, the analysis would indicate an improvement.

30 METER ACCELERATION TEST

The prime goal of this assessment is to determine how well an athlete is able to go from an absolute standstill to an all out pace in as little time as possible. The better the fast-twitch muscles are working in this individual, likely the better they will be able to perform.

The point of the 30 meter acceleration performance evaluation test is to help measure how fast your body can go from a complete standstill to top speed.

Objective

The objective of this test is to monitor the development of the athlete's ability to effectively and efficiently build up acceleration, from a standing start or from starting blocks, to maximum speed.

Required Resources

To undertake this test you will require:

- 400 meter track - with a 30 meter marked section on the straight
- Stop watch
- An assistant

How to Conduct the Test?

The test comprises of 3 × 30 meter runs from a standing start or from starting blocks and with a full recovery between each run. The assistant should record the time for the athlete to complete the 30 meters.

Normative Data for 30 Meter Test

The following are national norms for 16 to 19 year olds

Gender	Time (second)				
	Excellent	Above Average	Average	Below Average	Poor
Male	<4.0	4.2 - 4.0	4.4 - 4.3	4.6 - 4.5	>4.6
Female	<4.5	4.6 - 4.5	4.8 - 4.7	5.0 - 4.9	>5.0

Source: Davis et al, 2000

Sprint Time Predictions

From the result of the 30 meters acceleration test it is possible to predict times for the 60 meters, 100 meters and 200 meters.

30 METER SPRINT FATIGUE-POWER MAINTENANCE TEST

In many multi-sprint sports such basketball, hockey, rugby, soccer and so on, players often have to reproduce sprints in quick succession. The ability to recover between sprints and produce the same level of power over and over is a measure of **sprint fatigue**.

Objective

In sports such as basketball, hockey, rugby and soccer, players often have to reproduce sprints in quick succession. The ability to recover between sprints and produce the same level of power repeatedly is a measure of your sprint fatigue.

Required Resources

To undertake this test you will require:

- 40 meter section of a track.
- 12 Cones to mark out the course (see diagram).
- Stop watch.
- Assistant

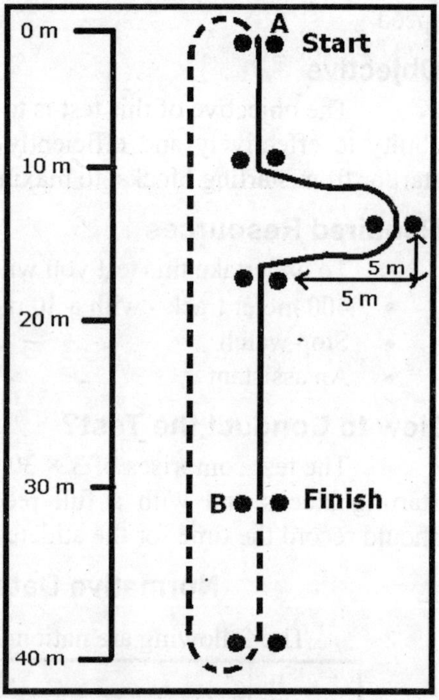

How to Conduct the Test?

- Set up a course as per the diagram.
- The athlete sprints from A to B between the cones deviating 5 m sideways in the middle of the sprint.
- The assistant records the time for the athlete to complete the sprint from A to B.
- The athlete jogs slowly back to point A (taking no longer than 30 seconds to do so) following the route on the diagram.
- When the athlete reaches point A repeat the sprint to point B.
- The athlete is to complete a total of 10 sprints.

Analysis

Analysis of the result is by comparing it with the results of previous tests. It is expected that, with appropriate training between each test, the analysis would indicate an improvement.

Performance Assessment

Enter the athlete's times for the ten sprints and then calculate.

1st Sprint	seconds	2nd Sprint	seconds
3rd Sprint	seconds	4th Sprint	seconds
5th Sprint	seconds	6th Sprint	seconds
7th Sprint	seconds	8th Sprint	seconds
9th Sprint	seconds	10th Sprint	seconds

Sprint Fatigue =	Assessment =
Power Maintenance =	

Sprint Fatigue

Using the 10 recorded sprint times subtract your fastest time from your slowest time. For example if your slowest sprint was 7.8 seconds and your fastest sprint was 6.9 seconds your sprint fatigue is 0.9 (7.8 - 6.9).

Power Maintenance

Determine the average speed of the first three trials and divide it by the average speed of the last three trials. So if your times were...

- 7.1 seconds, 6.9 seconds, 6.9 seconds
- 7.0 seconds, 7.2 seconds, 7.1 seconds, 7.3 seconds
- 7.3 seconds, 7.4 seconds, 7.5 seconds

The average of the first 3 times (7.1, 6.9, and 6.9) is 6.97 seconds and the average of the last 3 times (7.3, 7.4, and 7.5) is 7.40 seconds.

Power Maintenance = 6.97 ÷ 7.40 = 0.94 (Excellent)

- Excellent 0.9
- Good 0.85 to 0.899
- Average 0.80 to 0.849
- Poor <0.799

5 METER SPRINT SPEED TEST

Objective

The objective of the sprint speed test is to assess maximum running speed. It involves running a single maximum sprint over 35 meters.

Required Resources

To undertake this test you will require:

- Measuring tape or marked track
- Stopwatch
- Markers
- Assistant

How to Conduct the Test?

- The athlete undertakes a warm up.
- A cone/marker is placed at 35 meters from the start line.
- The athlete sprints the 35 meters from a sprint start.
- The assistance records the time the athlete takes to complete the 35 meters.
- The best of 3 x 35 meter sprints is recorded

Normative Data for 35 meter Sprint Speed Test

Rating	Time (seconds)	
	Male	Female
Excellent	< 4.80	< 5.30
Good	4.80 - 5.09	5.30 - 5.59
Average	5.10 - 5.29	5.60 - 5.89
Fair	5.30 - 5.60	5.90 - 6.20
Poor	> 5.60	> 6.20

40 METER MULTIPLE SPRINT TEST

Objective

The objective of this test is to monitor the athlete's level of sprint fatigue.

Required Resources

To undertake this test you will require:

- 400 meter track - with a 40 meter marked section on the straight
- Starting Blocks
- Stop watch
- An assistant

How to Conduct the Test?

The test comprises of 6 × 40 meter runs from a standing start or from starting blocks and with a 30 second recovery between each run. The assistant should record the time for the athlete to complete the 40 meters.

Analysis

The quickest sprint time is multiplied by 6 to give an optimal sprint time. The difference between the total and optimal times indicates the level of fatigue experienced in the performer.

Analysis of the result is by comparing it with the results of previous tests. It is expected that, with appropriate training between each test, the analysis would indicate an improvement.

Performance Assessment

For an evaluation of the athlete's performance enter the six 40m sprint times and then calculate.

1st 40 m time	seconds
2nd 40 m time	seconds
3rd 40 m time	seconds
4th 40 m time	seconds
5th 40 m time	seconds
6th 40 m time	seconds
Total time = seconds Optimal time = seconds	

Normative Data for 40 Meter Sprint Test

At the present time there is no normative data for this test. A difference between the total and optimal times of less than 0.8 seconds would be regarded as excellent for a senior player.

40 YARD SPRINT SPEED TEST

This test measures the ability of athlete to accelerate to full speed quickly as well as reaction time. This test is suitable for middle distance athletes

Objective

Frank Horwill's 40 yard (36.6 meters) test is used to predict an athlete's potential 400 meter time.

Required Resources

To undertake this test you will require:

- 400 meter track
- Stop watch
- An assistant

How to Conduct the Test?

- The athlete is required to run 40 yards (36.6 meters) from a crouch start.
- The assistance records the time.
- Repeat the test 2 or 3 times and note the best time

The athlete's potential 400 m time, in seconds, can be calculated as follows:

Male athletes = (Time for 40 yards × 10) + 2
Female athletes = (Time for 40 yards × 10) + 4

When to Use

To predict performance and monitor progress this test can be used at the:

- Beginning of the winter training to establish a baseline (September/October).
- Just prior to indoor racing (December/January).
- Just prior to the outdoor season (March/April)

60 METER SPEED TEST

Objective

To monitor the development of the athlete's acceleration and pick up to full flight

Required Resources

To undertake this test you will require:

- 400 meter track - 60 meter marked section on the straight
- Stop watch
- An assistant

How to Conduct the Test?

The test comprises of 3 × 60 meter runs from a standing start and with a full recovery between each run. The athlete is to use the first 30 meters to build up to maximum speed and then maintain speed through to 60 meters. The coach should record the time for the athlete to complete 30 meters and 60 meters. This test can be combined with the flying 30 meter test.

Analysis

Analysis of the result is by comparing it with the results of previous tests. It is expected that, with appropriate training between each test, the analysis would indicate an improvement.

60 meter Speed Test Calculator

Enter the Time and then calculate.

Predicted 100 meters time	seconds
Predicted 200 meters time	seconds

Predicted Times for the 60 Meter Test for 100 Meter's Athlete

The following calculator will predict the times for 0 meters to 30 meters, 0 meters to 60 meters and 30 meters to 60 meters based on the athlete's target 100 meter's time.

Athlete's target 100 meter's Time	seconds
Predicted 0 - 30 meter's Time	seconds
Predicted 0 - 60 meter's Time	seconds
Predicted 30 - 60 meter's Time	seconds

Enter the Athlete's target 100 meter's Time and then calculate.

150 METER ENDURANCE TEST

To ensure you finish strongly, it is important to train 'over-distance' - longer than your race. For 100 meter sprinters, the 150 meter Endurance Test is an excellent way to test their sprint endurance.

Objective

To monitor the development of the athlete's endurance for the 100 meters event

Required Resources

To undertake this test you will require:

- 400 meter track - 150 meter marked section
- Stop watch
- Assistant

How to Conduct the Test?

The test comprises of a 150 meter run from a standing start. The assistant records the time for the athlete to complete 150 meters.

Analysis

Analysis of the result is by comparing it with the results of previous tests. It is expected that, with appropriate training between each test, the analysis would indicate an improvement.

250 METER ENDURANCE TEST

Running over-distance allows you train your endurance for an event. If you are a 200 m runner, you can monitor your endurance with the 250 meter Endurance Test. The results will allow you to predict your time for the race itself.

Objective

To monitor the development of the athlete's endurance for the 200 meter's event

Required Resources

To undertake this test you will require:

- 400 meter track - 250 meter marked section.
- Stop watch.
- Assistant

How to Conduct the Test?

The test comprises of a 250 meter run from a standing start. The assistant records the time for the athlete to complete 250 meters

Analysis

Analysis of the result is by comparing it with the results of previous tests. It is expected that, with appropriate training between each test, the analysis would indicate an improvement.

300 YARD SHUTTLE TEST

The 300 yard shuttle test is also a good option for those who are required to do a lot of direction changing in their activity because you will constantly be moving in one direction, then switching to another. This makes it a good way to assess your agility ability as well.

The point of the 300 yard shuttle test is to help measure how fast your body can sprint given the chemicals your body creates whilst working hard, and also your agility when up to speed.

Objective

The objective of this test is to monitor the athlete's intermediate anaerobic power (lactate system).

Required Resources

To undertake this test you will require:

- Two cones placed 25 yard (22.8 meters) apart
- Stop watch
- An assistant

How to Conduct the Test?

- The athlete starts at one cone.
- The assistant gives the command to 'Go'.
- The athlete performs 12 shuttle runs between the cones.
- At each turn the athlete is to touch the cone.
- The assistant records the time taken to complete the 12 shuttle runs

Analysis

Analysis of the result is by comparing it with the results of previous tests. It is expected that, with appropriate training between each test, the analysis would indicate an improvement.

400 METER DROP OFF TEST

Objective

The objective of this test is to monitor the athlete's anaerobic efficiency

Required Resources

To undertake this test you will require:

- 400 meter track
- Stop watch
- An assistant

How to conduct the test

The test is conducted as follows:

- The athlete is timed running at full speed over 100 meters.
- The athlete takes a five-minute recovery.
- The athlete is timed running at full speed over 400 meters.
- The time for the 400 meters is converted to 100m splits by dividing the time by 4.
- The 100 meter sprint time is then subtracted from the split-time, giving the drop off time.

Analysis

Analysis of the result is by comparing it with the results of previous tests. It is expected that, with appropriate training between each test, the analysis would indicate an improvement.

Example

100 meter's time = 13.0 seconds, therefore, 400 meter's time = 60.0 seconds

$60 \div 4 = 15$ seconds, therefore, $15 - 13 =$ a drop off time of 2 seconds

The aim is always to reduce the 'drop off' time by increasing anaerobic efficiency. A top female 400 meter runner has a 'drop off' time of around 0.7 seconds.

400 METER CONTROL TEST

Objective

To monitor the speed, speed endurance, strength/general endurance of a 400 meter athlete

Required Resources

To undertake this test you will require:

- 400 meter track

- Cones to mark 150 meter, 300 meter and 600 meter points
- Stop watch
- Assistant

How to Conduct the Test?

The test comprises of three separate runs over 150 meters, 300 meters and 600 meters from a standing start and with a full recovery between each run. The assistant should record the time for the athlete to complete each distance.

400 Meter Control Test Calculations

Enter the athlete's times for 150 meters, 300 meters, and 600 meters and then calculate.

150 meter Time -	seconds	(Basis of 400 meter Speed)
300 meter Time -	seconds	(Speed Endurance)
600 meter Time -	seconds	(Strength & General Endurance)

Speed Endurance Index		Target Index Value	
Strength & General Endurance Index		Target Index Value	

Speed Endurance Index

If the athlete's speed endurance index is greater than the target index value, and provided the 150 meter time is in line with training targets, then more speed endurance work (lactic anaerobic) is indicated.

Strength & General Endurance Index

If the athlete's strength & general endurance index is greater than the target index value, and provided the 300 meter time is in line with training targets, then more strength and general endurance work (aerobic) is indicated.

Predicted Times for the 400m Control Tests

The following calculator will predict the times for each of the control tests based on the athlete's target 400 meter time. Enter the Athlete's target 400 meter Time and then calculate.

Athlete's target 400 meter time is	--------- seconds
Predicted 150 meter time	---------- seconds
Predicted 300 meter time	---------- seconds
Predicted 600 meter time	---------- seconds

FLYING 30 METER SPEED TEST

This test is suitable for sprinters.

Objective

To monitor the development of the athlete's maximum speed

Required Resources

To undertake this test you will require:

- 400 meter track - 60 meter marked section on the straight.
- Cone to mark 30 meter point.
- Stop watch.
- Assistant.

How to Conduct the Test?

The test comprises of 3 × 60 meter runs from a standing start and with a full recovery between each run. The athlete uses the first 30 meters to build up to maximum speed and then maintains the speed through to 60 meters. This test can be combined with the meter speed test. The assistant records the time for the athlete to complete the:

- First 30 meters
- Whole 60 meters

Normative Data for Flying 30 Meter Test

The following data has been obtained from the results of tests conducted with world class athletes.

% Rank	Time (seconds)	
	Females	Males
91-100	2.90 - 2.99	2.50 - 2.59
81 - 90	3.00 - 3.09	2.60 - 2.69
71 - 80	3.10 - 3.19	2.70 - 2.79
61 - 70	3.20 - 3.29	2.80 - 2.89
51 - 60	3.30 - 3.39	2.90 - 2.99
41 - 50	3.40 - 3.49	3.00 - 3.09
31 - 40	3.50 - 3.59	3.10 - 3.19
21 - 30	3.60 - 3.69	3.20 - 3.29
11 - 20	3.70 - 3.79	3.30 -3.39
1 - 10	3.80 - 3.89	3.40 - 3.49

Source: Chu, 1996

LACTIC VERSUS SPEED (LAS) TEST

The LAS (Lactic vs Speed) test, a speed endurance assessment for 400 meter athletes, has been provided by Les Archer - a coach from New Zealand. This test is suitable for male and female 400 meter runners.

Objective

The objective of this test is to monitor the 400 meter athlete's speed endurance.

Required Resources

To undertake this test you will require:

- 400 meter track
- Stop watch
- An assistant

How to Conduct the Test?

- Have the athlete perform a 500 meter time trial
- Record the time (T1)

  At least 48 hours later have the athlete perform the following sprints:
- 50 meters - record the time (T2)
- 4 minutes recovery
- 100 meters - record the time (T3)
- 4 minutes recovery
- 150 meters - record the time (T4)
- 4 minutes recovery
- 200 meters - record the time (T5)

Analysis

Sum the times $S1 = T2 + T3 + T4 + T5$

Compare the times T1 (time for the 500 meter run) and S1 (total time for the sprints). The difference should not exceed 5 seconds. If the difference is more than 5 seconds then this indicates a lack of endurance and a difference less than 5 seconds indicates a lack of speed.

Analysis of the result is by comparing it with the results of previous tests. It is expected that, with appropriate training between each test, the analysis would indicate an improvement.

LAS Test Calculator

Enter the time for each distance.

500 meter run -	seconds
50 meter run -	seconds
100 meter run -	seconds
150 meter run -	seconds
200 meter e run -	seconds
Result indicates -	

CYCLE TESTS

PWC-170 CYCLE TEST

This test is suitable for sprint cyclists and sprinters.

Objective

The primary purpose of the PWC-170 test is to predict the power output (watts) at a projected heart rate of 170 beats per minute (bpm).

Required Resources

To undertake this test you will require:

- Bicycle ergometer
- Heart rate monitor
- Stop watch
- An assistant

How to Conduct the Test?

The athlete performs two consecutive six minute bicycle ergometer rides in which the workloads are selected to produce a heart rate between 120 and 140 bpm on the first session and 150 and 170 bpm on the second session. For each session, the average Heart Rate (bpm) and Power Output (watts) are recorded.

Analysis

Analysis of the result is by comparing it with the result of previous tests. It is expected that, with appropriate training between each test, the analysis would indicate an improvement.

Calculations

Use a graph to plot the two points: X axis = Power (Watts) and Y axis = Heat Rate (bpm). Draw a straight line through the two points so that it is extended to 170 bpm. Draw a perpendicular line from the point plotted at a heart rate of 170 bpm to the X axis. Read off the projected power output at this point.

An alternative mathematical approach to determining the power output at 170 bpm is the Polynomial Approximation Method.

Example

An athlete produces the following test results:

- Session 1 - Average heart rate of 130 bpm at 100 watts (600 kg/minute)
- Session 2 - Average heart rate of 153 bpm at 150 watts (900 kg/minute)

Power output = (((P1 × HR2) - (P2 × HR1)) ÷ (HR2 - HR1)) + (170 × ((P1 - P2) ÷ (HR1 - HR2)))

Where:

- P1 = Power (watts) for session 1
- P2 = Power (watts) for session 2
- HR1 = Heart rate for session 1
- HR2 = Heart rate for session 2

Power output = (((100 × 153) - (150 × 130)) ÷ (153-130)) + (170 × ((100-150) ÷ (130-153))
Power output = ((15300 - 19500) ÷ 23) + (170 × (-50 ÷ -23))
Power output = -182.61 + 369.57
Power at 170 bpm = 186.96 watts

WINGATE ANAEROBIC 30 CYCLE TEST

The Wingate anaerobic 30 cycle test (WANT) was developed during the 1970s at the Wingate Institute in Israel. The WANT has been the most popular anaerobic test to date but as a cycle ergometer test it is more specific to cycle based sports. The most commonly used test length has been thirty seconds. This is a period for maximal efforts where the major fuel source is anaerobic. RAST provides a running based test of anaerobic performance.

The test is used to determine peak anaerobic power, anaerobic fatigue and total anaerobic capacity.

Anaerobic power is the ability to produce energy by the ATP-PC energy pathway. Anaerobic power reflects the ability of the adenosine triphosphate and phosphocreatine (ATP-PCr) energy pathways to produce energy.

In short... adenosine triphosphate (ATP) is created and stored in muscle cells. These muscle cells then generate mechanical work (i.e. running) from the energy produced in a naturally occurring chemical reaction that converts ATP into adenosine **di**phosphate (ADP) and a phosphate (P)...

ATP is stored in limited supplies that are quickly consumed by muscle cells during exercise.

So... the body uses an organic compound found in muscle tissue called phosphocreatine and the resulting ADP to re-synthesize ATP.

The ATP-PC energy pathway defines the energy created by a breakdown of PCr to a re-synthesized ATP.

Peak anaerobic power represents the highest mechanical power generated during any 3-5 second interval of the test

Anaerobic capacity is the combined ability of both anaerobic pathways to produce energy and so is shown as the average power output during the test.

Anaerobic fatigue is the percentage decline in power compared with the peak power output.

This test is suitable for sprint cyclists and sprinters.

How to Conduct the Test?

The testing device is a mechanically braked bicycle ergometer. After a 10 minute warm up the athlete begins pedaling as fast as possible without any resistance. Within 3 seconds, a fixed resistance is applied to the flywheel and the athlete continues to pedal "all out" for 30 seconds. An electrical or mechanical counter continuously records flywheel revolutions in 5 second intervals.

Resistance

Flywheel resistance equals 0.075 kg per kg body mass. For a 70 kg person, the flywheel resistance would equal 5.25 kg (70 kg X 0.075).

Resistance often increases to 1.0 kg X body mass or higher (up to 1.3 kg) when testing power and sprint athletes.

Peak Power Output (PP)

The highest power output, observed during the first 5 sec of exercise, indicates the energy generating capacity of the immediate energy system (intramuscular high energy phosphates ATP and PC). PP is calculated as follows:

PP in Watts = Force X Distance (number of revolutions X distance per revolution) / Time in minutes (5 secs = 0.0833 min).

Norms for Peak Power

Percentile norms for Peak Power for active young adults are:

% Rank	Males Watts	Females Watts
90	822	560
80	777	527
70	757	505
60	721	480
50	689	449
40	671	432
30	656	399
20	618	376
10	570	353

Source: Maud and Schultz, 1989

Relative Peak Power Output (RPP)

Peak power output relative to body mass is calculated as follows:

- RPP in Watts/ kg = PP / Body mass (kg)

Norms for Peak Power

Percentile norms for Relative Peak Power for active young adults are:

% Rank	Males Watts/kg	Females Watts/kg
90	10.89	9.02
80	10.39	8.83
70	10.20	8.53
60	9.80	8.14
50	9.22	7.65
40	8.92	6.96
30	8.53	6.86
20	8.24	6.57
10	7.06	5.98

Source: Maud and Schultz, 1989

Anaerobic Fatigue (AF)

AF represents the systems total capacity to produce ATP via the immediate and short-term energy systems. AF provides percentage decline in power output and is calculated as follows:

AF = ((Highest 5 sec PP - Lowest 5 sec PP) ÷ (Highest 5 sec PP)) x 100.

Anaerobic Capacity (AC)

Total work accomplished in 30 secs. AC is calculated as follows:

- AC = Sum of each 5 sec PP or
- AC = Force x Total distance in 30 secs.

Assessment of anaerobic performance can provide the coach with valuable information about the athlete's fitness status as well as allowing them to monitor progress through training. The test scores can reliably determine peak anaerobic power, anaerobic fatigue, and total anaerobic capacity.

POWER AND RUN TESTS

MARGARIA KALAMEN POWER TEST

A power test is one of the better assessments to perform if you are involved in activities that call upon you to move a large amount of weight in a short period of time. Whether it is your body weight that you need to transport over a given distance or a specified weight that you are lifting while in a stationary position, a power test will determine how quickly the muscles are able to respond and with how much force.

Objective

The objective of this test is to monitor the development of the athlete's power.

Required Resources

To undertake this test you will require:

- Stopwatch
- Assistant
- Flight of 12 steps with a starting line of 6 meters in front of the first step - each step is about 17.5 cm high with the 3rd , 6th and 9th step brightly coloured

How to Conduct the Test?

- The athlete's weight is determined (kg) and recorded.
- The vertical distance between the 3rd and 9th step is recorded.
- The athlete undertakes 2 or 3 practice runs up the steps to warm up.
- The athlete stands ready at the starting line. On the command "Go", the athlete sprints to the steps and up the flight of steps taking three steps at a time (3rd, 6th and 9th stairs).
- Assistant records the time to get from the 3rd step to the 9th step - the stopwatch is to be started with foot contact on the 3rd step and stopped with foot contact on the 9th step.
- Athlete repeats the test 2 more times - allow a 2-3 minute recovery between each test

Analysis

Power (Watts) is calculated from the formula:

$P = (M \times D) \times 9.8/t$

Where,

P = Power (Watts); M = Body mass (kg); D = Vertical distance (m) **; t = Time (s).

**The vertical distance (D) between the 3rd and 9th step must be accurately measured and used when calculating the power.

ROWING TEST

CONCEPT 2 ROWING STEP TEST

This test is only suitable for competitive rowers whose time for the 2000 meters is less than 8 minutes and 30 seconds

Objective

To monitor the development of the athlete's anaerobic threshold

Required Resources

To undertake this test you will require:

- Concept 2 Rowing Machine
- Heart rate monitor
- An assistant

How to conduct the test?

The test consists of five four minute rows, each rowed at a constant 500 meter pace. The pace is increased for each step and you have a 30 second recovery between each row. The 5th step is at 100 % (maximum) effort.

For each step, you need to record the set 500 meter/pace, distance rowed in 4 minutes, the stroke rate, the actual 500 meter pace and steady state heart rate. Heart rate reaches its steady state after approximately 3 minutes of rowing.

Analysis

Analysis of the results is by comparing it with the results of previous tests. Improvement in endurance is indicated when you find that the steady state heart rate is lower for any given 500 meter pace when compared to a previous test. It is expected that, with appropriate training between each test, the analysis would indicate an improvement in the athlete's anaerobic threshold.

Example

The following is an example of a test for an athlete whose best time for the 2000 meters is 6 minutes and 32 seconds, which is an average 500 meters split of 1 minute 38 seconds.

- Step 1 - 4 minutes at 1 minute 59 seconds/500 meters. 30 seconds recovery - record distance, stroke rate, set & actual 500 meter's pace and steady pace heart rate.
- Step 2 - 4 minutes at 1 minute 54 seconds/500 meters. 30 seconds recovery - record distance, stroke rate, set & actual 500 meter's pace and steady pace heart rate.
- Step 3 - 4 minutes at 1 minute 50 seconds/500 meters. 30 seconds recovery - record distance, stroke rate, set & actual 500 meter's pace and steady pace heart rate.
- Step 4 - 4 minutes at 1 minute 47 seconds/500 meters. 30 seconds recovery - record distance, stroke rate, set & actual 500 meter's pace and steady pace heart rate.
- Step 5 - 4 minutes at maximum effort. Record distance, stroke rate, actual 500 meter's pace and steady pace heart rate

500 Meter's Pace for each Step

To determine the pace for each of the 4 minute rows, enter current 2000 meter time.

2000 meter time	minutes	seconds
Step 1: 4 minutes at	minutes	seconds/500 meters
Step 2: 4 minutes at	minutes	seconds/500 meters
Step 3: 4 minutes at	minutes	seconds/500 meters
Step 4: 4 minutes at	minutes	seconds/500 meters
Step 5: 4 minutes at	minutes	seconds/500 meters

♦♦♦♦♦♦♦

16

PSYCHOLOGY EVALUATION TESTS

- **Anxiety, Task and Ego Orientation Tests**
    - Sport Competition Anxiety Test (SCAT)
    - Task and Ego Orientation in Sport Questionnaire (TEOSQ)
    - Sport Personality Questionnaire (SPQ20) Test

Sport psychology (or sports psychology) is the study of a people's behavior in sport. It is also a specialization within the brain psychology and kinesiology that seeks to understand psychological/mental factors that affect performance in sports, physical activity, and exercise and apply these to enhance individual and team performance. It deals with increasing performance by managing emotions and minimizing the psychological effects of injury and poor performance. Some of the most important skills taught are goal setting, relaxation, visualization, self-talk, awareness and control, concentration, confidence, using rituals, attribution training, and periodization

Sports has for long been considered the mainstay of muscle power. But the power of the mind that fuels those incredible sporting feats is no less potent.

ANXIETY, TASK AND EGO ORIENTATION TESTS

SPORT COMPETITION ANXIETY TEST (SCAT)

By analyzing an athlete's responses to a series of statements about how she/he feels in a competitive situation it is possible to determine their level of anxiety. A test that provides such functionality is the Sport Competition Anxiety Test (SCAT) that was developed by Martens, Vealey, and Burton in 1990.

Assessing Your Anxiety

Read each statement below, decide if you "Rarely", "Sometimes" or "Often" feel this way when competing in your sport and select the appropriate radio button to indicate your response.

Do not spend too long on each statement, as there are no right or wrong answers. Your SCAT score will range from a low of 10 to a high of 30 where 10 indicates a low level of anxiety and 30 a high level of anxiety (stressed).

SCAT Form

Read each statement below, decide if you "Rarely", "Sometimes" or "Often" feel this way when competing in your sport, and tick the appropriate box to indicate your response.

Q. No.	Questions	Rarely	Sometimes	Often
1	Competing against others is socially enjoyable			
2	Before I compete I feel uneasy			
3	Before I compete I worry about not performing well			
4	I am a good sportsman when I compete			
5	When I compete I worry about making mistakes			
6	Before I compete I am calm			
7	Setting a goal is important when competing			
8	Before I compete I get a queasy feeling in my stomach			
9	Just before competing I notice my heart beats faster than usual			
10	I like to compete in games that demand a lot of physical energy			
11	Before I compete I feel relaxed			
12	Before I compete I am nervous			
13	Team sports are more exciting than individual sports			
14	I get nervous wanting to start the game			
15	Before I compete I usually get uptight			

Analysis

The score for the response to each question is detailed below. Enter the score for each question in the "Athlete's Score" column and then total the column up to provide a SCAT score.

Note that question 1, 4, 7, 10 and 13 score zero regardless of the response.

Question Response to Scat Form

Question No.	Rarely	Sometimes	Often	Athlete's Score
1	0	0	0	0
2	1	2	3	
3	1	2	3	
4	0	0	0	0
5	1	2	3	
6	3	2	1	
7	0	0	0	0
8	1	2	3	
9	1	2	3	
10	0	0	0	0
11	3	2	1	
12	1	2	3	
13	0	0	0	0
14	1	2	3	
15	1	2	3	
Total				

SCAT Score:

Less than 17 - Low level of anxiety
17-24 - Average level of anxiety
More than 24 - High level of anxiety

TASK AND EGO ORIENTATION IN SPORT QUESTIONNAIRE (TEOSQ)

TEOSQ can be used to assess whether an individual defines success in a sporting context as mastery (task orientated) or outperforming others (ego orientated).

Questionnaire

TEOSQ is a 13 item questionnaire measuring task orientation (7 questions) and the other ego orientation (6 questions). Before completing the questionnaire, the individual is asked to think of a time when they felt most successful in their sport and answer the questions based on this. The answers are indicated on a 5 point scale, where 1 = strongly agree and 5 = strongly disagree. A mean score is calculated for each participant by adding all the scores for all the task orientated questions and dividing by 7 and doing the same for the ego orientated questions but dividing by 6. This gives a mean score between 1 (low) and 5 (high) for each orientation.

Questions: Consider the statement "I feel most successful in sport when..." and read each of the following statements listed below and indicate how much you personally agree with each statement by entering an appropriate score.

Where:

1 = Strongly Disagree   2 = Disagree

3 = Neutral   4 = Agree

5 = Strongly Agree

I feel most successful in sport when...

Question	Score
I am the only one who can do the play or skill	
I learn a new skill and it makes me want to practice more	
I can do better than my friends	
The others cannot do as well as me	
I learn something that is fun to do	
Others mess up "and" I do not	
I learn a new skill by trying hard	
I work really hard	
I score the most points/goals/hits, etc.	
Something I learn makes me want to go practice more	
I am the best	
A skill I learn really feels right	
I do my very best	

0 (Zero) is treated as 1 and a value above 5 is treated as 5

Ego Orientation		(1 = Low ..... 5 = High)
Task Orientation		(1 = Low ..... 5 = High)

Source: Duda, 1989

SPORT PERSONALITY QUESTIONNAIRE (SPQ20)

SPQ20 measures the mental factors that have a high impact on sports performance.

Take the leading edge SPQ20 sport psychology questionnaire to understand your mental approach and the behaviors and skills you need to develop in order to:

- Identify and reduce mental factors that impede your performance such as lapses in concentration, pre-performance anxiety and 'choking' under pressure.
- Improve your motivation, self-confidence and mental attitude.
- Increase your chances of playing in the zone, getting in the winner's circle and enjoying your sport.

- The online sport psychology assessment takes about 10-15 minutes to complete and you get an instant report covering twenty dimensions that have a high impact on sporting achievement

SPQ20 PROFILE SHEET

Lower			Average				Higher			Dimension	
1	2	3	4	5	6	7	8	9	10		
.	.	.	.	.	.	.	←	…	→	**Competitiveness** Enjoys competing and wants to get in the winner's circle	Dynamism
.	.	.	.	.	.	←	…	→	.	**Aggressiveness** Adopts an aggressive attitude, tends to intimidate opponents	Dynamism
.	.	.	.	.	.	.	←	…	→	**Self-Efficacy** Displays self-confidence and bounces back from setbacks	Dynamism
.	.	.	.	.	.	←	…	→	.	**Flow** Able to immerse himself/herself in performance and play in the zone	Dynamism
.	.	.	.	.	.	.	.	←	…	**Achievement** Trains hard and makes personal sacrifices to achieve excellence	Motives & Values
.	.	.	.	.	←	…	→	.	.	**Power** Enjoys having authority over people and aspires to leadership positions	Motives & Values
.	.	.	.	.	.	.	.	←	…	**Conscientiousness** Shows self-discipline, prepares thoroughly, stays with the plan	Motives & Values
.	.	.	.	.	.	.	←	…	→	**Ethics** Has strong principles, behaves ethically, shows sportsperson ship	Motives & Values
.	.	.	.	.	.	.	←	…	→	**Adaptability** Open to ideas and suggestions, keeps up with technical developments	Openness
.	.	.	.	.	.	←	…	→	.	**Self-Awareness** Aware of strengths and weaknesses, asks for feedback, reflective	Openness
.	.	.	.	.	.	←	…	→	.	**Intuition** Uses instincts and intuition to guide performance, sees things in advance	Openness
.	.	.	.	.	←	…	→	.	.	**Relationships** Builds relationships, engages in conversation, enjoys socializing	Sociability
.	.	.	.	.	←	…	→	.	.	**Empathy** Listens to other people's views, reinforces them, goes out of way to help	Sociability
.	.	.	.	.	.	.	←	…	→	**Emotions** Knows how to regulate feelings and emotions to maximize performance	Sociability
.	←	…	→	.	.	.	.	.	.	**Competition Anxiety** Experiences anxiety and tension before important events	Anxieties
←	…	→	.	.	.	.	.	.	.	**Fear of Failure** Afraid of failing and letting people down, not living up to expectations	Anxieties
.	←	…	→	.	.	.	.	.	.	**Burnout** Experiences apathy, fatigue, anxiety, isolation and feels like leaving sport	Anxieties
.	.	.	.	.	.	←	…	→	.	**Self-Talk** Talks positively to self to maintain motivation, stay calm, perform well	Techniques
.	.	.	.	.	.	←	…	→	.	**Visualization** Uses imagery to help play well, rehearse performances, stay calm	Techniques
.	.	.	.	.	.	.	.	←	…	**Goal Setting** Identifies priorities, sets goals, measures progress	Techniques

The term mental skills cover sets of behaviors other than physical skills that are instrumental in achieving success in sports. Ability to perform these sets of behaviors depends on a range of psychological factors. These include personality, motives, emotional intelligence, and performance improvement factors such as goal setting, imagery etc, and the athlete's values/ethics.

The SPQ measures 20 dimensions covering six key factors, which in the SPQ are referred to as dynamism, motives and values, openness, sociability, anxieties and performance techniques. The instrument also provides a measure of socially desirable responding. The table above shows the key psychometric properties of the instrument.

♦♦♦♦♦♦♦

17

TALENT EVALUATION TESTS

EVALUATION OF MALE AND FEMALE PHYSICAL TALENT

Recent studies conducted at Indiana University USA revealed that it is possible to accurately predict performance in selected track and field events using relatively simple tests.

Objectives

To assist coaches recognize potential Olympic athletes at a young age and predict their performance in selected track and field events.

The Tests

The following measurements and tests are undertaken in the order given:

- Male Athletes - Standing long jump, vertical jump, five bounds and standing 30 meters.
- Female Athletes - Weight, standing long jump, stride length and stride frequency

Standing Long Jump (Males & Females)

The athlete places their feet over the edge of the sandpit. The athlete crouches, leans forward, swings their arms backwards, the jumps horizontally as far as possible, jumping with both feet into the sandpit.

The coach should measure from the edge of the sandpit to the nearest point of contact. The start of the jump must be from a static position. Two trials are performed and the best performance used in the calculations. Result to be in meters.

Scores for Standing Long Jump Test

Distance in meters					
Gender	Poor	Below Average	Average	Good	Excellent
Males	<2.0	2.3	2.5	2.7	>3.0
Females	<1.7	1.9	2.2	2.5	>2.8

Vertical Jump (Males)

The athlete chalks the end of his finger tips stands side onto the wall, keeping both feet remaining on the ground, reaches up as high as possible with one hand and marks the wall with the tips of the fingers (M1). From a static position the athlete jumps as high as possible and marks the wall with the chalk on his finger tips (M2). The coach then measures the distance from M1 to M2. Two trials are performed and the best performance used in the calculations. Result to be in cm.

Scores for Vertical Jump Test

Distance in meters					
Gender	Poor	Below Average	Average	Good	Excellent
Males	<46	50	55	60	>65
Females	<36	40	45	50	>55

Jump height can be converted into a power using the following formula:

Power = body mass (kg) x (4.9 x height jumped in meters)2

So for example if you weigh 80 kg and jumped 50 cm (0.5m) your score would be........

$$= 80 \text{ x } (4.9 \text{ x } 0.5)2 = 80 \text{ x } 2.45 \text{ x } 2.45 = 480 \text{ kg-m}$$

Five Bounds for Distance (Males)

From a stationary position with both feet together the athlete executes 4 bounds and a jump into the sandpit. Measurement is made from the start point to the landing point nearest to the starting line. Two trials are performed and the best performance used in the calculations. Result to be in meters.

Standing 30 Meters (Males)

From a standing start the athlete runs 30 meters. Two trials are performed and the fastest time is used in the calculations. Result to be in seconds.

Stride Frequency (Females)

From a standing start the athlete runs 60 meters. The time is recorded for athlete to compete 30 meters and 60 meters. The number of strides taken from 30 meters to 60 meters is recorded. The number of strides is divided by the time for the last 30 meters (60 meters time - 30 meters time) to give stride frequency. Result to be strides/second.

Stride Length (Females)

From a standing start the athlete runs 60 meters. The number of strides taken from 30 meters to 60 meters is recorded. The number of strides is divided by 30 to give stride length. Result to be in meters.

Weight (Females)

Wearing running clothes, not shoes, measure the athlete's weight. Result to be in pounds. Enter the test results and then calculate.

Vertical Jump	meters
Standing Long Jump	meters
Five Bounds	meters
Standing 30 meters	seconds
Total	points
90 % confidence level	to points

Analysis

The IAAF Scoring Tables for Combined Events are used to estimate performance in a selected event. On the appropriate male event table locate the number of points and read off the distance or time. The 90 % confidence levels for each event are detailed below.

Males

100 meters	to seconds	High Jump	to meters
200 meters	to seconds	Pole Vault	to meters
400 meters	to seconds	Long Jump	to meters
1500 meters	to seconds	Shot	to meters
110 meters Hurdles	to seconds	Discus	to meters
		Javelin	to meters

Females

Enter the event results and then calculate.

Weight	pounds (lbs)
Standing Long Jump	meters
Stride Length	meters
Stride Frequency	strides/second
	points
90 % confidence level	to points

Analysis

The IAAF Scoring Tables for Combined Events are used to estimate performance in a selected event. On the appropriate female event table locate the number of points and read off the distance or time. The 90 % confidence levels for each event are detailed below.

100 meters	to seconds	High Jump	to meters
200 meters	to seconds	Pole Vault	to meters
400 meters	to seconds	Long Jump	to meters
800 meters	to seconds	Shot	to meters
1500 meters Hurdles	to seconds	Discus	to meters
		Javelin	to meters

♦♦♦♦♦♦♦♦

SECTION – I

Part IV

BODY COMPOSITION ASSESSMENT

Body composition refers primarily to the distribution of muscle and fat in the body, and its measurement plays an important role in both sports and health. In sports, excess fat hinders performance as it does not contribute to muscular force production, and it is additional weight that requires energy to move about.

Body fat and the calculation of its amount in the human body has become one of the most widely used measurements. There is a number of different techniques, such as dual-energy x-ray absorptiometry, isotope dilution, and air displacement plethysmography, performed in order to study and monitor body reactions to certain changes. These techniques are often used for research work, but generally are too expensive, time consuming, and impractical for use in field evaluations, gym environments and healthcare settings. A number of field techniques solve the problems and have the added benefits of being portable, are relatively simplistic to use and are noninvasive. They do, however, have limitations of lower accuracy and validity. Field methods such as skinfold tests, bioelectrical impedance analysis, circumference measures, and near infra-red interactance are all doubly indirect, and are based upon regression models devised by comparing measure to criterion measurements.

There are a number of ways to assess body composition. These procedures differ in the time, expense, and expertise required and in accuracy of the results they provide. All of these procedures are subject to some error and can only provide an estimate of the actual percent body fat. Errors in body composition estimates can result from either the actual measurement procedures, from the equations selected to calculate percent body fat, or from both.

What is Percent Body Fat?

Percent body fat is the percentage of the total body that is fat. Thus someone who weighs 150 pounds and is 10 % fat has 15 pounds of fatty tissue and 135 pounds of other, so called lean tissue.

How does Exercise Affect Body Fat?

An increase in regular exercise will help to increase calorie expenditure. The more physical activity one does the more calories one will burn.

Body composition is often represented as a two compartment system; lean body weight and fat weight. The fat weight is then expressed as a percentage of total body weight, where percent body fat = (fat weight / total body weight) X 100. The table below gives general guidelines for body fat percentage levels.

Guidelines for Body Fat Level

Categories	General population		Athletes	
	Males	Females	Males	Females
Lean	< 12	< 17	< 7	< 12
Acceptable	12 - 21	17 - 28	7 - 15	12 - 25
Moderately Overweight	21 - 26	28 - 33	-	-
Overweight	> 26	> 33	> 15	> 25

Sourcr: www.sport-fitness-advisor.com/calculatebodyfat.html

How To Calculate Body Fat... The Best and Worst Techniques

What is **the single, most effective** way to calculate body fat? That's a tough one. Accuracy? Reliability? Cost? Availability? They are **all** important factors to think about. Fortunately there are quite a few techniques to choose from.

BODY COMPOSITION TESTS

- Anthropometric Tests (Body Size and Body Circumferences)
- Skinfold Measurement
- Hydrostatic Weighing(Hydro densitometry or underwater weighing)
- Bioelectric Impedance
- Dual-Energy X-Ray Absorptiometry (DEXA)
- Near Infrared Interactance
- Total Body Potassium (TBK)
- Whole-body Air-Displacement Plethysmography (BodPod)
- Magnetic Resonance Imaging (MRI)
- Total Body Electrical Conductivity (TOBEC)
- Computed Tomography (CT)
- Total Body Protein (TBP)

♦♦♦♦♦♦♦

18

ANTHROPOMETRIC TESTS

Besides body composition, tests of anthropometry include measurements of body size and structure. For most sports body size is important, whether it is advantageous to be short, tall, heavy or light. A measure which uses both body composition and body size is somatotype.

Measuring Somatotype

Somatotyping is a system of classifying body types in terms of three categories: endomorphy, mesomorphy and ectomorphy. In each category someone can be classified on a scale from 1 to 7, though you cannot score highly on all three. The three numbers together give a somatotype number, with the endomorphy score first, then mesomorphy and finally ectomorphy. The scores may also be plotted in a shield diagram, representing the somatotype on a two dimensional scale.

Endomorphy

An endomorphic person would be stocky, with a large round body, a short thick neck, short arms and legs, and with a tendency to store body fat. Sports people tend not to be in this category, being either more mesomorphic or ectomorphic. Generally, endomorphs rate poorly on physical fitness tests and so make poor athletes.

Mesomorphy

A mesomorphic person would be strongly built, with a broad muscular chest and shoulders, very muscular arms and legs, and little body fat. An example of a mesomorphic person in the sporting world would be a typical weightlifter or shot putter. In general, mesomorphs rank high on strength, endurance, power and agility.

Ectomorphy

An ectomorphic person would be tall and thin, with a narrow body, thin arms and legs, little body fat and wiry muscles. An example of an ectomorphic person in the sporting world would be a typical long distance runner or basketball player. In general, ectomorphs rank high on endurance, flexibility and agility.

Body Size can be determined by measuring standing height, body mass/weight, sitting height, arm length, hand span, arm span, shoulder width and body girths/circumferences.

STANDING HEIGHT

Description/Procedure: Measure the maximum distance from the floor to the highest point on the head, when the subject is facing directly ahead. Shoes should be off, feet together, and arms by the sides. Heels, buttocks and upper back should also be in contact with the wall.

Equipment Required: Stadiometer or steel ruler placed against a wall

Reliability: Height measurement can vary throughout the day, being higher in the morning, so it should be measured at the same time of day each time.

Advantages: Low costs, quick test

Other Comments: Height or lack of height is an important attribute for many sports.

Note: Figure is presented in Section II.

BODY MASS / WEIGHT

The most accurate assessment of your ideal weight takes into account the composition of your body - how much of your weight is lean body mass (muscle and bone) and how much is body fat. For optimum health, body fat should be no more than 20 % of total body weight for men and 30 % for women.

Purpose: Measuring body mass can be valuable for monitoring body fat or muscle mass changes, or for monitoring hydration level.

Equipment Required: Scales, which should be calibrated for accuracy using weights authenticated by a government department of weights and measures.

Description/Procedure: The person stands with minimal movement with hands by their side. Shoes and excess clothing should be removed.

Reliability: To improve reliability, weigh routinely in the morning (12 hours since eating). Body weight can be affected by fluid in the bladder (weigh after voiding the bladder). Other factors to consider are the amount of food recently eaten, hydration level, the amount of waste recently expelled from the body, recent exercise and clothing. If you are monitoring changes in body mass, try and weigh at the same time of day, under the same conditions, and preferably with no clothes on. Always compare using the same set of scales.

Advantages: Quick and easy measurement when testing large groups, with minimal costs.

Other Comments: Measuring weight can be used as a measure of changes in body fat, but as it does not take into account changes in lean body mass it is better to use other methods of body composition measurement.

Note: Figure is presented in Section II.

Weight for Height and Age for Males and Females

Age (years)	Boys		Girls	
	Height (cm)	Weight (kg)	Height (cm)	Weight (kg)
0	50.5	3.3	49.9	3.2
¼ (3 months)	61.1	6.0	60.2	5.4
½ (6 months)	67.8	7.8	66.6	7.2
¾ (9 months)	72.3	9.2	71.1	8.6
1.0	76.1	10.2	75.0	9.5
1.5	82.4	11.5	80.9	10.8
2.0	85.6	12.3	84.5	11.8
3.0	94.9	14.6	93.9	14.1
4.0	102.9	16.7	101.6	16.0
5.0	109.9	18.7	108.4	17.7
6.0	116.1	20.7	114.6	19.5
7.0	121.7	22.9	120.6	21.8
8.0	127.0	25.3	126.4	24.8
9.0	132.2	28.1	132.2	28.5
10.0	137.5	31.4	138.3	32.5
11+	140.0	32.2	142.0	33.7
12+	147.0	37.0	148.0	38.7
13+	153.0	40.9	155.0	44.0
14+	160.0	47.0	159.0	48.0
15+	166.0	52.6	161.0	51.4
16+	171.0	58.0	162.0	53.0
17+	175.0	62.7	163.0	54.0
18+	177.0	65.0	164.0	54.4

Source: NCHS

Estimates of Ideal Body Weight in Adults

The ideal body weight for an individual can be estimated from the person's height and gender.

Equations of Devine and McCarron

According to Robinson et al, these equations were proposed by Devine based on the empirical estimates of his mentor Dr Margaret McCarron.

Ideal Body Weight in kilograms for Males

= 50 + (2.3 X ((height in inches) - 60))

Ideal Body Weight in kilograms for Females

= 45.5 + (2.3 X ((height in inches) - 60))

Where:

• "60" indicates inches in 5 feet.

• Handling of patients with height under 5 feet is unclear.

• According to Robinson et al., these equations underestimate the slope and overestimate the intercept in the approximation line. These cancel each other out for people of average height but may introduce errors for those who are tall or short.

Equations of Robinson et al.

Ideal Body Weight in kilograms for Males

= 51.65 + (1.85 X ((height in inches) - 60))

Ideal Body Weight in kilograms for Females

= 48.67 + (1.65 X ((height in inches) - 60))

Where,

• "60" indicates inches in 5 feet.

• Handling of patients with height under 5 feet is unclear. Robinson indicates that the equation for women is valid to at least 4 feet 10 inches.

Hamwi Method

For a medium sized adult:

Ideal Body Weight for Males in pounds

= 106 + (6 X ((height in inches) - 60))

Ideal Body Weight for Females in pounds

= 100 + (5 X ((height in inches) - 60))

If the body frame is light, then the calculated weight should be reduced by 10 %.

If the frame is heavy, then the calculated weight should be increased by 10 %.

BODY MASS INDEX (BMI)

BMI stands for Body Mass Index. It is a simple measure of body composition.

BMI = Body mass in kilograms ÷ (Height x Height in meters) (Divide weight in lbs by 2.2046 to get weight in kg's)

So as an example a **150 lb** (68 kg) woman who is **165 cm** (1.65 m) tall...

BMI = 68 ÷ (1.65 x 1.65)
= 68 ÷ 2.7
= 25 kg/m2

This person has a Body Mass Index of **25**. What exactly does this mean?

The higher the figure the more overweight you are.

Assessment of BMI Score

Body Mass Index Classifications		
Classification	**Risk**	**BMI Score (kg/m^2)**
Underweight	Moderate	Less than 18.5
Normal	Very low	18.5 - 24.9
Overweight	Low	25.0 - 29.9
Obese Class 1	Moderate	30.0 - 34.9
Obese class 2	High	35.0 - 39.9
Extrcmc obcsity	Vcry high	Greater than 40.0

Like any of these types of measures it is only an indication and other issues such as body type and shape have a bearing as well. Remember, BMI is just a guide - it does not accurately apply to elderly populations, pregnant women or very muscular athletes such as weightlifters.

BMI will be **inaccurate** for many athletes. BMI doesn't calculate body fat so it can't make allowances for muscular development. Athletes such as bodybuilders, football players, throwing athletes and anyone on a weight training program should **avoid** using BMI as a way to calculate body fat.

Growing children and very elderly, sedentary adults should also avoid using BMI as a way to calculate body fat.

Along with height-weight tables, BMI has serious limitations. Neither can be used to calculate body fat.

A BMI of between 20 and 25 is considered to be an ideal. One can use the table given in *Appendix II* to determine the acceptable weight range for the height (in cm), by finding the weight corresponding to a BMI level of 20, 25 and 30 kg/m^2.

A BMI of between 20 and 25 is considered to be an ideal, which corresponds to the green band on the graph below. You can use this table to determine your rating by determining where the lines from your current height and weight intersect.

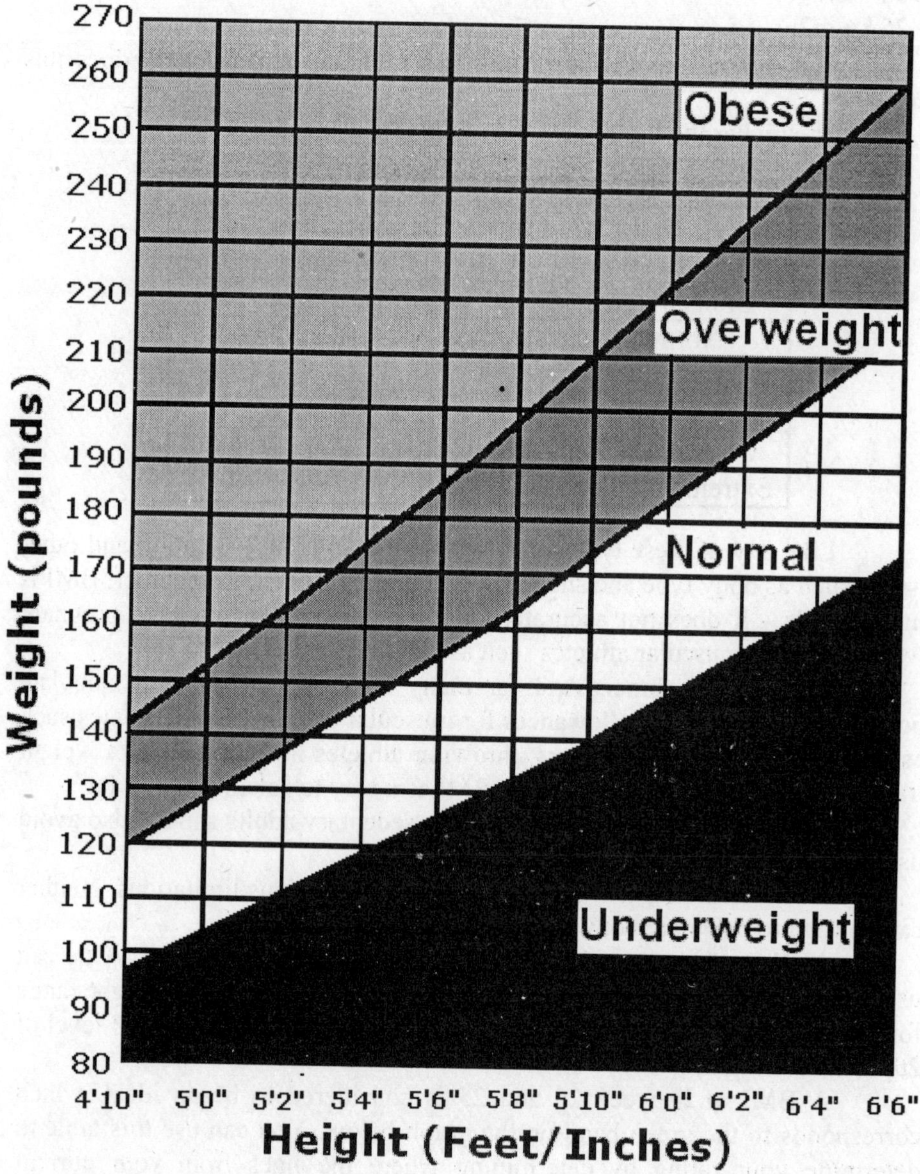

Source: www.topendsports.com

SITTING HEIGHT

Description/Procedure: Sitting height gives a measure of the length of the trunk. It is a measurement of the distance from the highest point on the head to the base sitting surface. The subject sits with both feet on the floor, the lower back and shoulders against the wall, looking straight ahead. Distance can be measured from the floor, and the height of the box measured and subtracted from the total distance.

Equipment Required: Stadiometer or ruler placed against a wall, box or chair.

Reliability: Height measurement can vary throughout the day, being higher in the morning, so should be measured at a consistent time of day.

Advantages: Low costs, quick test

Other Comments: Upper body length or proportionally long legs is an important attribute for many sports.

ARM LENGTH

Purpose: Long arms are advantageous for some sports which involve reaching and tackling.

Equipment Required: Ruler or tape measure

Description/Procedure: A measurement is made from the point of the shoulder to the tip of the little finger.

Advantages: Very low cost, simple and quick test

Other Comments: It is important for the subject to fully stretch out the fingers to get the maximum length (www.astm.org/Standards/D6829.htm).

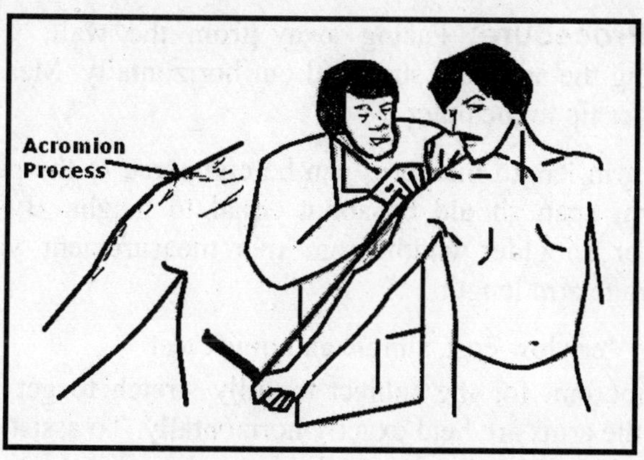

HAND SPAN

Purpose: The size of the hand is advantageous for some sports which involve catching, gripping or tackling.

Equipment Required: Flat surface and ruler or tape measure

Description/Procedure: The hand is placed palm down on a flat surface. The fingers are outstretched as far as possible. Measure the linear distance between the outside of the thumb to the outside of the little finger.

Advantages: Very low cost, simple and quick test

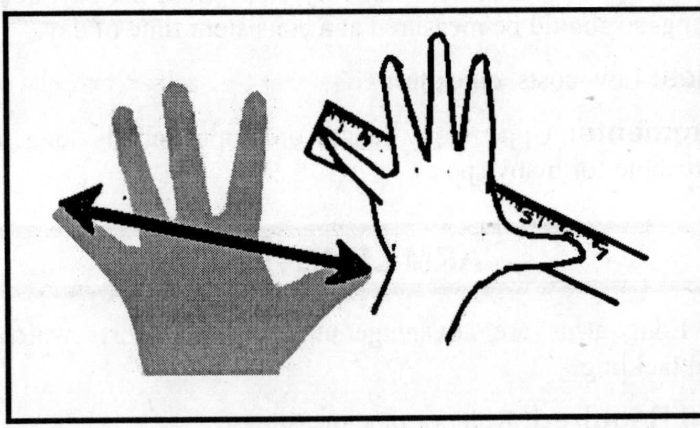

ARM SPAN

Purpose: Long arms are advantageous for some sports which involve reaching and tackling.

Equipment Required: Ruler or tape measure, wall.

Description/Procedure: Facing away from the wall, with back and buttocks touching the arms are stretched out horizontally. Measure from one furthermost finger tip to the other.

Results: The arm length measures can be compared to the person's height. On average, arm span should be about equal to height. By subtracting a measurement for shoulder width from this measurement you can get a measure of average arm length.

Advantages: Very low cost, simple and quick test

It is important for the subject to fully stretch to get the maximum reach, and that the arms are held exactly horizontally. To assist in keeping the outstretched arms horizontal, use a wall that has horizontal lines already on it such as a brick wall. Also measure out from a corner or wall protrusion so that one hand can be stable and all measurements are away from it.

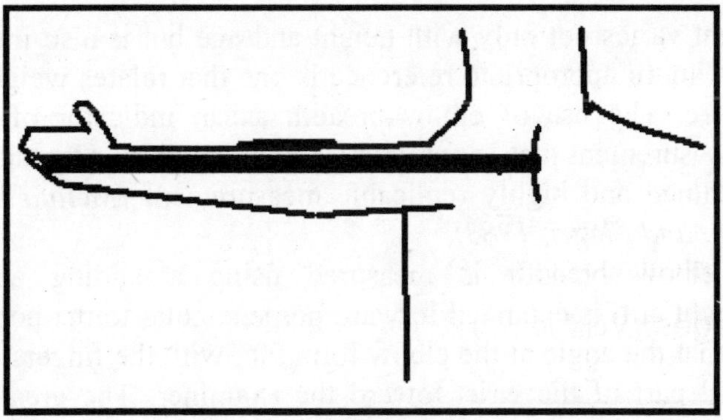

SHOULDER WIDTH

Purpose: Shoulder width can be used as a measure of development.

Equipment Required: Ruler or tape measure

Description/Procedure: The measurement is taken as the distance between the two bones at the ends of the shoulders.

Advantages: Very low cost, simple and quick test.

Disadvantages: This measure can be difficult to do accurately. It is important to measure only to the point of the bony structure, not to the extent of the muscle bulk.

By taking this score away from a measure of arm span, the average arm length can be determined.

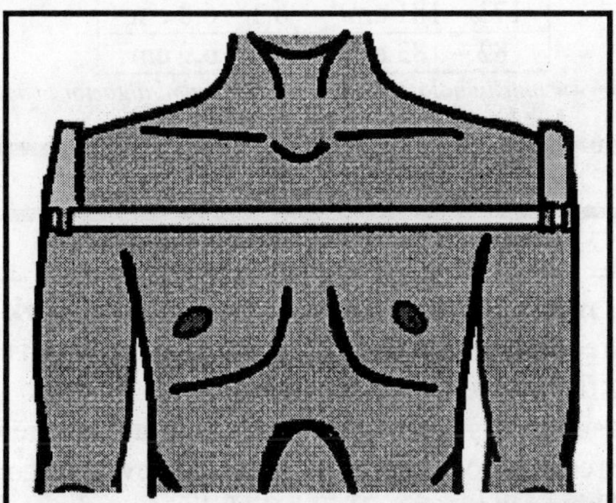

ELBOW BREADTH

Weight varies not only with height and age but is also influenced by body build. A more appropriate reference is one that relates weight to height and frame size. The use of elbow breadth as an indicator of frame size provides a measurement that is not drastically affected by adiposity. It is also an easily obtained and highly replicable measurement *(Melina et al., 1973 and Frisancho and Flegel, 1983).*

The elbow breadth is measured using a sliding caliper. The examinee's right arm is extended forward perpendicular to the body, with the arm bend so that the angle at the elbow form 90°, with the fingers pointing up and the dorsal part of the wrist toward the examiner. The greatest breadth across the elbow joint is measured.

Note: Figure is presented in Section II.

Normal Elbow Breadth for Men and Women

Men	
Height	**Ellbow Breadth**
158 - 161 cm	6.4 – 7.2 cm
162 – 171 cm	6.7 – 7.4 cm
172 – 181 cm	6.9 – 7.6 cm
182 – 191 cm	7.1 – 7.8 cm
192 – 193 cm	7.4 – 8.1 cm
Women	
Height	**Ellbow Breadth**
148 – 151 cm	5.6 – 6.4 cm
152 – 161 cm	5.8 – 6.5 cm
162 – 171 cm	5.9 – 6.6 cm
171 – 181 cm	6.1 – 6.8 cm
182 – 183 cm	6.2 – 6.9 cm

Adapted from:www.nutritionalassessment.english.azm.nl/algoritme+na/onderzoek/

BODY GIRTHS

Girths are circumference measures at standard anatomical sites around the body, measured with a tape measure. First mark the sites to be measured. When recording, you need to make sure the tape is not too tight or too loose, is lying flat on the skin, and is horizontal.

Girth measurements are sometimes used as a measure of body fat, but is not a valid predictor of this. They are however a good measure of proportionality. Things that may affect reliability are changes to the testers, constant and even tension on the tape, and correct landmarking (finding the correct anatomical sites for measurement). Low costs involved in the testing procedure, and for many sites the measurement can be self administered. Girth measurements combined with skinfold measurements can give a clearer picture of changes in muscle and fat compositions and distribution. A common girth measure is the waist measure, used in determining waist to hip ratio (WHR).

Equipment Required: Flexible metal tape measure and pen suitable for marking the skin. If a plastic or cloth tape is used, it should be checked regularly against a metal tape as they may stretch over time.

Reliability: Factors that may affect reliability include changes to the testing personnel, constant and even tension on the tape, and correct landmarking (finding the correct anatomical site for measurement).

Advantages: Low costs involved in the testing procedure, and ease of self testing

Comments: Girth measurements combined with skinfold measurements can give a clearer picture of changes in tissue composition and distribution of muscle and fat

Clothing over the site should be removed if possible to make sure measuring tape is positioned correctly and that the correct circumference is determined

Below are some common sites used for girth measurements.

HEAD GIRTH

Purpose: To measure the circumference of the head, as one of the many measurements of body size.

Description/Procedure: The subject may stand or sit for this measurement. The head circumference measurement is taken at the level immediately above the brow. When recording, you need to make sure the tape compresses the hair and is kept horizontal. Also make sure there are no ties or clips in the hair, and that the ears are not included.

Note: Figure is presented in Section II.

NECK GIRTH

Purpose: To measure the circumference of the neck, as one of the many measurements of body size.

Description/Procedure: The neck measurement is taken immediately above the thyroid cartilage (the Adam's Apple). The subject should keep their head up and looking straight ahead. When recording, you need to make sure the tape is not too tight or too loose, is lying flat on the skin.

Note: Figure is presented in Section II.

ARM RELAXED GIRTH

Purpose: To measure the circumference of the arm, as a measure of the underlying musculature and adipose tissue. Girth measurements combined with skinfold measurements can give a clearer picture of changes in tissue composition and distribution of muscle and fat.

Description/Procedure: First mark the site to be measured. This girth measurement is usually taken on the right side of the body. The arm is relaxed and hanging by the side, and the circumference is taken at the level of the mid-point between the acromial (boney point of shoulder) and the olecranon (boney point of elbow) processes. When recording, you need to make sure the tape is not too tight or too loose, is lying flat on the skin, and is horizontal.

Note: Figure is presented in Section II.

ARM FLEXED GIRTH

Purpose: To measure the circumference of the arm, as a measure of the underlying musculature and adipose tissue. Girth measurements combined with skinfold measurements can give a clearer picture of changes in tissue composition and distribution of muscle and fat.

Description/Procedure: This girth measurement is usually taken on the right side of the body. The arm is raised to a horizontal position in the sagittal (forward) plane, with the elbow at about 45 degrees. The subject maximally contracts the biceps muscle, and the largest circumference is measured. When recording, you need to make sure the tape is not too tight or too loose, is lying flat on the skin, and is kept vertical. The maximal girth is not always obvious, and the tape may need to be moved along to find the point of maximum circumference.

Note: Figure is presented in Section II.

FOREARM GIRTH

Purpose: To measure the circumference of the forearm, as a measure of the underlying musculature and adipose tissue. Girth measurements combined with skinfold measurements can give a clearer picture of changes in tissue composition and distribution of muscle and fat.

Description/Procedure: This girth measurement is usually taken on the right side of the body. The subject holds the arm out with the palm facing upwards. The measurement is taken along the forearm at the point of the largest circumference. The maximal girth is not always obvious, and the tape may need to be moved up and down along the forearm to find the point of maximum circumference, which will usually be found closer to the elbow. When recording, you need to make sure the tape is not too tight or too loose and is lying flat on the skin.

Note: Figure is presented in Section II.

WRIST GIRTH

Purpose: To measure the circumference of the wrist, as one of the many measurements of body size.

Description/Procedure: This girth measurement is usually taken on the right arm, at a point just distal (away from the body) to the styloid processes. This is usually the minimum circumference in this region, though the tape should be moved around to make sure you have recorded the minimum girth measurement. When recording, you need to make sure the tape is not too tight or too loose, and is lying flat on the skin.

Note: Figure is presented in Section II.

CHEST GIRTH

Purpose: To measure the circumference of the chest, as a measure of the chest muscles and lung size.

Description/Procedure: This measure is taken at the level of the middle of the sternum (breast-bone), with the tape passing under the arms. After the tape is in position, the arms should be relaxed by the side, and the measurement taken at the end of a normal expiration. When recording, you need to make sure the tape is not too tight or too loose, is lying flat on the skin, and is horizontal, particularly around the back.

Note: Figure is presented in Section II.

WAIST / ABDOMINAL GIRTH

Purpose: The purpose of determining waist girth is to gain a measure of the amount of abdominal fat (visceral fat), which has been linked to increased risk of coronary heart disease and diabetes.

Description/Procedure: The waist measurement is taken at the narrowest waist level, or if this is not apparent, at the mid point between the lowest rib and the top of the hip bone (iliac crest). When recording, you need to make sure the tape is not too tight or too loose, is lying flat on the skin, and is horizontal.

Note: Figure is presented in Section II.

The health risk may not be accurate in those individuals with thick waist musculature or those that are particularly tall or short. For women who deposit fat primarily lower on the body (hips, buttocks, and thighs), waist measurements in isolation are have a poor relationship with health factors *Pouliot et al. (1995).*

Factors that may affect reliability include changes to the testing personnel, constant and even tension on the tape, and correct landmarking (finding the correct anatomical site for measurement).

Scoring for Waist Girth

Risk	Men		Women	
	cm	Inches	cm	Inches
Very High	> 120	> 47	> 110	> 43.5
High	100 - 120	39.5 - 47	90 - 109	35.5 - 43
Low	80 - 99	31.5 - 39	70 - 89	28.5 - 35
Very Low	<80	< 31.5	< 70	< 28.5

Source: ACSM (2005)

HIP GIRTH

Purpose: To measure the circumference of the hip area, as a measure of the underlying hip structure, musculature and adipose tissue. When combined with the measure of abdominal girth in the Waist-Hip Ratio (WHR), has been shown to be related to the risk of coronary heart disease

Description/Procedure: The hip girth measurement is taken over minimal clothing, at the level of the greatest protrusion of the gluteal (buttock) muscles. The subject stands erect with their weight evenly distributed on both feet and legs slightly parted, making sure not tense the gluteal muscles. When recording, you need to make sure the tape is not too tight or too loose, is lying flat and is horizontal. It may help to have the subject stand on a box to make the measurement easier.

Note: Figure is presented in Section II.

WAIST TO HIP RATIO

Purpose: The purpose of this test to determine the ratio of waist circumference to the hip circumference, as this has been shown to be related to the risk of coronary heart disease.

It is a simple calculation of the measurements of the waist girth divided by the hip girth.

Waist to Hip Ratio (WHR) = Gw / Gh,

Where, Gw = waist girth, Gh = hip girth

Scoring: The table below gives general guidelines for acceptable levels for hip to waist ratio. You can use any units for the measurements (e.g. cm or inches), as it is only the ratio that is important.

Scoring for Waist Hip Ratio

Gender	Acceptable		Unacceptable		
	Excellent	Good	Average	High	Extreme
Male	< 0.85	0.85 - 0.90	0.90 - 0.95	0.95 - 1.00	> 1.00
Female	< 0.75	0.75 - 0.80	0.80 - 0.85	0.85 - 0.90	> 0.90

UPPER / GLUTEAL THIGH GIRTH

Purpose: To measure the circumference of the upper thigh, as a measure of the underlying musculature and adipose tissue. Girth measurements combined with skinfold measurements can give a clearer picture of changes in tissue composition and distribution of muscle and fat.

Description/Procedure: This girth measurement is usually taken on the right side of the body. The subject stands erect with their weight evenly distributed on both feet and legs slightly parted. The circumference measure is taken 1 cm below the gluteal line or fold (buttock crease) with the tape held horizontal. When recording, you need to make sure the tape is not too tight or too loose, and is lying flat on the skin.

Note: Figure is presented in Section II.

For this girth measurement, due to the location of the measure, care should be taken to maintain personal privacy of the subject, and sometimes it is appropriate to measure over clothing. If so, this should be recorded with the results. It may help to have the subject stand on a box to make the measurement easier.

CALF GIRTH

Purpose: To measure the circumference of the calf, as a measure of the underlying musculature and adipose tissue. Girth measurements combined with skinfold measurements can give a clearer picture of changes in tissue composition and distribution of muscle and fat.

Description/Procedure: This girth measurement is usually taken on the right side of the body. The subject stands erect with their weight evenly distributed on both feet and legs slightly apart. The measurement is taken at the level of the largest circumference of the calf. The maximal girth is not always obvious, and the tape may need to be moved up and down to find the point of maximum circumference. When recording, you need to make sure the tape is not too tight or too loose, is lying flat on the skin, and is horizontal. It may help to have the subject stand on a box to make the measurement easier.

Note: Figure is presented in Section II.

ANKLE GIRTH

Purpose: To measure the circumference of the ankle, as one of the many measurements of body size.

Description/Procedure: This girth measurement is usually taken on the right side of the body, at the level of the narrowest point of the ankle. The minimal girth point is not always obvious, and the tape may need to be moved up and down to find the point of least circumference. When recording, you need to make sure the tape is not too tight or too loose, is lying flat on the skin, and is horizontal. It may help to have the subject stand on a box to make the measurement easier.

Note: Figure is presented in Section II.

♦♦♦♦♦♦♦

19

ARM AND FAT DISTRIBUTION

It is assumed that there is an equal distribution of fat around the arm and that there is a constant amount of bone compared to the muscle area.

Upper arm fat mass (F), also measured by upper arm circumference measured together with the triceps skinfold (T), provides a better determination of the total body fat mass than a single skinfold measurement. The thickness of the triceps skinfold and the area of the upper arm diminish if the person has malnutrition. Repeated measurements can give an indication about changes in body composition and nutritional state of the person.

Frisancho (1981) has published some tables with percentiles, which can be used to compare the measured values with the values of a general population. As a person can be compared to the low percentiles, than he or she belongs to the skinny people.

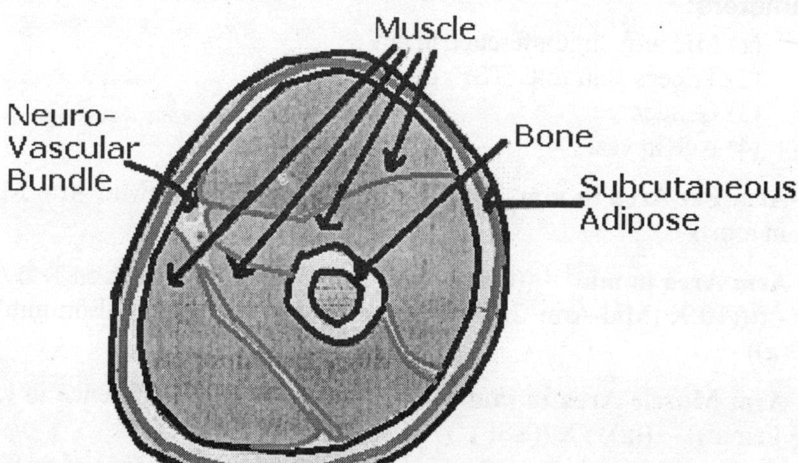

Fat and Muscle in the Arm Area

One of the ways to measure body fat percentage is with anthropometric measurements. Measurements are taken with a measuring tape at sites where fat is usually distributed, such as the waist and thigh. Specific equations are used to calculate the body fat percentage. These measurements are less costly and easier to do than the use of skin fold calipers.

Circumferences can be used as indicators for the quantity of fat and muscle mass in the body. The upper arm muscle circumference is a measure for muscle mass in the body measured together with the triceps skinfold. In this method the assumption is that the measured muscle circumference is representative for the rest of the body.

Following are the equations for prediction of mid arm fat area, mid arm area, mid arm muscle area, upper arm muscle circumference and area and ratio of the upper and lower body segments and trunk frame size and index.

EQUATIONS FOR PREDICTION OF ARM FAT AREA, ARM MUSCLE CIRCUMFERENCE AND BODY FRAME SIZE

Predicting Mid-Arm Fat Area Using the Equations of Frisancho

Parameters:

(1) Mid arm circumference in cm
(2) Triceps skin fold (TSF) in mm
(3) Gender
(4) Age in years

Mid-Arm Fat Area in mm^2 = (Mid Arm Area in mm^2) - (Mid Arm Muscle Area in mm^2)

Mid Arm Area in mm^2 = (((10 X (Mid-Arm Circumference in cm)) ^{2}) / (4 X (π))) - ((((10 X (Mid-Arm Circumference in cm)) - ((π) X (TSF in mm)) ^{2}) / (4 X (π))

Mid Arm Muscle Area in mm^2 = (5 X (Mid-Arm Circumference in cm) X (TSF in mm)) - (((π)^2) X ((TSF)^2) / (4 X (π)))

Data on percentiles of upper arm fat area, upper arm circumference and triceps skinfold is shown in *Appendix III.*

Predicting Upper Arm Muscle Circumference Using the Equations of McWhirter

c = upper arm circumference in mm; T = triceps skinfold in mm
p = 3.14

Upper Arm Muscle Circumference in mm = c - (T X 3.14)

Upper Arm Area in mm² = c^2 / 12.56

Upper Arm Muscle Area in mm² = (Upper arm muscle circumference in mm) ^{2} / 12.56

Upper Arm Fat Area in mm² = Upper Arm Area - Upper Arm Muscle Area

Arm Muscle Area in cm² for men = ((((midarm circumference in cm) - (π X (triceps skin fold thickness in cm))) ^{2}) / (4 X π)) - 10

Arm Muscle Area in cm² for women = ((((midarm circumference in cm) - (π X (triceps skin fold thickness in cm))) ^{2}) / (4 X π)) - 6.5

Total Body Muscle Mass (in kilograms) = (height in centimeters) X (0.0264 + (0.0029 X (corrected arm muscle area in cm^2)))

Notations: The triceps skin fold thickness is typically measured in millimeters. It is converted to centimeters for these equations.

Data on percentiles of upper arm muscle area is shown in *Appendix III.*

Predicting Body Frame Size Using Equations

In order to refine and define theoretical weights, researchers added frame size as a factor. The sizes are categorized into three categories, small frame, medium frame and large frame. The reason for this is that obviously bone structures vary in size and density from person to person. Equally obviously men and women have different structures. Bone mass and muscle mass all play a part in determining your optimal weight. There are two simple methods of determining frame size:-

- Measuring the circumference of your wrist. This is by far the most straight forward.
- Measuring the breadth of your elbow. This is a little more complex but provides a greater results range for the purposes of accuracy. Compare the value with the tables below.

Wrist Measurement in Females

Female Wrist Measurements			
Body Frame	Height less than 5' 2" (Less than 155 cm)	Height 5' 2" - 5' 5" (155 cm-163 cm)	Height more than 5' 5" (More than 163 cm)
Small	Less than 5.5" (140mm)	Less than 6.0" (152mm)	Less than 6.25" (159mm)
Medium	5.5" - 5.75" (140-146 mm)	6"-6.25" (152-159 mm)	6.25"-6.5" (159-165 mm)
Large	More than 5.75" (146 mm)	More than 6.25" (159 mm)	More than 6.5" (165 mm)

(Source: *www.am-i-fat.com/body_frame_size.html* and *www.medindia.net/patients/calculators/framesize1.asp*)

Elbow Measurement in Females

Female Elbow Measurements Medium Frame			
(If your elbow breadth is less than those in the table for a specific height, you are small framed. Similarly, if your elbow breadth is bigger than those in the table, you are large framed)			
Height Feet and Inches	Elbow Breadth Inches	Height cm	Elbow Breadth mm
4' 10" - 4' 11"	21/4" - 21/2"	146 - 148	57 - 64
5' 0" - 5' 3"	21/4" - 21/2"	150 - 158	57 - 64
5' 4" - 5' 7"	23/8" - 25/8"	160 - 168	60 - 67
5' 8" - 5' 11"	23/8" - 25/8"	170 - 178	60 - 67
6' 0" - 6' 4"	21/2" - 23/4"	180 - 190	63 - 70

(Source: *www.am-i-fat.com/body_frame_size.html* and *www.medindia.net/patients/calculators/framesize1.asp*)

Wrist Measurement in Males

Male Wrist Measurements	
Body Frame	Height more than 5' 5" (More than 163cms)
Small	5.5" - 6.5" (140 – 165 mm)
Medium	6.5" - 7.5" (165 - 191mm)
Large	More than 7.5" (191 mm)

(Source: *www.am-i-fat.com/body_frame_size.html* and *www.medindia.net/patients/calculators/framesize1.asp*)

Elbow Measurement in Females

Male Elbow Measurements Medium Frame			
Height Feet and Inches	Elbow Breadth Inches	Height cm	Elbow Breadth mm
5' 2" - 5' 3"	21/2" - 27/8"	155 - 158	64 - 73
5' 4" - 5' 7"	25/8" - 27/8"	160 - 168	67 - 73
5' 8" - 5' 11"	23/4" - 3"	170 - 178	70 - 75
6' 0" - 6' 3"	23/4" - 31/8"	180 - 188	70 - 79
6' 4" - 6' 7"	27/8" - 31/4"	190 - 198	73 - 83

(Source: *www.am-i-fat.com/body_frame_size.html* and *www.medindia.net/patients/calculators/framesize1.asp*)

Frame size can be calculated using following formula:

$$\textbf{Frame Size (r)} = \frac{\text{Height (cm)}}{\text{Wrist Circumference (cm)}}$$

Frame Size can be determined as follows:

Body Frame Size Guide

Males	Females
r >10.4 small	r >11.0 small
r = 9.6 – 10.4 medium	r = 10.1 – 11.0 medium
r < 9.6 large	r < 10.1 large

(Source: Anderson et al., 1982)

Body frame size can be determined by a person's wrist circumference in relation to his/her height. For example, a man whose height is over 5' 5" and wrist is 6" would fall into the small-boned category.

Determining Frame Size: To determine the body frame size, measure the wrist with a tape measure and use the following chart to determine whether the person is small, medium, or large boned.

Women:

- Height under 5' 2"
  - Small = wrist size less than 5.5"
  - Medium = wrist size 5.5" to 5.75"
  - Large = wrist size over 5.75"
- Height 5' 2" to 5' 5"
  - Small = wrist size less than 6"
  - Medium = wrist size 6" to 6.25"
  - Large = wrist size over 6.25"
- Height over 5' 5"
  - Small = wrist size less than 6.25"
  - Medium = wrist size 6.25" to 6.5"
  - Large = wrist size over 6.5"

Men:

- Height over 5' 5"
  - Small = wrist size 5.5" to 6.5"
  - Medium = wrist size 6.5" to 7.5"
  - Large = wrist size over 7.5"

(Source: *www.nlm.nih.gov/medlineplus/ency/imagepages/17182.htm*)

Predicting Ratio of the Upper and Lower Body Segments Using the Equations of Hall et al.

The ratio of the upper and lower body segments can be used to describe a person's bodily proportions. The subject should stand perfectly straight with eyes forward. Bending forward can lower the ratio.

Segment	Definition
Upper	From top of head to the midportion of the pubic bone
Lower	From the midportion of the pubic bone to the sole of the foot

Total Body Height = (Length of the Upper Body Segment) + (Length of the Lower Body Segment)

Ratio of the Upper to Lower Body Segment = (Length of the Upper Body Segment) / (Length of the Lower Body Segment)

Interpretation:

The ratio is approximately 1.0 at age 10. It is usually > 1 in children and < 1 in adolescents and adults.

Adult males tend to have longer legs than women, so the ratio in adult males is lower.

Predicting Trunk Frame Size from Sitting Height, Bi-iliac Breadth and Standing Height Using the Equations of Ruff and Jamison

Ruff and Jamison described the trunk frame size as a measure appropriate for comparing people with different body proportions. Trunk frame size may be more appropriate than stature for calculating body mass indices.

Parameters:

(1) Sitting height in cm
(2) Bi-iliac breadth (as a measure of relative body breadth) in cm
(3) Standing height (stature) in cm

Relative Sitting Height = (Sitting Height in cm) / (Stature in cm)

Relative Bi-Iliac Body Breadth = (Bi-iliac Breadth in cm) / (Stature in cm)

Trunk Frame Size in square cm = (Sitting Height in cm) X (Bi-iliac Breadth in cm)

Predicting Trunk Frame Index (TFI) from Sitting Height, Bi-iliac Breadth and Body Weight Using the Equations of Ruff and Jamison

Ruff and Jamison described the Trunk Frame Index (TFI) as a measure appropriate for comparing people with different body proportions. Trunk frame size is more appropriate than stature for calculating body mass indices. The TFI shows less systematic bias than the body mass index (BMI), which tends to overestimate obesity in certain racial groups. It shows a better correlation with skinfold measurements in children than the BMI.

Parameters:

(1) Trunk frame size derived from:
(a) Sitting height in cm
(b) Bi-iliac breadth (as a measure of relative body breadth) in cm
(2) Body weight in kilograms

Trunk Frame Size in square cm = (Sitting Height in cm) X (Bi-iliac Breadth in cm)

Trunk Frame Index = (Body Weight in kg) / Trunk Frame Size in square cm) X 1000

♦♦♦♦♦♦♦♦

20

SKINFOLD MEASUREMENT

Skinfold measurements indirectly measure the thickness of the subcutaneous adipose tissue, and must be taken by a trained individual; at the correct sites. The summation of skinfolds can be used into a prediction equation to calculate body density. The body density value may then be used in the equation to predict body fat. The prediction equations, used to predict body fat need to be population specific, in terms of gender, race, age, and activity level. Skinfold measurement method has been recommended for use on athletes and sports people. This has led to over many specific equations.

Skinfold methods are based upon two basic assumptions; that there is a relationship between total body fat and subcutaneous fat, and that skinfold measurements can accurately measure subcutaneous fat. Skinfold measurement method is susceptible to many sources of error; for example, skinfold sites need to be exactly located, and only the subcutaneous fat measured. The calipers compress the fatty tissue, therefore if sufficient time isn't given before re-measuring then the data will be inaccurate.

Good athletes almost never have a high body fat percentage. And if they do, there is a lot of room for improvement. This is particularly true for middle distance athletes, but top sprinters have a low percentage as well.

VO_2max is an athlete's maximum oxygen uptake ability, and is one of the most important factors in determining distance athletes' aerobic performance. When the racing distance gets longer, the VO_2max usually plays a bigger role. Research has shown that there is a direct correlation between an athlete's body fat percentage and his VO_2max. In other words, the lower his body fat percentage, the better his oxygen uptake.

Skinfold Measurement...The Most Economical Way to Calculate Body Fat

Skinfold thickness is an indicator of musculature and fatness that can be objectively tracked over time. Approximately one half of the body's total fat content is located in the tissues beneath the skin. The procedure for taking the fatfold measurements as well as the precise location of the skinfold sites must be standardized if the results are to be reliable and used for comparative purposes.

There are two ways to use fatfolds:

The **first** is to use individual fatfold score or add the scores from the various measurements and use this value as an indication of the relative degree of fatness among subjects. The sum of fatfolds can be used to reflect changes in fatness before and after a physical conditioning or weight reduction programme.

A **second** way to use fatfold is in conjugation with the mathematical equations that have been developed to predict body density or percent body fat. These equations are often quite useful in ranking or ordering individuals within a group in terms of relative fatness.

While the fatfold technique has been widely used in the fields of physical education, nutrition and sports and medicine, it presents a major drawback in that the person taking the measurements must have considerable expertise with the proper techniques to obtain consistent and accurate fatfold values.

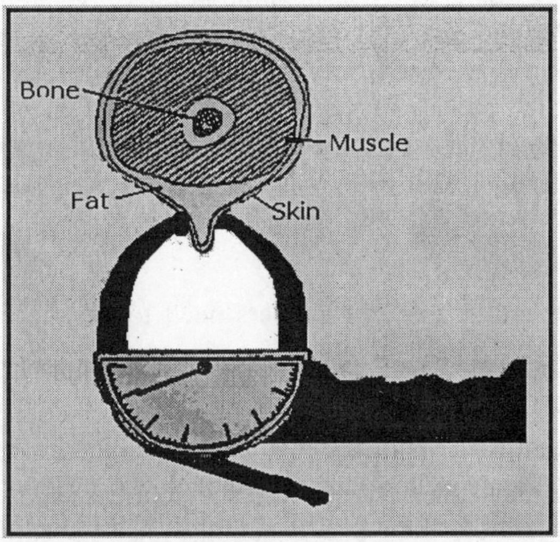

Fatfold Measurement

Advantages of Using Skin Fold Calipers:

- Unlike Height-Weight tables and BMI they actually **calculate body fat percentage**.
- They are very easy to use. The hardest part is finding the **right locations** to pinch.
- They are relatively **inexpensive** and once you have a set they should last a lifetime.
- They can be used to calculate body fat in the **privacy** of your own home.
- They are **portable**. You can test others in the most convenient place for them.
- Used correctly they are an **accurate** and **reliable** way to calculate body fat.
- It can be a quick way to calcualte body fat percentages for a large number of people in a short space of time.

Disadvantages of Using Skin Fold Calipers:

- For accurate results an **experienced examiner** is needed... it really is hard to find the precise locations!
- There are different equations used for different people to calculate body fat percentage from skinfolds. Choosing the **wrong** equation makes a world of difference.
- It is very difficult to test yourself. You may have to ask a friend or family member and this is when skinfold testing becomes unreliable.
- Really cheap calipers won't stay very accurate for long. They aren't as accurate as the more expensive ones to start with.

The major source of error in anthropometry lies in the actual skinfold measurement. Making accurate skinfold measurement is more than simply pinching the skin somewhere around a particular area and measuring the thickness. There are precise sites on which the measurements are to be taken.

Unfortunately, most people who take skinfold measurements are not well trained. Obtaining consistently accurate skinfold measurements requires training and experience.

Use Good Quality Calipers

To be accurate body fat calipers need to exert a certain amount of **constant pressure** (10 gm./sq. mm).

The Top 5 Body Fat Calipers

Harpenden Skinfold Caliper: The Harpenden is the most accurate skinfold caliper made. It has been the standard research caliper for many years. Virtually all the data and equations relating skinfold thickness to bodyfat are based on studies done with the Harpenden.

Lafayette Skinfold Caliper: The Lafayette Skinfold Caliper is one of the most accurate and durable calipers available today. It was designed with the assistance of Dr. Andrew Jackson, co-author of the widely used Jackson-Pollock skinfold formulas.

Lange Caliper: This is the best selling of the higher priced body fat calipers. It has been manufactured since 1962 and is widely used in schools, colleges and fitness centers. The Lange is one of the lower cost professional calipers.

Accu-Measure Body Fat Calipers: At the moment these are the only body fat calipers that reliably let one test oneself. They are extremely simple to use and a recent study has shown very positive results for accuracy. Recommended in Body-for-LIFE and endorsed by the World Natural Bodybuilding Federation.

Slim Guide Skinfold Caliper: Much lower priced than any of the above body fat calipers yet will produce results that are almost as accurate. This is the only low cost caliper accurate enough to be used for professional measurements and is the most widely used professional caliper in the world.

Figures of various skinfold calipers are shown in *Appendix VI.*

How to Take Skinfold Measurement?

- Take skinfold measurement while standing.
- Take all skinfold measurements on the same side of the body, preferably the right side.
- Pinch between the forefinger and the thumb. Pinch deep enough to get the fat but not so deep that you start pulling muscle up. Pulling muscle up is pretty much impossible. With the skinfold in hand, pinch hard to get the water out. This is hard enough as it causes minor discomfort.
- Place the body fat calipers less than 1/2 inch from the pinch, midway between the crest and the base.
- For each of the skinfold site, take three measurements and use the average of those three. But don't take the three measurements consecutively, instead run through all the sites three times. This will allow the skin to regroup between skinfold measurements.

One can refer to the body fat interpretation chart or can compare the readings with the reference standards or can use the equations to predict body fat percentage. Following figures depict how to lift and pinch the skinfold at the chosen site.

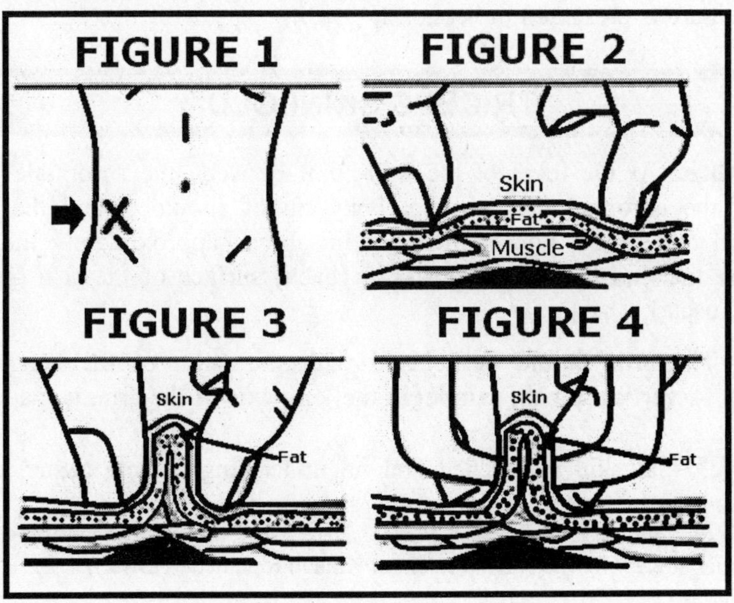

SKINFOLD MEASUREMENT SITES

There are many sites at which the skinfold pinch can be taken. The following are the most common. It is important to find the correct location to take the skinfold pinch, and anatomical terms are used to describe the landmarks (Retrieved from http://www.brianmac.co.uk/eval).

Common skinfold Measurement Sites

- Biceps
- Triceps
- Subscapular
- Suprailiac
- Chest
- Abdominal
- Thigh
- Calf

BICEPS SKINFOLD

Landmark: With the arm resting comfortably at the side, take a vertical fold halfway between the elbow and top of the shoulder on the front of the upper arm.

Note: Figure is presented in Section II.

TRICEPS SKINFOLD

Landmark: At the level of the mid-point between the acromiale (lateral edge of the acromial process, e.g. bony tip of shoulder) and the radiale (proximal and lateral border of the radius bone, approximately the elbow joint), on the mid-line of the posterior (back) surface of the arm (over the triceps muscle).

Pinch: The arm should be relaxed with the palm of the hand facing forwards. A vertical pinch, parallel to the long axis of the arm, is made at the landmark.

If it is felt that skin is pinched and no underlying muscle tissue, ask the subject to flex the muscle while holding the pinch.

(From *International Standards for Anthropometric Assessment* (2001) published by The International Society for the Advancement of Kinanthropometry (ISAK))

Note: Figure is presented in Section II.

SUBSCAPULAR SKINFOLD

Landmark: The lower angle of the scapula (bottom point of shoulder blade).

If there is difficulty finding this landmark, get the subject to reach behind their back with their right arm, while feeling for the movement of the scapula.

Pinch: The pinch is made following the natural fold of the skin, approximately on a line running laterally (away from the body) and downwards (at about 45 degrees).

(From *International Standards for Anthropometric Assessment* (2001) published by The International Society for the Advancement of Kinanthropometry (ISAK))

Note: Figure is presented in Section II.

SUPRAILIAC SKINFOLD

Landmark: The intersection of a line joining the spinale (front part of iliac crest) and the anterior (front) part of the axilla (armpit), and a horizontal line at the level of the iliac crest.

Pinch: The pinch is directed medially (towards the centerline) and downward, following the natural fold of the skin (at an approximate angle of 45 degrees). This site is called supraspinale.

(From *International Standards for Anthropometric Assessment* (2001) published by The International Society for the Advancement of Kinanthropometry (ISAK))

Note: Figure is presented in Section II.

CHEST SKINFOLD

Landmark: Between the axilla and nipple as high as possible on the anterior axillary fold

Pinch: A diagonal pinch.

This measurement is usually only performed on males only due to the difficulty in modestly obtaining a measure on females.

(From *International Standards for Anthropometric Assessment* (2001) published by The International Society for the Advancement of Kinanthropometry (ISAK))

Note: Figure is presented in Section II.

ABDOMINAL SKINFOLD

Landmark: 5 cm adjacent to the umbilicus (belly-button), to the right side.

Pinch: The vertical pinch is made

Do not place the caliper or fingers inside the navel

(From *International Standards for Anthropometric Assessment* (2001) published by The International Society for the Advancement of Kinanthropometry (ISAK))

Note: Figure is presented in Section II.

THIGH SKINFOLD

Landmark: The mid-point of the anterior (front) surface of the thigh, midway between patella (knee cap) and inguinal fold (crease at top of thigh).

Pinch: A vertical pinch

This measurement is normally taken with the subject sitting and the knee bent at right angles. If there is difficulty in lifting a fold of skin, it may be easier with the leg extended, or with the thigh supported from below by the subject. (From *International Standards for Anthropometric Assessment* (2001) published by The International Society for the Advancement of Kinanthropometry (ISAK))

Note: Figure is presented in Section II.

CALF SKINFOLD

Landmark: A point on the medial (inside) surface of the calf, at the level of the largest circumference.

Pinch: A vertical pinch parallel to the long axis of the leg

The subject should place their foot on a chair or box so that the knee is at approximately 90 degrees.

(From *International Standards for Anthropometric Assessment* (2001) published by The International Society for the Advancement of Kinanthropometry (ISAK))

Note: Figure is presented in Section II.

Body stature, weight, circumferences and skinfold measurement at various sits can be used to predict body density, body fat and lean body mass.

Tips When Using Body Fat Calipers

- For greater accuracy, monitor changes with **skinfold measurements** rather than converting them into a body fat percentage and using that to judge progress.

- Have an **experienced examiner** test the case if possible. At the very least have the same person test the case each time.
- Take the reading **within 4 seconds** of applying the body fat calipers to the skinfold. A prolonged delay has been shown to significantly underestimate the actual skinfold value.
- Take measurements at the **same time of day** for each test.
- Don't have a test immediately **after exercising**.
- If the chance arises, compare the results to a hydrostatic weighing test or any other test like the **Bod Pod**.

♦♦♦♦♦♦♦♦

SECTION - II

Part V

PREDICTION OF BODY DENSITY, BODY FAT PERCENTAGE AND LEAN BODY MASS BASED ON SKIN FOLD, BODY MASS AND BODY CIRCUMFERENCES

Measuring body fat percentage is an easy method of discovering correct body weight and composition. Beneath the skin is a layer of subcutaneous fat and the percentage of total body fat can be measured by taking the girth measurements at selected points on the body with a measuring tape.

The development of skinfold and body measurements came as the result of investigations for simpler and less expensive method for determining body composition. Body mass, circumferences and/or skinfold thickness are used in a regression equation, of which there are many available, for prediction of body composition.

Hydrostatic weighing is one of the most accurate indirect methods available to assess the body density and then, body fat content. However, proper measurement with this technique requires equipment and facilities are not normally available. Thus, alternative but simple procedures to predict body density and body fatness have been developed. These are measurement of fatfold and girth or circumferences at selected sites on the body.

♦♦♦♦♦♦♦♦

21

EQUATIONS FOR ESTIMATION OF BODY DENSITY

Predicting Body Density Using the Equation of Brozek

Percent Fat = [(4.570 / Body Density) - 4.142] X 100

Predicting Body Density of Adults from Skinfold Thickness Using the Equations of Durnin and Rahaman

Skinfold Measurements:

- Measurements taken on the right side with the subject in a relaxed condition.
- Sites measured: biceps, triceps, subscapular region, supra-iliac region.
- The skinfold thickness taken with a caliper tension of 9.8 X 104 Newton's per square meter.
- Measurements ≤ 5 mm taken to the nearest 0.5 mm; measurements > 5 mm taken to the nearest mm.

Sum of 4 Skinfolds = (thickness of biceps skinfold in mm) + (thickness of triceps skinfold in mm) + (thickness of subscapular skinfold in mm) + (thickness of supra-iliac skinfold in mm)

For Boys:

Body Density = 1.1533 – 0.0643 (log of the sum of skinfold thicknesses at four sites)

For Men:

Body Density = 1.1610 – 0.0632 (log of the sum of skinfold thicknesses at four sites)

For Girls:

Body Density = 1.1369 – 0.0598 (log of the sum of skinfold thicknesses at four sites)

For Women:

Body Density = 1.1581 – 0.0720 (log of the sum of skinfold thicknesses at four sites)

Predicting Body Density and Body Fat Percentage of Adults from Skinfold Thickness Using the Equations of Durnin and Womersley

Skinfold Measurements:

- Measurements taken on the right side with the subject in a relaxed condition.
- Sites measured: biceps, triceps, subscapular region, and supra-iliac region.
- The skinfold thickness taken with a caliper tension of 9.8 X 104 Newton's per square meter.
- Measurements ≤ 5 mm taken to the nearest 0.5 mm; measurements > 5 mm taken to the nearest mm.
- The researchers found that subtracting 1.8 mm from each skinfold to take into account two layers of skin thickness during skinfold measurement did not improve results.

Sum of 4 Skinfolds = (thickness of biceps skinfold in mm) + (thickness of triceps skinfold in mm) + (thickness of subscapular skinfold in mm) + (thickness of supra-iliac skinfold in mm)

Body Density in 1000 kg per cubic meter = c – (m X (log of (total skinfolds in mm)))

Where:

1 g per cc = 1000 kg per cubic meter

Data for Males and Females

Age in Years	c	m
Males		
17-19	1.1620	0.0630
20-29	1.1631	0.0632
30-39	1.1422	0.0544
40-49	1.1620	0.0700
50-72	1.1715	0.0779
Females		
16-19	1.1549	0.0678
20-29	1.1599	0.0717
30-39	1.1423	0.0632
40-49	1.1333	0.0612
50-68	1.1339	0.0645

Percent Body Fat for Males

Total Sum Skinfolds mm	Percent Body Fat Males with Age in Years			
	17-29	30 – 39	40 – 49	50 - 72
15	4.8	-	-	-
20	8.1	12.2	12.2	12.6
25	10.5	14.2	15.0	15.6
30	12.9	16.2	17.7	18.6
35	14.7	17.7	19.6	20.8
40	16.4	19.2	21.4	22.9
45	17.7	20.4	23.0	24.7
50	19.0	21.5	24.6	26.5
55	20.1	22.5	25.9	27.9
60	21.2	23.5	27.1	29.2
65	22.2	24.3	28.2	30.4
70	23.1	25.1	29.3	31.6
75	24.0	25.9	30.3	32.7
80	24.8	26.6	31.2	33.8
85	25.5	27.2	32.1	34.8
90	26.2	27.8	33.0	35.8
95	26.9	28.4	33.7	36.6
100	27.6	29.0	34.4	37.4
105	28.2	29.6	35.1	38.2
110	28.8	30.1	35.8	39.0
115	29.4	30.6	36.4	39.7
120	30.0	31.1	37.0	40.4
125	30.5	31.5	37.6	41.1
130	31.0	31.9	38.2	41.8
135	31.5	32.3	38.7	42.4
140	32.0	32.7	39.2	43.0
145	32.5	33.1	39.7	43.6
150	32.9	33.5	40.2	44.1
155	33.3	33.9	40.7	44.6
160	33.7	34.3	41.2	45.1
165	34.1	34.6	41.6	45.6
170	34.5	34.8	42.0	46.1
175	34.9			
180	35.3			
185	35.6			
190	35.9			
195				
200				
205				
210				

Source: Durnin and Womersley, 1974

Percent Body Fat for Females

Total Sum Skinfolds mm	Percent Body Fat Females with Age in Years			
	16-29	30 – 39	40 – 49	50 - 68
15	10.5	-	-	-
20	14.1	17.0	19.8	21.4
25	16.8	19.4	22.2	24.0
30	19.5	21.8	24.5	26.6
35	21.5	23.7	26.4	28.5
40	23.4	25.5	28.2	30.3
45	25.0	26.9	29.6	31.9
50	26.5	28.2	31.0	33.4
55	27.8	29.4	32.1	34.6
60	29.1	30.6	33.2	35.7
65	30.2	31.6	34.1	36.7
70	31.2	32.5	35.0	37.7
75	32.2	33.4	35.9	38.7
80	33.1	34.3	36.7	39.6
85	34.0	35.1	37.5	40.4
90	34.8	35.8	38.3	41.2
95	35.6	36.5	39.0	41.9
100	36.4	37.2	39.7	42.6
105	37.1	37.9	40.4	43.3
110	37.8	38.6	41.0	43.9
115	38.4	39.1	41.5	44.5
120	39.0	39.6	42.0	45.1
125	39.6	40.1	42.5	45.7
130	40.2	40.6	43.0	46.2
135	40.8	41.1	43.5	46.7
140	41.3	41.6	44.0	47.2
145	41.8	42.1	44.5	47.7
150	42.3	42.6	45.0	48.2
155	42.8	43.1	45.4	48.7
160	43.3	43.6	45.8	49.2
165	43.7	44.0	46.2	49.6
170	44.1	44.4	46.6	50.0
175		44.8	47.0	50.4
180		45.2	47.4	50.8
185		45.6	47.8	51.2
190		45.9	48.2	51.6
195		46.2	48.5	52.0
200		46.5	48.8	52.4
205			49.1	52.7
210			49.4	53.0

Source: Durnin and Womersley, 1974

Males with Sum of Skinfolds ≤ 90 mm

Percent fat for males 17-29 years old with skinfold 15-90 mm
= (0.000041 X ((total skinfold) 3)) – (0.00932 X ((total skinfold) 2)) + (0.866067 X (total skinfold)) – 6.00107

Percent fat for males 30-39 years old with skinfold 20-90 mm
= (0.0000241 X ((total skinfold) 3)) – (0.006048 X ((total skinfold) 2)) + (0.6400706 X (total skinfold)) + 1.6609664

Percent fat for males 40-49 years old with skinfold 20-90 mm
= (0.0000365 X ((total skinfold) 3)) – (0.008677 X ((total skinfold) 2)) + (0.8749747 X (total skinfold)) – 2.002712

Percent fat for males 50-72 years old with skinfold 20-90 mm
= (0.0000429 X ((total skinfold) 3)) – (0.010065 X ((total skinfold) 2)) + (0.99782 X (total skinfold)) – 3.637384

Males with Sum of Skinfolds ≥ 90 mm

Percent fat for males 17-29 years old with skinfold 90-190 mm
= (0.0000015 X ((total skinfold) 3)) – (0.001 X ((total skinfold) 2)) + (0.285045 X (total skinfold)) + 7.5579898

Percent fat for males 30-39 years old with skinfold 90-170 mm
= (0.0000026 X ((total skinfold) 3)) – (0.0014 X ((total skinfold) 2)) + (0.3141237 X (total skinfold)) + 8.9496

Percent fat for males 40-49 years old with skinfold 90-170 mm
= (0.0000014 X ((total skinfold) 3)) – (0.000961 X ((total skinfold) 2)) + (0.2892191 X (total skinfold)) + 13.707379

Percent fat for males 50-72 years old with skinfold 90-170 mm
= (0.0000002 X ((total skinfold) 3)) – (0.000594 X ((total skinfold) 2)) + (0.274175 X (total skinfold)) + 15.78274

Females with Sum of Skinfolds ≤ 90 mm

Percent fat for females 16-29 years old with skinfold 15-90 mm
= (0.0000426 X ((total skinfold) 3)) – (0.009878 X ((total skinfold) 2)) + (0.94845 X (total skinfold)) – 1.432143

Percent fat for females 30-39 years old with skinfold 20-90 mm
= (0.0000323 X ((total skinfold) 3)) – (0.00782 X ((total skinfold) 2)) + (0.797252 X (total skinfold)) + 3.9435567

Percent fat for females 40-49 years old with skinfold 20-90 mm
= (0.0000351 X ((total skinfold) 3)) – (0.008319 X ((total skinfold) 2)) + (0.8182132 X (total skinfold)) + 6.4602618

Percent fat for females 50-68 years old with skinfold 20-90 mm
= (0.0000368 X ((total skinfold) 3)) – (0.008741 X ((total skinfold) 2)) + (0.8658072 X (total skinfold)) + 7.3191546

Females with Sum of Skinfolds ≥ 90 mm

Percent fat for females 16-29 years old with skinfold 90-170 mm
= (0.0000021 X ((total skinfold) 3)) – (0.001291 X ((total skinfold) 2)) + (0.3404369 X (total skinfold)) +13.092466

Percent fat for females 30-39 years old with skinfold 90-200 mm
= (0.0000005 X ((total skinfold) 3)) – (0.000519 X ((total skinfold) 2)) + (0.2163384 X (total skinfold)) + 20.274699

Percent fat for females 40-49 years old with skinfold 90-200 mm
= (0.0000009 X ((total skinfold) 3)) – (0.000711 X ((total skinfold) 2)) + (0.2388038 X (total skinfold)) + 21.965364

Percent fat for females 50-68 years old with skinfold 90-210 mm
= (0.0000011 X ((total skinfold) 3)) – (0.000801 X ((total skinfold) 2)) + (0.2600804 X (total skinfold)) + 23.492094

Following is the classification of body fat based on skinfold measurements at triceps, scapular and abdomen:

Classification of Body Fat from Skinfold Thicknesses for Male and Female Athletes

Male Athletes ■					
Classification	Body Fat	Skinfold Thicknesses (mm)			
		Triceps	Scapular	Abdomen	Sum
Lean	<7 %	<7	<8	<10	<25
Acceptable	7-15 %	7-13	8-15	10-20	25-48
Overfat	>15 %	>13	>15	>20	>48
Female Athletes #					
Classification	Body Fat	Skinfold Thicknesses (mm)			
		Triceps	Scapular	Abdomen	Sum
Lean	<12 %	<9	<7	<7	<23
Acceptable	12-25 %	9-17	7-14	7-15	23-46
Overfat	>25 %	>17	>14	>15	>46

■ From Buskirk (1974) # Based on data from Hall (1977)

Predicting Body Density from Skinfold Thickness Using the Equations of Goldman and Becklake

$$\text{Body Density (g/cm3)} = \frac{P}{[\{(W - Ww)/Wd\} - (RV + 0.0)]}$$

Where,

W –Body Mass in kg on air
Ww – Weight in water in kg
Wd – Water Density (corrected by temperature)
RV – Residual Volume
0.1 – Gastrointestinal Gs Constant (100 ml)

Residual Volume = 0.017 (Age in yrs) + 0.027 (height in cm) - 3.477

Predicting Body Density from Skinfold Thickness Using the Equations of Guedes

Body Density = 1.17136 – 0.06706 X log (AB SF + SS SF + TR SF)
Where,

AB SF – Abdominal Skinfold
SS SF – Subscapular Skinfold
TR SF – Tricipital Skinfold

Predicting Body Density in Adults Using the Equations of Hodgdon and Beckett

Parameters:

(1) Gender
(2) Height in centimeters with subject standing tall.
(3) Abdomen circumference at the level of the umbilicus in centimeters (abdomen II)
(4) Abdomen circumference at the narrowest point between the lower sternum and umbilicus in centimeters (abdomen I)
(5) Hip circumference in centimeters at the level of greatest protrusion of the buttocks
(6) Neck circumference in centimeters below the larynx (Adam's apple)

Measurement Instructions:

(1) The tape measure should be non elastic without stretch.
(2) Height recorded to the nearest half inch.
(3) Measurements of the abdomen, hips and waist rounded down to the nearest half inch.
(4) Measurements of the neck are rounded up to the nearest half inch.
(5) The person's arms to be hanging naturally at the sides.

For Males

Body Density = (-0.191 X log 10((abdomen II) - (neck circumference))) + (0.155 X log 10(height)) + 1.032

For Females

Body Density = (-0.350 X log 10((abdomen I) + (hip circumference) - (neck circumference))) + (0.221 X log 10(height)) + 1.296

Predicting Body Density of Men from Body Measurements Using the Equations of Jackson, Pollock and Ward

The body density of young to middle aged women can be estimated from body measurements using the generalized equations developed by Jackson, Pollock and Ward.

Measurements:

- Skinfold thicknesses measured in mm using a Lange skinfold fat caliper.
- Gluteal circumference measured in centimeters using a Lufkin steel tape.

Sites of Skinfold Thickness Measurement:

(1) Chest
(2) Axilla
(3) Triceps
(4) Subscapula
(5) Abdomen
(6) Suprailium
(7) Thigh

Sum of 7 Skinfolds = (Sum of skinfold thickness from all 7 sites in mm)

Sum of 4 Skinfolds = (skinfold thickness triceps in mm) + (skinfold thickness abdomen in mm) + (skinfold thickness suprailium in mm) + (skinfold thickness thigh in mm)

Sum of 3 Skinfolds = (skinfold thickness triceps in mm) + (skinfold thickness thigh in mm) + (skinfold thickness suprailium in mm)

Equations using Sum of 7 Sites

Equation 1

Body Density in g per mL = 1.0970 - (0.00046971 X (sum of 7 skinfolds in mm)) + (0.00000056 X ((sum of 7 skinfolds in mm) 2)) - (0.00012828 X (age in years))

Equation 2

Body Density in g per mL = 1.23173 - (0.03841 X (log (sum of 7 skinfolds in mm))) - (0.00015 X (age in years))

Equation 3

Body Density in g per mL = 1.1470 - (0.00042359 X (sum of 7 skinfolds in mm)) + (0.00000061 X ((sum of 7 skinfolds in mm) 2)) - (0.0006520 X (gluteal circumference in cm))

Equation 4

Body Density in g per mL = 1.25475 - (0.03100 X (log (sum of 7 skinfolds in mm))) - (0.00068 X (gluteal circumference in cm))

Equation 5

Body Density in g per mL = 1.1470 - (0.00042930 X (sum of 7 skinfolds in mm)) + (0.00000065 X ((sum of 7 skinfolds in mm) 2)) - (0.00009975 X (age in years)) - (0.00062415 X (gluteal circumference in cm))

Equation 6

Body Density in g per mL = 1.25186 - (0.03048 X (log (sum of 7 skinfolds in mm))) - (0.00011 X (age in years)) - (0.00064 X (gluteal circumference in cm))

Equations using Sum of 4 Sites

Equation 1

Body Density in g per mL = 1.0960950 - (0.0006952 X (sum of 4 skinfolds in mm)) + (0.0000011 X ((sum of 4 skinfolds in mm) 2)) - (0.0000714 X (age in years))

Equation 2

Body Density in g per mL = 1.21993 - (0.03936 X (log (sum of 4 skinfolds in mm))) - (0.00011 X (age in years))

Equation 3

Body Density in g per mL = 1.1443913 - (0.0006523 X (sum of 4 skinfolds in mm)) + (0.0000014 X ((sum of 4 skinfolds in mm) 2)) - (0.0006053 X (gluteal circumference in cm))

Equation 4

Body Density in g per mL = 1.24374 - (0.03162 X (log (sum of 4 skinfolds in mm))) - (0.00066 X (gluteal circumference in cm))

Equation 5

Body Density in g per mL = 1.1454464 - (0.0006558 X (sum of 4 skinfolds in mm)) + (0.0000015 X ((sum of 4 skinfolds in mm) 2)) - (0.0000604 X (age in years)) - (0.0005981 X (gluteal circumference in cm))

Equation 6

Body Density in g per mL = 1.241721 - (0.031069 X (log (sum of 4 skinfolds in mm))) - (0.000077 X (age in years)) - (0.000635 X (gluteal circumference in cm))

Equations using Sum of 3 Sites

Equation 1

Body Density in g per mL = 1.0994921 - (0.0009929 X (sum of 3 skinfolds in mm)) + (0.0000023 X ((sum of 3 skinfolds in mm) 2)) - (0.0001392 X (age in years))

Equation 2

Body density in g per mL = 1.21389 - (0.04057 X (log (sum of 3 skinfolds in mm))) - (0.00016 X (age in years))

Equation 3

Body Density in g per mL = 1.1466399 - (0.000930 X (sum of 3 skinfolds in mm)) + (0.0000028 X ((sum of 3 skinfolds in mm) 2)) - (0.0006171 X (gluteal circumference in cm))

Equation 4

Body Density in g per mL = 1.23824 - (0.03248 X (log (sum of 3 skinfolds in mm))) - (0.00067 X (gluteal circumference in cm))

Equation 5

Body Density in g per mL = 1.1470292 - (0.0009376 X (sum of 3 skinfolds in mm)) + (0.0000030 X ((sum of 3 skinfolds in mm) 2)) - (0.0001156 X (age in years)) - (0.0005839 X (gluteal circumference in cm))

Equation 6

Body Density in g per mL = 1.23530 - (0.03192 X (log (sum of 3 skinfolds in mm))) - (0.00013 X (age in years)) - (0.00062 X (gluteal circumference in cm))

Predicting Body Density of Men from Body Measurements Using the Equations of Jackson and Pollock

The body density in young and middle aged males can be estimated from body measurements using generalized equations developed by Jackson and Pollock (1978).

Measurements:

- Skinfold thicknesses measured in mm using a Lange skinfold fat caliper.
- Waist and forearm circumferences measured in meters using a Lufkin steel tape.

Sites of Skinfold Thickness Measurement:

(1) Chest
(2) Axilla
(3) Triceps
(4) Subscapula
(5) Abdomen
(6) Suprailium
(7) Front thigh

Sum of 7 Skinfolds = (Sum of skinfold thickness from all 7 sites in mm)
Sum of 3 Skinfolds = (skinfold thickness of chest in mm) + (skinfold thickness of abdomen in mm) + (skinfold thickness of thigh in mm)

Equations using Sum of 7 Sites

Equation 1

Body Density in g per mL = 1.112 - (0.00043499 X (sum of 7 skinfolds in mm)) + (0.00000055 X ((sum of 7 skinfolds in mm) 2)) - (0.00028826 X (age in years))

Equation 2

Body Density in g per mL = 1.101 - (0.00041150 X (sum of 7 skinfolds in mm)) + (0.00000069 X ((sum of 7 skinfolds in mm) 2)) - (0.00022631 X (age in years)) - (0.0059239 X (waist circumference in meters)) + (0.0190632 X (forearm circumference in meters))

Equation 3

Body Density in g per mL = 1.21394 - (0.03101 X (log (sum of 7 skinfolds in mm))) - (0.00029 X (age in years))

Equation 4

Body Density in g per mL = 1.17615 - (0.02394 X (log (sum of 7 skinfolds in mm))) - (0.00022 X (age in years)) - (0.0070 X (waist circumference in m)) + (0.02120 x (forearm circumference in m))

Equations using Sum of 3 Sites

Equation 1

Body Density in g per mL = 1.10938 - (0.0008267 X (sum of 3 skinfolds in mm)) + (0.0000016 X ((sum of 3 skinfolds in mm) 2)) - (0.0002574 X (age in years))

Equation 2

Body Density in g per mL = 1.0990750 - (0.0008209 X (sum of 3 skinfolds in mm)) + (0.0000026 X ((sum of 3 skinfolds in mm) 2)) - (0.0002017 X (age in years)) - (0.005675 X (waist circumference in m)) + (0.018586 X (forearm circumference in m))

Equation 3

Body Density in g per mL = 1.18860 - (0.03049 X (log (sum of 3 skinfolds in mm))) - (0.00027 X (age in years))

Equation 4

Body Density in g per mL = 1.15737 - (0.02288 X (log (sum of 3 skinfolds in mm))) - (0.00019 X (age in years)) - (0.0075 X (waist circumference in m)) + (0.0223 X (forearm circumference in m))

Predicting Body Density from Skinfold Thickness Using the Equations of Katch and McArdle

Body Density = 1.09665 – 0.00103 X (TR SF) – 0.00056 X (SS SF) – 0.00054 X (AB SF)

Where,

TR SF – Tricipital Skinfold
SS SF – Subscapular Skinfold
AB SF – Abdominal Skinfold

Predicting Body Density from Skinfold Thickness Using the Equations of Lohman

Body Density = 1.0982 – 0.000815 X (TR SF + SS SF + AB SF) +0.0000084 X (TR SF + SS SF + AB SF) 2

Where,

TR SF – Tricipital Skinfold
SS SF – Subscapular Skinfold
AB SF – Abdominal Skinfold

Predicting Body Density from Skinfold Thickness Using the Equations of Thorland et al.

Body Density = 1.1136 – 0.00154 X (TR SF + SS SF + MUA SF) + 0.00000516 X (TR SF + SS SF + MUA SF) 2

Where,

TR SF – Tricipital Skinfold   SS SF – Subscapular Skinfold

MUA SF – Mid Upper Arm Skinfold

Estimating Body Density in Young Women Using the Equations of Wilmore and Behnke

Wilmore and Behnke derived several equations to estimate the body density in young women (age 17.8 to 47.8 years).

Measurements:

(1) All skin fold thicknesses taken with the subject standing.

(2) All circumferences except for the upper extremity measured with the subject standing.

(3) All diameters taken with the person seated.

(4) Skin fold thickness taken with a Lange skin-fold caliper with a caliper pressure of 10 grams per square mm.

(5) Diameters except for the wrist measured with a broad-blade Bayer-Rue anthropometer. The wrist measured with a vernier caliper.

Estimates of Body Density

Equation 1

Body Density in grams per cubic cm =1.06234 - (0.00068 X (scapula skin fold thickness in mm)) - (0.00039 X (triceps skin fold thickness in mm)) - (0.00025 X (thigh skin fold thickness in mm))

Equation 2

Body Density in grams per cubic cm = 1.065551 + (0.0112 X (wrist diameter in cm)) - (0.00055 X (maximum abdominal circumference in cm)) - (0.00082 X (hip circumference in cm)) - (0.00159 X (extended biceps circumference in cm) + (0.00362 X (forearm circumference in cm))

Equation 3

Body Density in grams per cubic cm = 1.07685 - (0.00063 X (scapula skin fold thickness in mm)) - (0.00336 X (knee diameter in cm)) + (0.00227 X (neck circumference in cm)) - (0.00049 X (minimum abdominal circumference in cm)) - (0.00043 X (maximum abdominal circumference in cm))

♦♦♦♦♦♦♦♦

22

EQUATIONS FOR ESTIMATION OF PERCENT BODY FAT

Predicting Subcutaneous Abdominal Adipose Tissue (SAT) Using the Equations of Bonora et al.

Parameters:

(1) Gender
(2) Waist circumference in cm (maximum circumference between the xyphoid process and iliac crests, usually at the level of the navel)
(3) Age
(4) Body mass index (BMI)
(5) Hip circumference in cm (at the level of the greater trochanters)

Area of Subcutaneous Abdominal Adipose Tissue in square cm for Males = (5.51 X (hip circumference in cm)) + (9.37 X (BMI in kg per sq m)) - 621

Area of Subcutaneous Abdominal Adipose Tissue in square cm for Females = (2.26 X (age in years)) + (24.5 X (BMI in kg per sq m)) - 332.9

Predicting Percent Body Fat Using Bioelectrical Impedance and the Equations of Bunc et al.

For Boys Under 10 Years of Age

Percent Body Fat = 39.2649 – (5.4577 X (age in years)) – (9.2044 X ((height in meters) 2)) + (0.4177 X (mass in kilograms)) + (0.0442 X (resistance in Ohms))

For Boys 10 to 15 Years of Age

Percent Body Fat = 6.4649 – (0.0577 X (age in years)) – (9.2044 X ((height in meters) 2)) + (0.4077 X (mass in kilograms)) + (0.0084 X (resistance in Ohms))

For Girls Under 10 Years of Age

Percent Body Fat = 14.6812 – (0.1105 X (age in years)) + (0.5938 X (mass in kilograms)) – (4.9063 X ((height in meters) 2) / (resistance in kilo Ohms))

For Girls 10 to 15 Years of Age

Percent Body Fat = 10.8852 – (0.0968 X (age in years)) + (0.5634 X (mass in kilograms)) – (5.0603 X ((height in meters) 2) / (resistance in kilo Ohms))

Predicting Percent Body Fat from Age, Gender and Body Mass Index Using the Equations of Deurenberg et al.

Parameters:

(1) Age in years
(2) Gender
(3) Body mass index in kg per meter squared

Gender	Points
Female	0
Male	1

For ≤ 15 years

Percent Body Fat as a Number from 0 to 100 = (1.51 X (body mass index)) - (0.70 X (age in years)) - (3.6 X (points for gender)) + 1.4

For > 15 years

Percent Body Fat as a Number from 0 to 100 = (1.2 X (body mass index)) + (0.23 X (age in years)) - (10.8 X (points for gender)) -5.4

Predicting Percent Body in Adults Using the Equations of Marriott and Grumstrup-Scott and Wright et al.

Researchers developed equations for predicting the percent body fat in adults based on anthropometric measurements. This has been used by the U.S. Marine Corps for evaluating its personnel.

Parameters:

(1) Gender
(2) Abdomen circumference at the level of the umbilicus in centimeters (abdomen II)
(3) Neck circumference in centimeters below the larynx (Adam's apple)
(4) Biceps circumference in centimeters (arm abducted at 90° to body with hand supinated upwards; measurement taken at largest part of the biceps/triceps group)
(5) Forearm circumference in centimeters (arm abducted at 90° to body with hand supinated upwards; measurement taken at largest part of the forearm)

(6) Thigh circumference in centimeters (taken just below the gluteal fold with the subject standing evenly on both legs)

For Males

Percent Body Fat = (0.740 X (abdomen II)) - (1.249 X (neck circumference)) + 0.528

For Females

Percent Body Fat = (1.051 X (biceps circumference)) - (1.522 X (forearm circumference)) - (0.879 X (neck circumference)) + (0.326 X (abdomen II)) + (0.597 X (thigh circumference)) + 0.707

Predicting Percent Body in Adults Using the Equations of Gallagher et al.

Parameters:

(1) Body mass index in kilograms per square meter
(2) Age in years
(3) Gender
(4) Race

Parameter	Finding	Points
Gender	Male	1
	Female	0
Race	Black	1
	White	0

Body Fat as Percent of Body Weight Independent of Race = (1.46 X (BMI)) + (0.12 X (age in years)) - (11.61 X (points for gender)) - 10.02

Body Fat as Percent of Body Weight Independent of Race = (1.47 X (BMI)) + (0.12 X (age in years)) - (11.61 X (points for gender)) - (0.22 X (points for race)) - 10.13

Predicting Percent Body Fat in Adults from Anthropometric Measurements Using the Equations of Hodgdon and Friedl (DoD Body Composition Equations)

Parameters:

(1) Gender
(2) Height in inches with subject standing tall.
(3) Abdomen circumference at the level of the umbilicus in inches (abdomen II)

(4) Abdomen circumference at the narrowest point between the lower sternum and umbilicus in inches (abdomen I)
(5) Hip circumference in inches at the level of greatest protrusion of the buttocks
(6) Neck circumference in inches below the larynx (Adam's apple)

Measurement Instructions:

(1) The tape measure should be non elastic without stretch.
(2) Height recorded to the nearest half inch.
(3) Measurements of the abdomen, hips and waist rounded down to the nearest half inch.
(4) Measurements of the neck rounded up to the nearest half inch.
(5) The person's arms to be hanging naturally at the sides.

For Males

Percent Body Fat = (86.010 X log 10((abdomen II) - (neck circumference))) - (70.041 X log 10(height)) + 36.76

For Females

Percent Body Fat = (163.205 X log 10((abdomen I) + (hip circumference) - (neck circumference))) - (97.684 X log 10(height)) - 78.387

Predicting Body Fat Percent Using the Equations of McArdle et al.

One can determine the best combination of circumference measures for predicting body fatness.

Following girth measures predict body fat content.

Gender and Age	Young Women (17 – 26 yrs)	Older Women (27 – 50 yrs)	Young Men (17 – 26 yrs)	Older Men (27 – 50 yrs)
Girth	Abdomen	Abdomen	Right Upper Arm	Buttocks
	Right Thigh	Right Thigh	Abdomen	Abdomen
	Right Forearm	Right Calf	Right Forearm	Right Forearm

Abdomen = one inch above the umbilicus

Buttocks = maximum protrusion with the heels together

Right Thigh = upper thigh just below the buttocks

Right Upper Arm = arm straight, palm up and extended in front of the body (measure at the mid point between the shoulder and elbow)

Right Forearm = maximum circumference with the arm extended in front of the body with palm up

Right Calf = widest circumference midway between the ankle and knee

Percent body fat can be calculated directly by use of the three constants **A**, **B** and **C** presented in the tables given in *Appendix IV* (Source: McArdle et al., 1981).

Percent body fat is obtained after performing the two additions and two subtractions in the formulas given for each age group of males and females. It should be emphasized that the equations to predict percent body fat from circumferences may not be valid all the time.

For Young Women

Percent Fat = Constant A + Constant B - Constant C - 19.6

For athletic people, age correction is 22.6

For Older Women

Percent Fat = Constant A + Constant B - Constant C - 18.4

For athletic people, age correction is 21.4

For Young Men

Percent Fat = Constant A + Constant B - Constant C - 10.2

For athletic people, age correction is 14.2

For Older Men

Percent Fat = Constant A + Constant B - Constant C - 15.0

For athletic people, age correction is 19.0

Example: 24 year old woman, weight is 57 kg.

Circumferences:

Abdomen - 28.0 inches (71.12 cm)
Right Thigh - 20.0 inches (50.8 cm)
Forearm - 8.0 inches (20.3 cm)

Three constants for the case:

Constant **A,** corresponding to 28.0 inches = 37.43
Constant **B,** corresponding to 20.0 inches = 41.61
Constant **C,** corresponding to 8.0 inches = 34.48

Percent Body Fat = Constant A + Constant B - Constant C - 19.6
= 37.43 + 41.61 – 34.48 – 19.6
= 79.04 – 34.48 – 19.6
= 44.56 – 19.6
= 24.96 %

Similarly, one can predict percent body fat for athletic person using these tables.

Predicting Percent Body Fat from Skinfold Thickness Using the Equations of Ledesma

Sum of 4 Skinfolds = (thickness of biceps skinfold in mm) + (thickness of triceps skinfold in mm) + (thickness of subscapular skinfold in mm) + (thickness of supra-iliac skinfold in mm)

Percent Body Fat in Men from 17-74 years = (14.83 X (log (SUM of 4 skinfolds in mm))) – 36.45

Percent Body Fat in Women from 17-74 years = (14.71 X (log (SUM of 4 skinfolds in mm))) – 29.04

Predicting Percent Body Fat in Adults Using the Formulas of YMCA

The YMCA uses a simple equation to estimate the body fat in adults.

Parameters:

(1) Waist circumference at the level of the umbilicus (navel) in inches
(2) Weight in pounds
(3) Gender

For Males

Body Fat in pounds = (4.15 X (waist circumference in inches)) - (0.082 X (body weight in pounds)) - 98.42

For Females

Body Fat in pounds = (4.15 X (waist circumference in inches)) - (0.082 X (body weight in pounds)) - 76.76

Percent Body Fat = (body fat in pounds) / (body weight in pounds)

Predicting Body Fat Percentage Using the Equation of Siri

The amount of body fat can be calculated for athletes using Siri's (1956) equation.

After calculating or estimating body density, body fat content can be derived using this formula.

Fat (%) = [(4.95/density) - 4.5] x 100

Predicting Percent Body Fat from Skinfold Thickness Using the Equations of Yuhasz

For Males

% Body Fat = (0.1051 X sum of skinfolds at triceps, subscapular, supraspinale, abdominal, thigh, calf) + 2.585

For Females

% Body Fat = (0.1548 X sum of skinfolds at triceps, subscapular, supraspinale, abdominal, thigh, calf) + 3.580

Typical % Body Fat

The average man has 15 to 17 % body fat, while the average woman is between 18 % and 22 %.

Typical values for elite athletes are 6 % to 12 % for men and 12 % to 20 % for women.

Percentage Body Fat for Male and Female Athletes for Variety of Sports

Sport	Males	Females
Baseball	12-15 %	12-18 %
Basketball	6-12 %	20-27 %
Canoe/Kayak	6-12 %	10-16 %
Cycling	5-15 %	15-20 %
Field & Ice Hockey	8-15 %	12-18%
Gymnastics	5-12 %	10-16 %
Rowing	6-14 %	12-18 %
Swimming	9-12 %	14-24 %
Tennis	12-16 %	16-24 %
Track - Runners	8-10 %	12-20 %
Track - Jumpers	7-12 %	10-18 %
Track - Throwers	14-20 %	20-28 %
Triathlon	5-12 %	10-15 %
Volleyball	11-14 %	16-25 %

Source: Yuhasz, 1974

Predicting Body Fat Mass and Fat Free Mass Using the Equations of Keys et al. and VanItallie et al.

Fat free or lean body mass is estimated or measured using a method such as bio-impedance, body density, or skinfold measures.

Body Fat Mass in kilograms = (total body mass in kilograms) – (fat free mass in kilograms)

Fat Free Mass Index (FFMI) = (fat free body mass in kilograms) / ((body height in meters) ^{2})

Body Fat Mass Index (BFMI) = (body fat mass in kilograms) / ((body height in meters) ^{2})

Because **(Body Mass)** = (fat free mass) + (body fat mass)

Body Mass Index (BMI) = FFMI + BFMI

Interpretation:

• A FFMI or BBMI below the 5th percentile for a reference population was associated with protein-energy malnutrition.

Parameters	**50th percentile**	**5th percentile**
FFMI	20 kg per square meter	17 kg per square meter
BFMA	4.4 kg per square meter	2.45 kg per square meter

♦♦♦♦♦♦♦♦

23

EQUATIONS FOR ESTIMATION OF LEAN BODY MASS

Predicting Lean Body Mass Using the Equations of Behnke

Fat Free Body Mass & Lean Body Mass

The fat-free body mass (FFBM) represents the body mass devoid of all fat whereas lean body mass (LBM) contains a small percentage of essential fat. LBM is a theoretical value developed by Behnke. For men Behnke considered it to be FFBM +3 % essential fat and for females FFBM +12 % fat (3 % essential fat + 9 % sex specific essential fat).

Fat and Fat Free Tissue Density

The density of fat and fat free tissue remains relatively constant: fat = 0.9 gm/cm³ and fat free tissue = 1.1 gm/cm³.

Lean body mass is simply an estimation of how much you weigh without the body fat - how much is the weight of the bones, organs and muscles. As the other factors are assumed to be relatively static, by monitoring your LBM one can get a fairly accurate estimate of the amount of muscle one is gaining or losing.

Body Fat in pounds = (Total Body Weight) (Body Fat Percentage (in decimal form))

Lean Body Mass =Total Body Weight - Body Fat in lbs.

So someone who weighs 173 pounds with a body fat percentage of 17.5 % would calculate as follows:

(173)(0.175) = 30.0 pounds of body fat

173 – 30.3 = 142.7 as LBM

The accuracy of LBM number is dependant on the accuracy of inputs - weight and body fat percentage.

Predicting Fat Free Mass from Anthropometric Measurements Using the Equations of Brennan and Fuchs et al.

Parameters:

(1) Gender

(2) Circumference of the flexed biceps in centimeters

(3) Height in centimeters
(4) Forearm circumference in centimeters
(5) Body weight in kilograms

Measurements:

(1) Flexed biceps circumference: Clench the fists and bend the elbow to 90°. Measure the maximum circumference of the upper arm.
(2) Forearm circumference: Bend the elbow to 90°. Mark a point on the forearm 0.25 inches from the skin fold. Extend the elbow straight. Measure the circumference of the forearm at the mark.

For Males

Fat Free Body Mass in kilograms = (0.018 X ((circumference of flexed biceps) 2)) + (0.514 X (height)) - 49.67

For Females

Fat Free Body Mass in kilograms = (1.619 X (forearm circumference)) + (0.311 X (height)) - 47.76

Percent Body Fat = ((body weight) - (fat free mass)) / (body weight) X 100%

Predicting Lean Body Mass Using Bioelectrical Impedance and the Equations of Bunc et al.

Lean Body Mass in kilograms = (body mass in kilograms) X (100 – (percent body fat)) / 100

Predicting Fat Free Mass from Quetelet Index Using the Equations of Garrow and Webter

Parameters:

(1) Body height in meters
(2) Body weight in kilograms

Fat Free Mass in kilograms = (body weight in kilograms) - (fat mass in kilograms)

Fat Mass in kilograms = ((A X (weight) / ((height) 2)) - B) X ((height) 2)
Where:

- A = 0.715 for males and 0.713 for females
- B = 12.1 for males and 9.74 for females

If the equations are rearranged:

Fat Free Mass for Males in kilograms = (0.285 X (weight in kilograms)) + (12.1 X ((height in meters) 2))

Fat Free Mass for Females in kilograms = (0.287 X (weight in kilograms)) + (9.74 X ((height in meters) 2))

Predicting Lean Body Mass from Height and Weight Using Equations of Hume

"Muscle weighs more than fat." This is true. While a pound of muscle weighs the same as a pound of fat, the volume is different. Muscle is denser than fat.

For men over the age of 16:

Lean Body Mass in kilograms = (0.32810 X (body weight in kilograms)) + (0.33929 X (height in centimeters)) - 29.5336

For women over the age of 30:

Lean Body Mass in kilograms = (0.29569 X (body weight in kilograms)) + (0.41813 X (height in centimeters)) - 43.2933

Predicting Lean Body Mass from Height and Weight Using the Equation of James

For Males:

Lean Body Mass in kilograms = (1.10 X (body weight in kilograms)) – (128 X ((body weight in kilograms) 2) / ((body height in cm) 2))

For females:

Lean Body Mass in kilograms = (1.07 X (body weight in kilograms)) – (148 X ((body weight in kilograms) 2) / ((body height in cm) 2))

Predicting Lean Body Mass Using the Equations of Katch and McArdle

LBM = Actual body weight (kg) - Body fat (kg)

When the weight of body fat is subtracted from the total body weight, the remaining weight is referred to as fat free weight or lean body mass. FFW reflects mainly the skeletal muscle mass but also includes the weight of other tissues & organs such as bones & skin. The less body fat the more the fat free mass. The average FFW of college going men is about 85 % of their total body weight and that of college aged women about 75 % of their total body weight.

Data on relative body fat values in male and female athletes is given in *Appendix V.*

Relative FFW refers to the percentage of total body weight that is lean body weight. Absolute FFW refers to the actual weight of the lean body mass & is calculated by the following formula:

Actual FFW = (Total Body Weight x Relative FFW) ÷ 100

For example, if an average college man has a total body weight of 160 pounds (72.6 kg), then his absolute FFW would be

= (160 pounds x 85 %) ÷ 100 = 136 pounds or (72.6 kg x 85 %) ÷ 100 = 61.7 kg.

FFW is usually considered to be positively related to athletic performance, because a larger FFW component means a large muscle mass and thus greater force potential.

Predicting Lean Body Mass Using Bioelectrical Impedance and the Equations of Segal et al.

Fat free mass can be estimated using several variables including bioelectrical impedance analysis. The precision can be enhanced by using equations specific for gender and fatness.

Parameters:

(1) Age in years
(2) Gender
(3) Body weight in kilograms
(4) Height in centimeters
(5) Resistance from bioelectrical impedance in ohms (0-1000 ohm scale)

Bioelectrical Impedance Measurement:

(1) Total body resistivity measured with a 4 terminal impedance analyzer.

(2) The individual lying down comfortably with limbs abducted.

(3) Current injector electrodes: (1) just below the phalangeal-metacarpal joint in the middle of the dorsal side of the right hand, (2) just below the transverse arch on the superior side of the right foot.

(4) Detector electrodes: (1) posterior side of the right wrist in the midline, with the prominent pisiform bone on the medial (fifth phalangeal) side, (2) ventrally across the medial ankle bone of the right ankle with foot semiflexed.

(5) Resistance to the flow of a 50 kHz (800 μA) injected current is measured on a 0-1000 ohm scale.

(6) Reactance is measured on a 0-200 ohm scale.

Criteria for Separating Normal from Obese (Anthropometric and Independent of Body Density):
(1) Men are considered obese if body fat is ≥ 20 %
(2) Women are considered obese if body fat ≥ 30 %

Estimated Lean Body Mass in kilograms = ((height variable) X ((height in cm) 2)) - ((resistance variable) X (resistance in ohms)) + ((weight variable) X (weight in kilograms)) - ((age variable) X (age in years)) + (intercept)

Variables	Men Normal	Men Obese	Women Normal	Women Obese
Height	0.00066360	0.00088580	0.00064602	0.00091186
Resistance	0.02117	0.02999	0.01397	0.01466
Weight	0.62854	0.42688	0.42087	0.2999
Age	0.12380	0.07002	0	0.07012
Intercept	9.33285	14.52435	10.43485	9.37938

Variation in hydration can affect the accuracy of the equations

Predicting Fat Free Mass from Anthropometric Measurements Using the Equation of von Dobeln

Parameters:

(1) Body height in meters
(2) Sum of left and right femoral condylar breadths in decimeters
(3) Sum of left and right radioulnar bistyloid breadths in decimeters

Where:

- A measurement in decimeters = (measurement in centimeters) / 10.
- The femoral condylar breadth measured at the knee, from the medial to lateral femoral condyles.
- The radioulnar bistyloid breadth measured at the wrist.
- Measurements of the condylar and bistyloid breadths require special calipers.

Fat Free Weight in kilograms = 15.1 X ((((height in meters) 2) X (sum of femoral condylar breadths in dm) X (sum of radioulnar bistyloid breadths in dm)) 2 (0.712))

Estimating Lean Body Mass in Young Women Using the Equations of Wilmore and Behnke (Age: 17.8 to 47.8 Years)

Measurements:

(1) All skin fold thicknesses taken with the subject standing.

(2) All circumferences except for the upper extremity measured with the subject standing.

(3) Skin fold thickness taken with a Lange skin-fold caliper with a caliper pressure of 10 grams per square mm.

(4) Diameters except for the wrist measured with a broad-blade Bayer-Rue anthropometer. The wrist measured with a vernier caliper.

Equation 1

Lean Body Weight in kilograms = 8.629 + (0.680 X (body weight in kilograms)) - (0.163 X (scapula skin fold in mm)) - (0.1 X (triceps skin fold in mm)) - (0.054 X (thigh skin fold in mm))

Equation 2

Lean Body Weight in kilograms = 8.987 + (0.732 X (body weight in kilograms)) + (3.786 X (wrist diameter in cm)) - (0.157 X (maximum abdominal circumference in cm)) - (0.249 X (hip circumference in cm)) + (0.434 X (forearm circumference in cm))

Equation 3

Lean Body Weight in kilograms = 1.661 + (0.668 X (body weight in kilograms)) - (0.158 X (scapula skin fold in mm)) - (0.081 X (triceps skin fold in mm)) + (0.555 X (neck circumference in cm)) - (0.141 X (maximum abdominal circumference in cm))

♦♦♦♦♦♦♦

Part VI

OTHER METHODS FOR CALCULATION OF BODY FAT CONTENT

The finding that women lower maximal aerobic capacity than men of an essentially equal training status can be attributed to a large extent to the fact that women possess more body fat (and less muscle mass) than men.

The fat and lean components of the human body have been determined by two general procedures. One procedure measures body composition directly by chemical analysis. The second approach assesses body composition indirectly with hydrostatic weighing or with simple circumferences or fatfold measurements. While direct methods form the basis for indirect techniques and are useful in animal research and for human cadaver analysis, the use of indirect procedures enables the scientists to assess the body composition of living people accurately.

BODY VOLUME DETERMINATION

About two thousand years ago the Greek mathematician Archimedes discovered a basic principle that is currently applied in the evaluation of body composition. An itinerant scholar of that time described the very interesting circumstances surrounding this event:

King Hieron of Syracuse suspected that his pure gold crown had been altered by substitution of silver for gold. The king directed Archimedes to device a method for testing the crown for its gold content without dismantling it. Archimedes pondered over this problem for many weeks without succeeding until one day he stepped into a bath filled to the top with water and observed the overflow of water. He thought about this for a moment, and then, wild with joy, jumped from the bath and ran naked through the streets of Syracuse shouting "Eureka! Eureka! I have discovered a way to solve the mystery of King's golden crown. Archimedes reasoned that a substance such as gold must have a volume proportionate to its weight, and the way to measure the volume of an irregular object such as the crown was to submerge it in water and collect the overflow. Archimedes took a lump of gold and silver, each having the same weight as the crown, and submerged each in a container full of water, and to his delight discovered that the crown displaced more water than the lump of gold and less than the lump of silver. What this meant was that the crown was indeed composed of silver and gold as the king had suspected (Katch and McArdle, 1983).

Essentially, what Archimedes evaluated was the specific gravity of the crown (ratio of the weight of the crown to the weight of an equal volume of water) compared to the specific gravities of gold and silver. Archimedes probably also reasoned that an object submerged in water must be buoyed up by a counterforce that equals the weight of the water it displaces. This buoyancy force helps to support an object in water against the downward pull of gravity. Thus, the object is said to lose weight in water. Because the object's loss of weight in water equals the weight of the volume of water it displaces, one can redefine specific gravity as the ratio of the weight of an object in air divided by its loss of weight in water.

$$\textbf{Specific Gravity} = \frac{\text{Weight of an object in air}}{\text{Loss of weight in water or (weight in air – weight in water)}}$$

The physical principle Archimedes discovered can be applied directly to the assessment of body composition in humans. This is achieved by determining the volume of the body by water submersion in relation to the total body mass. Because, density is mass per unit volume, it becomes a relatively simple matter to compute the body density once the mass and volume are known *(Katch and McArdle, 1983).*

HYDROSTATIC WEIGHING /HYDRODENSITOMETRY

Hydrostatic weighing (under water weighing) is a method of determining body fat percentage from body density. Density is the ratio of body weight to body volume. Volume is determined by submerging the person in water and calculating their weight on dry land compared to their weight in water. Lung volume must also be measured during the actual weighing. Hydrostatic weighing is a fairly accurate way to measure body fat, but it can be very expensive and it is not practical for use on a regular basis.

Purpose: The aim of underwater weighing is to measure the density of the body and from that figure calculate percentage body fat

Equipment Required: Hydrostatic stainless steel weighing tank, including underwater mounted chair and scale, weighted belt and nose clip. A more simple set up may include a chair and scale suspended from a diving board over a pool or hot tub.

Description/Procedure: The dry weight of the subject is first determined. The subject, in minimal clothing, then sits on a specialized seat, expels all the air from their lungs, and is lowered into the tank until all body parts are emerged. The person must remain motionless underwater while the underwater weight is recorded. This procedure is repeated several times to get a dependable underwater weight measure.

Scoring: Body density = Wa / (((Wa - Ww) / Dw) - (RV + 100cc)), where Wa = body weight in air (kg), Ww = body weight in water (kg), Dw = density of water, RV = residual lung volume, and 100cc is the correction for air trapped in the gastrointestinal tract. The body density (D) can be converted to percent body fat (% BF) using the Siri equation.

Advantages: Underwater weighing is the most widely used test of body density and in the past was the criterion measure for other indirect measures.

Disadvantages: The equipment required to do underwater weighing is expensive and time consuming. The tanks are mostly located at university or other research institutions and there is generally not easy access for the general population.

Validity: This method may underestimate body fat percentage of athletes as they tend to have denser bones and muscles than non-athletes, and may overestimate body fat percentage of elderly patients suffering from osteoporosis.

Other Comments: Residual lung volume (RV) is required for the calculation. For more accuracy it should be physically measured, though there are calculations for RV estimation. One estimation of residual volume is one third of forced vital capacity (FVC). This method is also known as Hydrodensitometry or underwater weighing.

BIOELECTRIC IMPEDANCE ANALYSIS (BIA)

Equipment Required: A Bioelectric Impedance Analyzer is a sophisticated scientific instrument, used in research and analysis. On a budget level, many bathroom type weighing scales are also available with a Bioelectric Impedance Analyzer, which is two built-in footpad electrodes on the base of the scale which the person stands on.

Description/Procedure: As the bioelectric impendence device measures the resistance of body tissues to the flow of a small electrical signal, the person being measured should not be in contact with any other non conducting surface, with legs apart and arms away from the body. Some devices require a pair of electrodes are placed on the hand and wrist, and another pair placed on the ankle and foot (usually opposite sides of the body), while other devices simply require you to stand on two foot plates. Follow the instructions of your particular device.

How it Works: Bioelectrical impedance measures the resistance of body tissues to the flow of a small, harmless electrical signal. The proportion of body fat can be calculated as the current flows more easily through the parts of the body that are composed mostly of water (such as blood, urine &

muscle) than it does through bone, fat or air. It is possible to predict how much body fat a person has by combining the bioelectric impendence measure with other factors such as height, weight, gender, fitness level and age.

Advantages: This method of body composition analysis is very simple and quick to perform, and if you have the right equipment can be done at home.

Disadvantages: The equipment is relatively expensive (units on the low end of the scale are available for about $100), with prices ranging up to thousands of dollars.

Reliability: The impedance measure is affected by body hydration status, body temperature, time of day, and therefore requires well controlled conditions to get accurate and reliable measurements. If a person is dehydrated, the amount of fat will likely be overestimated

Other Comments: Bioelectric impedance analysis is based on the principle that the resistance to an applied electric current is inversely related to the amount of fat-free mass within the body. This method does not take into account the location of body fat.

Contraindications: People with pacemakers should not use Bioelectrical Impendence for body composition analysis.

DUAL-ENERGY X-RAY ABSORPTIOMETRY (DEXA)

Equipment Required: DEXA machine, which differentiates body weight into the components of lean soft tissue, fat soft tissue and bone, based on the differential attenuation by tissues of two levels of x-rays.

Description/Procedure: The person lays on the whole body scanner, with the x-ray sources mounted beneath a table and a detector overhead. The person is scanned with photons that are generated by two low-dose x-rays at different energy levels. The body's absorption of the photons at the two levels is measured. The ratios can be then used to predict total body fat, fat-free mass and total body bone mineral. The procedure can take about 10 - 20 minutes.

Advantages: This method is precise, accurate, and reliable. DEXA measurements are based on a three compartmental model (total body mineral (from bones), fat-free soft (lean) mass and fat tissue mass) rather than two compartments as in most other methods. DEXA can also distinguish regional as well as whole body parameters of body composition. As such, it is considered a reference standard, and the latest body composition research uses this method.

Disadvantages: The equipment is expensive, and often requires trained radiology personnel to operate.

Other Comments: If not for the limiting price of measurement, DEXA would be considered the criterion method of body composition analysis.

NEAR INFRARED INTERACTANCE

Equipment Required: Near Infrared Interactance is measured using a computerized spectrophotometer, which has a single, rapid scanning monochromator and fiber optic probe.

Description/Procedure: This method uses the principles of light absorption and reflection to measure body fat. The measurement is taken on the person's dominant arm. A monochromator, or light "wand", sends a low-energy beam of near-infrared light into the biceps and penetrates the underlying tissue to a depth of one centimeter. The energy is either reflected, absorbed, or transmitted, depending on the scattering and absorption properties of the biceps. A detector within the wand measures the intensity of the re-emitted light. Shifts in the wavelength of the reflected beam and a prediction equation are used to compute the percent body fat.

Advantages: The measurement is safe and the equipment is portable and lightweight. It requires little training to use.

Disadvantages: This technique still lacks validation in humans, and may not accurately predict body fat across a broad range of fat levels. It assumes fat in the arm is proportional to total body fat, which may not be true.

Other Comments: This method is based on what was developed by the United States Department of Agriculture to measure the body composition of livestock and the fat content of various grains.

TOTAL BODY POTASSIUM (TBK)

Aim: This procedure accurately determines the body's total cell mass (that is, the active growing tissues in the body), which in turn can be used to estimate fat-free or lean body mass. When this measurement is combined with measurements from the Total Body Protein, you can determine total organ and muscle mass.

Equipment Required: Extremely sensitive equipment which measures the gamma rays emitted from the naturally occurring radioactive isotope of potassium known as 40K.

Description/Procedure: The subject must first be shielded from naturally occurring radiation in the environment, using concrete, lead or steel. Once the external radiation is minimized, the subject's natural radiation as 40K is measured through the use of scintillation counters. The radiated 40K is measured over a specified time period and from this TBK is estimated.

Advantages: Other than the initial outlay cost for equipment, this method is relatively simple to carry out, safe, and operational expenses are relatively small.

Disadvantages: The required instrument is very expensive to install and has limited availability.

Comments: The determination of TBK is based on the fact that the proportion of total potassium found in human tissues as 40K is constant at 0.0118% of total potassium. Therefore, by measuring 40K you can calculate total-body potassium. As potassium is distributed almost entirely within the intracellular compartment of fat-free mass, and using the ratio of total-body potassium to fat-free mass, once TBK is known you can calculate fat-free mass and total-body fat.

Use: TBK is a classical method of quantifying total-body fat. It has mostly been replaced by newer more accurate techniques.

Source: Burmeister (1965); Rosin and Shulov (1961) and Gilbert et al (1961) – Retrieved from www.sport-fitness-advisor.com

TOTAL BODY PROTEIN (TBP)

Aim: This technique measures the amount of nitrogen in the body, which is a direct indicator of total body protein (TBP).

Equipment Required: Prompt Gamma Activation Analyzer.

Description/Procedure: Before the scan begins, the subject undergoes measures of chest, arm, waist, and leg widths and thickness. These measurements are used to adjust the nitrogen scan data for a subject's size and shape. The subject then lies fairly still in the supine position as three separate body sections (legs, waist and chest) are measured for 10 minutes each. The scan involves irradiation of the subject with neutrons, and causes them to give off characteristic gamma rays. The gamma rays are collected from detectors placed on either side of the subject, and analyzed using conventional spectroscopy.

Results: Total protein can be estimated from the ratio of nitrogen to hydrogen counts. Nitrogen and protein are closely linked with each other because of a stable chemical combination (protein is 16% nitrogen) and because over 98% of the total body nitrogen is in the form of protein.

Advantages: When this measurement is combined with measurements from the Total Body Potassium Counter, it is possible to determine total organ and muscle mass.

Disadvantages: the required instrument is very expensive to install and has limited availability.

Comments: The system is called a *prompt gamma* system as the gammas are produced immediately, and stop appearing as soon as the neutron source is removed.

Use: Prompt Gamma Activation Analysis is the gold-standard method for measuring the amount of nitrogen in the body, which in turn is a direct indicator of total body protein (TBP).

WHOLE BODY AIR DISPLACEMENT PLETHYSMOGRAPHY

Aim: Using air displacement technology for measuring and tracking body fat and lean mass.

Equipment Required: Bod Pod by Life Measurements Instruments, Concord, CA

Description/Procedure: The Bod Pod system measures body composition by determining body volume and body weight. The subject should not have exercises for the previous two hours, as they must be fully rested and hydration status and increases in muscle temperature can adversely affect the results. Body weight is measured using scales. Body volume is measured by first measuring the volume of the chamber while empty. Then the volume of the subject chamber is measured with the subject inside. By subtraction, the volume of the subject is determined. Once those body volume and weight are determined, body density can be computed and inserted into an equation to provide percent fat measurements.

Method: Volume is determined by monitoring changes in pressure within a closed chamber. These pressure changes are achieved by oscillating a speaker mounted between the front testing chamber and a rear reference chamber, which causes complementary pressure changes in each chamber. The pressure changes are very small and are not noticed by the individual being tested.

Advantages: High level of accuracy, ease-of-use, and fast test time. Compared to underwater weighing, the Bod Pod does not require getting wet, and is well suited for special populations such as children, obese, elderly, and disabled persons.

Disadvantages: The Bod Pod unit is very expensive ($30,000 - $40,000) and only a few facilities have it. Some research or academic institutions may offer tests for a fee.

Accuracy: The manufacturers indicate that the general error range of the BOD POD is 1-2 % (the same as hydrostatic weighing).

Comments: The Bod Pod technology is fundamentally the same as underwater (hydrostatic) weighing, but uses air instead of water.

Source: Dempster and Aitkens (1995); McCrory et al. (1995) and Fields et al. (2002) Retrieved from www.sport-fitness-advisor.com

MAGNETIC RESONANCE IMAGING (MRI)

Magnetic resonance imaging (MRI), also called Nuclear magnetic resonance imaging (NMRI), is a noninvasive, painless medical imaging technique used commonly in radiology. MRI provides detailed images of the body in any plane, and is used to visualize the structure and function of the body for the diagnosis and treatment of human conditions. Due to the detailed images that can be provided using this technique, it is possible to get accurate measurements of the composition of body tissue.

Aim: MRI that is used to diagnose and treat medical conditions. In terms of body composition, the high-quality images can be processed to differentiate and measure the amounts of fat and lean body tissue and their distribution.

Equipment Required: MRI Scanner

Method: Simply, a magnetic field 'excites' water and fat molecules in the body, producing a measurable signal.

Description/Procedure: A person lies within the magnet as a computer scans the body, which can take about 30 minutes. High-quality images show the amount of fat and where it is distributed.

Advantages: This is a noninvasive method for body composition analysis

Disadvantages: The use of MRI is limited due to the high cost of equipment and analysis.

Other Comments: This technique uses no ionizing radiation (unlike CT scans), so is very safe.

TOTAL BODY ELECTRICAL CONDUCTIVITY (TOBEC)

Equipment Required: TOBEC device

Method: TOBEC is based on lean tissue being a better conductor of electricity than fat.

Description/Procedure: The subject lies in a cylinder that generates a very weak electromagnetic field. The strength of the field depends on the electrolytes found in the person's body water. In about 10 seconds, TOBEC makes 10 conductivity readings that estimate lean body mass.

Advantages: Very accurate noninvasive method for body composition analysis

Disadvantages: Equipment is costly.

COMPUTED TOMOGRAPHY (CT SCAN)

Aim: CT scanning is a noninvasive, painless medical test, which is used to diagnose and treat medical conditions. In terms of body composition, the high quality images can be processed to differentiate and measure the amounts of fat and lean body tissue, and further distinguish between intra-abdominal fat to extra-abdominal fat

Equipment Required: CT Scanner, which is typically a large machine with a tunnel in the center. A moveable examination table, on which the patient lies, slides into and out of this tunnel.

Description/Procedure: An x-ray tube rotates around the subject and sends a beam of photons toward a detector opposite. The data is collected, stored, and applied to complex algorithms to build cross-sectional images of the body, which can further be processed into 3D images.

Results: CT is particularly useful in giving a ratio of intra-abdominal fat to extra-abdominal fat

Advantages: This is a noninvasive method for body composition analysis

Disadvantages: The potential of CT analysis is limited by exposure to radiation and high equipment cost.

Other Comments: Also known as computed axial tomography or CAT Scans.

♦♦♦♦♦♦♦♦

APPENDIX I

RM-1 (1- RM) ASSESSMENT

One Repetition Max (One Rep Max)

The heaviest weight you can lift for a single repetition, on a given exercise. Often abbreviated to RM-1 or 1-RM. Ten rep max can also be used. Ensure you are fully warmed up prior to attempting to lift your estimated 1RM. If you feel you could have lifted more, do not attempt to do so on the same day as your muscles will be fatigued and so reduce the reliability of the test.

The 1-RM bench press assesses the maximum muscular strength of the major muscles of the upper body. Your 1-RM can be determined by using following guidelines.

After each successful lift, increase the weight by 2 to 5 kg until the maximum lift is achieved. Allow 3-5 minutes rest between each lift.

Maximum Load /Maximum Strength Assessment (1-RM)

Strength tests to measure **maximal strength** are suitable for many athletes. For the reasons why maximal strength is important to athletic performance. The one repetition maximum (1-RM) is still considered the 'gold standard' of strength assessment by most coaches. The procedure usually consists of the **bench press** and **back squat** or **leg press**. These are **compound movements** incorporating most of the large muscle groups in the upper and lower body.

Either free weights or resistance machines can be used for the testing procedure but the choice should be determined by what the athlete intends to use during training. The specific adaptation to imposed demands means that a barbell back squat will more accurately determine the effectiveness of a free weights strength program than a machine leg press for example.

Testing Procedure

The protocol for 1-RM testing as set out by the National Strength & Conditioning Association is given below:

1-RM Testing Protocol

1	Instruct the athlete to warm up with a light resistance that easily allows 5-10 repititions
2	Provide a 1 minute rest period
3	Estimate a warm up load that will allow the athlete to complete 3-5

	repititions by adding • 10-20 pounds (4-9 kg) or 5-10 % for upper body exercise or • 30-40 pounds (13-18 kg) or 10-20 % for lower body exercise
4	Provide a 2 minute rest period
5	Estimate a conservative, near maximum load that will allow the athlete to complete 2-3 repitions by adding • 10-20 pounds (4-9 kg) or 5-10 % for upper body exercise or • 30-40 pounds (13-18 kg) or 10-20 % for lower body exercise
6	Provide a 2-4 minute rest period
7	Make a load increase • 10-20 pounds (4-9 kg) or 5-10 % for upper body exercise or • 30-40 pounds (13-18 kg) or 10-20 % for lower body exercise
8	Instruct the athlete to attempt a 1-RM
9	If the athlete was successful provide a 2-4 minute rest period, decrease the load by subtracting • 5-10 pounds (2-4 kg) or 2-5 % for upper body exercises or • 15-20 pounds (7-9 kg) or 5-10 % for lower body exercises And then go back to step 8 Continue increasing or decreasing the load until the athlete can complete one repition with proper exercise technique. Ideally the athlete's 1-RM will be measured within five testing sets

Results

Take your 1-RM weight for the bench press and leg press and **divide it** by your **body weight**. So for example, if you were able to lift **300 lbs (136 kg)** on the leg press and you weigh **175 lbs (80 kg)**, that equates to a score of **1.7**. Compare your score with the chart below...

1-RM Scores

1-RM Scores					
Bench Press	**Poor**	**Fair**	**Good**	**Very good**	**Excellent**
Men	0.6	0.8	1.0	1.2	1.4
Women	0.3	0.4	0.5	0.6	0.7
Leg Press	**Poor**	**Fair**	**Good**	**Very good**	**Excellent**
Men	1.4	1.8	2.0	2.4	2.8
Women	1.2	1.4	1.8	2.0	2.2

The table below gives typical 1-RM scores for various groups of athletes:

Normative Data for 1-RM Bench Press and Back Squat for Various Groups of Athletes

Groups	1-RM Bench Press		1-RM Back Squat	
	lb	kg	lb	kg
College Football Players	385	175	531	241
Offensive Linemen	377	171	502	228
Defensive Linemen	358	163	476	216
Offensive Backs	355	152	471	214
Tight Ends	333	151	464	211
Defensive Backs	307	140	415	189
Wide Receivers	280	127	390	177
Quarter Backs	277	126	379	172
College Baseball Players (Men)	233	106	308	140
College Basketball Players (Men)	225	102	302	137
College Track (Men)	207	94	233	106
College Track (Women)	103	47	150	68
College Basketball Players (Women)	113	51	182	83

Source: Berg et al., 1992; Baechle and Earle, 2000 and Schweigert, 1996

If you need to determine your maximum load (1-RM) for a weight training exercise then there is a way of obtaining an approximate value based on a weight and the number of repetitions you can perform to exhaustion for that exercise. The following equations provide a good estimate of the maximum load providing the number of repetitions does not exceed 12.

Brzycki's Equation to Determine Max Load (1-RM Score)

- Weight ÷ (1.0278 - (0.0278 × Number of repetitions))

Alternative Equation to Determine Max Load (1-RM Score)

The alternative equation is as follows:

- Weight × (1 + (0.033 × Number of repetitions))

♦♦♦♦♦♦♦♦

APPENDIX II

ACCEPTABLE WEIGHT RANGE FOR HEIGHT TO FIND WEIGHT CORRESPONDING TO BMI LEVELS

Height (cm)	Minimum Weight (BMI = 20 kg/m^2)	Maximum Weight (BMI = 25 kg/m^2)	Obesity (BMI = 30 kg/m^2)
150	45.0	56.3	67.5
151	45.6	57.0	68.4
152	46.2	57.8	69.3
153	46.8	58.5	70.2
154	47.4	59.3	71.1
155	48.1	60.1	72.1
156	48.7	60.8	73.0
157	49.3	61.6	73.9
158	49.9	62.4	74.9
159	50.6	63.2	75.8
160	51.2	64.0	76.8
161	51.8	64.8	77.8
162	52.5	65.6	78.7
163	53.1	66.4	79.7
164	53.8	67.2	80.7
165	54.5	68.1	81.7
166	55.1	68.9	82.7
167	55.8	69.7	83.7
168	56.4	70.6	84.7
169	57.1	71.4	85.7
170	57.8	72.3	86.7
171	58.5	73.1	87.7
172	59.2	74.0	88.8
173	59.9	74.8	89.8
174	60.6	75.7	90.8
175	61.3	76.6	91.9
176	62.0	77.4	92.9
177	62.7	78.3	94.0
178	63.4	79.2	95.1
179	64.1	80.1	96.1
180	64.8	81.0	97.2
181	65.5	81.9	98.3
182	66.2	82.8	99.4

183	67.0	83.7	100.5
184	67.7	84.6	101.6
185	68.5	85.6	102.7
186	69.2	86.5	103.8
187	69.9	87.4	104.9
188	70.7	88.4	106.0
189	71.4	89.3	107.2
190	72.2	90.3	108.3
191	73.0	91.2	109.4
192	73.7	92.2	110.6
193	74.5	93.1	111.7
194	75.3	94.1	112.9
195	76.1	95.1	114.1
196	76.8	96.0	115.2
197	77.6	97.0	116.4
198	78.4	98.0	117.6
199	79.2	99.0	118.8
200	80.0	100.0	120.0

Source: www.topendsports.com

♦♦♦♦♦♦♦♦

APPENDIX III

PERCENTILES OF UPPER ARM FAT AREA (SQUARE MILLIMETERS)

Age (yrs)	Men			Women		
	5th %	50th %	95th %	5th %	50th %	95th %
1-1.9	452	741	1176	401	706	1140
2-2.9	434	737	1148	469	747	1173
3-3.9	464	736	1151	473	822	1158
4-4.9	428	722	1085	490	766	1236
5-5.9	446	713	1299	470	812	1536
6-6.9	371	678	1519	464	827	1436
7-7.9	423	758	1511	491	920	1644
8-8.9	410	725	1558	527	1042	2482
9-9.9	485	859	2081	642	1219	2524
10-10.9	523	982	2609	616	1141	3005
11-11.9	536	1148	2574	707	1301	3690
12-12.9	554	1172	3580	782	1511	3369
13-13.9	475	1096	3322	726	1625	4150
14-14.9	453	1082	3508	981	1818	3765
15-15.9	521	937	3100	839	1886	4195
16-16.9	542	1078	3041	1126	2006	4236
17-17.9	598	1096	2888	1042	2104	5159
18-18.9	560	1264	3928	1003	2104	3733
19-24.9	594	1406	3652	1046	2166	4896
25-34.9	675	1752	3786	1173	2548	5560
35-44.9	703	1792	3624	1336	2898	5847
45-54.9	749	1741	3928	1459	3244	6140
55-64.9	658	1645	3466	1345	3369	6152
65-74.9	573	1621	3327	1363	3063	5530

Source:Frisancho, 1981

PERCENTILES OF UPPER ARM CIRCUMFERENCE (MILLIMETERS)

Age (yrs)	Men			Women		
	5th %	50th %	95th %	5th %	50th %	95th %
1-1.9	142	159	183	138	156	177
2-2.9	141	162	185	142	160	184
3-3.9	150	167	190	143	167	189
4-4.9	149	171	192	149	169	191
5-5.9	153	175	204	153	175	211
6-6.9	155	179	228	156	176	211
7-7.9	162	187	230	164	183	231
8-8.9	162	190	245	168	195	261
9-9.9	175	200	257	178	211	260
10-10.9	181	210	274	174	210	265
11-11.9	186	223	280	185	224	303
12-12.9	193	232	303	194	237	294
13-13.9	194	247	301	202	243	338
14-14.9	220	253	322	214	252	322
15-15.9	222	264	320	208	254	322
16-16.9	244	278	343	218	258	334
17-17.9	246	285	347	220	264	350
18-18.9	245	297	379	222	258	325
19-24.9	262	308	372	221	265	345
25-34.9	271	319	375	233	277	368
35-44.9	278	326	374	241	290	378
45-54.9	267	322	376	242	299	384
55-64.9	258	317	369	243	303	385
65-74.9	248	307	355	240	299	373

Source:Frisancho, 1981

PERCENTILES OF TRICEPS SKINFOLD (MILLIMETERS)

Age (yrs)	Men			Women		
	5th %	50th %	95th %	5th %	50th %	95th %
1-1.9	6	10	16	6	10	16
2-2.9	6	10	15	6	10	16
3-3.9	6	10	15	7	11	15
4-4.9	6	9	14	7	10	16
5-5.9	6	9	15	6	10	18
6-6.9	5	8	16	6	10	16
7-7.9	5	9	17	6	11	18
8-8.9	5	8	16	6	12	24
9-9.9	6	10	18	8	13	22
10-10.9	6	10	21	7	12	27
11-11.9	6	11	24	7	13	28
12-12.9	6	11	28	8	14	27
13-13.9	5	10	26	8	15	30
14-14.9	4	9	24	9	16	28
15-15.9	4	8	24	8	17	32
16-16.9	4	8	22	10	18	31
17-17.9	5	8	19	10	19	37
18-18.9	4	9	24	10	18	30
19-24.9	4	10	22	10	18	34
25-34.9	5	12	24	10	21	37
35-44.9	5	12	23	12	23	38
45-54.9	6	12	25	12	25	40
55-64.9	5	11	22	12	25	38
65-74.9	4	11	22	12	24	36

Source:Frisancho, 1974

PERCENTILES OF UPPER ARM MUSCLE AREA (SQUARE MILLIMETERS)

Age (yrs)	Men			Women		
	5th %	50th %	95th %	5th %	50th %	95th %
1-1.9	956	1278	1720	885	1221	1621
2-2.9	973	1345	1787	973	1269	1727
3-3.9	1095	1484	1853	1014	1396	1846
4-4.9	1207	1579	2008	1058	1475	1958
5-5.9	1298	1720	2285	1238	1598	2159
6-6.9	1360	1815	2493	1354	1683	2323
7-7.9	1497	2027	2886	1330	1815	2469
8-8.9	1550	2089	2788	1513	2034	2996
9-9.9	1811	2288	3257	1723	2227	3112
10-10.9	1930	2575	3882	1740	2296	3093
11-11.9	2016	2670	4226	1784	2612	3953
12-12.9	2216	3022	4640	2092	2904	3847
13-13.9	2363	3553	4794	2269	3130	4568
14-14.9	2830	3963	5530	2418	3220	4850
15-15.9	3138	4481	5900	2426	3248	4756
16-16.9	3625	4951	6980	2308	3248	4946
17-17.9	3998	5286	7736	2442	3336	5251
18-18.9	4070	5552	8355	2398	3243	4767
19-24.9	4508	5913	8200	2538	3406	4940
25-34.9	4694	6214	8436	2661	3573	5541
35-44.9	4844	6490	8488	2750	3783	5877
45-54.9	4546	6297	8458	2784	3858	5964
55-64.9	4422	6144	8419	2784	4045	6247
65-74.9	3973	5716	7453	2737	4019	6214

Source:Frisancho, 1974

♦♦♦♦♦♦♦♦

APPENDIX IV

CONVERSION CONSTANTS TO PREDICT PERCENT BODY FAT FOR YOUNG WOMEN

ABDOMEN			THIGH			FOREARM		
Inches	cm	Constant A	Inches	cm	Constant B	Inches	cm	Constant C
20.00	50.80	26.74	14.00	35.56	29.13	6.00	15.24	25.86
20.25	51.43	27.07	14.25	36.19	29.65	6.25	15.87	26.94
20.50	52.07	27.41	14.50	36.83	30.17	6.50	16.51	28.02
20.75	52.70	27.74	14.75	37.46	30.69	6.75	17.14	29.10
21.00	53.34	28.07	15.00	38.10	31.21	7.00	17.78	30.17
21.25	53.97	28.41	15.25	38.73	31.73	7.25	18.41	31.25
21.50	54.61	28.74	15.50	39.37	32.25	7.50	19.05	32.33
21.75	55.24	29.08	15.75	40.00	32.77	7.75	19.68	33.41
22.00	55.88	29.41	16.00	40.64	33.29	8.00	23.32	34.48
22.25	56.51	29.74	16.25	41.27	33.81	8.25	20.95	35.56
22.50	57.15	30.08	16.50	41.91	34.33	8.50	21.59	36.64
22.75	57.78	30.41	16.75	42.52	34.85	8.75	22.22	37.72
23.00	58.42	30.75	17.00	43.18	35.37	9.00	22.86	38.79
23.25	59.05	31.08	17.25	43.81	35.89	9.25	23.49	39.87
23.50	59.69	31.42	17.50	44.45	36.41	9.50	24.13	40.95
23.75	60.32	31.75	17.75	45.08	36.93	9.75	24.76	42.03
24.00	60.96	32.08	18.00	45.72	37.45	10.00	25.40	43.10
24.25	61.59	32.42	18.25	46.35	37.97	10.25	26.03	44.18
24.50	62.23	32.75	18.50	46.99	38.49	10.50	26.67	45.26
24.75	62.86	33.09	18.75	47.62	39.01	10.75	27.30	46.34
25.00	63.50	33.42	19.00	48.26	39.53	11.00	27.94	47.41
25.25	64.13	33.76	19.25	48.89	40.05	11.25	28.57	48.49
25.50	64.77	34.09	19.50	49.53	40.57	11.50	29.21	49.57
25.75	65.40	34.42	19.75	50.16	41.09	11.75	29.84	50.65
26.00	66.04	34.76	20.00	50.80	41.61	12.00	30.48	51.73
26.25	66.67	35.09	20.25	51.43	42.13	12.25	31.11	52.80
26.50	67.31	35.43	20.50	52.07	42.65	12.50	31.75	53.88
26.75	67.94	35.76	20.75	52.70	43.17	12.75	32.38	54.96
27.00	68.58	36.10	21.00	53.34	43.69	13.00	33.02	56.04
27.25	69.21	36.43	21.25	53.97	44.21	13.25	33.65	57.11
27.50	69.85	36.76	21.50	54.61	44.73	13.50	34.29	58.19
27.75	70.48	37.10	21.75	55.24	45.25	13.75	34.91	59.27
28.00	71.12	37.43	22.00	55.88	45.77	14.00	35.56	60.35
28.25	71.75	37.77	22.25	56.51	46.29	14.25	36.19	61.42
28.50	72.39	38.10	22.50	57.15	46.81	14.50	36.83	62.50
28.75	73.02	38.43	22.75	57.78	47.33	14.75	37.46	63.58
29.00	73.66	38.77	23.00	58.42	47.85	15.00	38.10	64.66
29.25	74.29	39.10	23.25	59.05	48.37	15.25	38.73	65.73
29.50	74.93	39.44	23.50	59.69	48.89	15.50	39.37	66.81
29.75	75.56	39.77	23.75	60.32	49.41	15.75	40.00	67.89
30.00	76.20	40.11	24.00	60.96	49.93	16.00	40.64	68.97

30.25	76.83	40.44	24.25	61.59	50.45	16.25	41.27	70.04
30.50	77.47	40.77	24.50	62.23	50.97	16.50	41.91	71.12
30.75	78.10	41.11	24.75	62.86	51.49	16.75	42.52	72.20
31.00	78.74	41.44	25.00	63.50	52.01	17.00	43.18	73.28
31.25	79.37	41.78	25.25	64.13	52.53	17.25	43.81	74.36
31.50	80.01	42.11	25.50	64.77	53.05	17.50	44.45	75.43
31.75	80.64	42.45	25.75	65.40	53.57	17.75	45.08	76.51
32.00	81.28	42.78	26.00	66.04	54.09	18.00	45.72	77.59
32.25	81.91	43.11	26.25	66.67	54.61	18.25	46.35	78.67
32.50	82.55	43.45	26.50	67.31	55.13	18.50	46.99	79.74
32.75	83.18	43.78	26.75	67.94	55.65	18.75	47.62	80.82
33.00	83.82	44.12	27.00	68.58	56.17	19.00	48.26	81.90
33.25	84.45	44.45	27.25	69.21	56.69	19.25	48.89	82.98
33.50	85.09	44.78	27.50	69.85	57.21	19.50	49.53	84.05
33.75	85.72	45.12	27.75	70.48	57.73	19.75	50.16	85.13
34.00	86.36	45.45	28.00	71.12	58.26	20.00	50.80	86.21
34.25	86.99	45.79	28.25	71.75	58.78	20.25	51.43	87.29
34.50	87.63	46.12	28.50	72.39	59.30	20.50	52.07	88.34
34.75	88.26	46.46	28.75	73.02	59.82	20.75	52.70	92.42
35.00	88.90	46.79	29.00	73.66	60.34	21.00	53.34	93.50
35.25	89.53	47.12	29.25	74.29	60.86			
35.50	90.17	47.46	29.50	74.93	61.38			
35.75	90.80	47.79	29.75	75.56	61.90			
36.00	91.44	48.13	30.00	76.20	62.42			
36.25	92.07	48.46	30.25	76.83	62.94			
36.50	92.71	48.80	30.50	77.47	63.46			
36.75	93.34	49.13	30.75	78.10	63.98			
37.00	93.98	49.46	31.00	78.74	64.50			
37.25	94.61	49.80	31.25	79.37	65.02			
37.50	95.25	50.13	31.50	80.01	65.54			
37.75	95.88	50.47	31.75	80.64	66.06			
38.00	96.52	50.80	32.00	81.28	66.58			
38.25	97.15	51.13	32.25	81.91	67.10			
38.50	97.79	51.47	32.50	82.55	67.62			
38.75	98.42	51.80	32.75	83.18	68.14			
39.00	99.06	52.14	33.00	83.82	68.66			
39.25	99.69	52.47	33.25	84.45	69.18			
39.50	100.33	52.81	33.50	85.09	69.70			
39.75	100.96	53.14	33.75	85.72	70.22			
40.00	101.60	53.47	34.00	86.36	70.74			

Source: McArdle et al., 1981

CONVERSION CONSTANTS TO PREDICT PERCENT BODY FAT FOR OLDER WOMEN

ABDOMEN			THIGH			CALF		
Inches	cm	Constant A	Inches	cm	Constant B	Inches	cm	Constant C
25.00	63.50	29.69	14.00	35.56	17.31	10.00	25.40	14.46
25.25	64.13	29.98	14.25	36.19	17.62	10.25	26.03	14.82
25.50	64.77	30.28	14.50	36.83	17.93	10.50	26.67	15.18
25.75	65.40	30.58	14.75	37.46	18.24	10.75	27.30	15.54
26.00	66.04	30.87	15.00	38.10	18.55	11.00	27.94	15.91
26.25	66.67	31.17	15.25	38.73	18.86	11.25	28.57	16.27
26.50	67.31	31.47	15.50	39.37	19.17	11.50	29.21	16.63
26.75	67.94	31.76	15.75	40.00	19.47	11.75	29.84	16.99
27.00	68.58	32.06	16.00	40.64	19.78	12.00	30.48	17.35
27.25	69.21	32.36	16.25	41.27	20.09	12.25	31.11	17.71
27.50	69.85	32.65	16.50	41.91	20.40	12.50	31.75	18.08
27.75	70.48	32.95	16.75	42.52	20.71	12.75	32.38	18.44
28.00	71.12	33.25	17.00	43.18	21.02	13.00	33.02	18.80
28.25	71.75	33.55	17.25	43.81	21.33	13.25	33.65	19.16
28.50	72.39	33.84	17.50	44.45	21.64	13.50	34.29	19.52
28.75	73.02	34.14	17.75	45.08	21.95	13.75	34.91	19.88
29.00	73.66	34.44	18.00	45.72	22.26	14.00	35.56	20.24
29.25	74.29	34.73	18.25	46.35	22.57	14.25	36.19	20.61
29.50	74.93	35.03	18.50	46.99	22.87	14.50	36.83	20.97
29.75	75.56	35.33	18.75	47.62	23.18	14.75	37.46	21.33
30.00	76.20	36.62	19.00	48.26	23.49	15.00	38.10	21.69
30.25	76.83	35.92	19.25	48.89	23.80	15.25	38.73	22.05
30.50	77.47	36.22	19.50	49.53	24.11	15.50	39.37	22.41
30.75	78.10	36.51	19.75	50.16	24.42	15.75	40.00	22.77
31.00	78.74	36.81	20.00	50.80	24.73	16.00	40.64	23.14
31.25	79.37	37.11	20.25	51.43	25.04	16.25	41.27	23.50
31.50	80.01	37.40	20.50	52.07	25.35	16.50	41.91	23.86
31.75	80.64	37.70	20.75	52.70	25.66	16.75	42.52	24.22
32.00	81.28	38.00	21.00	53.34	25.97	17.00	43.18	24.58
32.25	81.91	38.30	21.25	53.97	26.28	17.25	43.81	24.94
32.50	82.55	38.59	21.50	54.61	26.58	17.50	44.45	25.31
32.75	83.18	38.89	21.75	55.24	26.89	17.75	45.08	25.67
33.00	83.82	39.19	22.00	55.88	27.20	18.00	45.72	26.03
33.25	84.45	39.48	22.25	56.51	27.51	18.25	46.35	26.39
33.50	85.09	39.78	22.50	57.15	27.82	18.50	46.99	26.75
33.75	85.72	40.08	22.75	57.78	28.13	18.75	47.62	27.11
34.00	86.36	40.37	23.00	58.42	28.44	19.00	48.26	27.47
34.25	86.99	40.67	23.25	59.05	28.75	19.25	48.89	27.84
34.50	87.63	40.97	23.50	59.69	29.06	19.50	49.53	28.20
34.75	88.26	41.26	23.75	60.32	29.37	19.75	50.16	28.56
35.00	88.90	41.56	24.00	60.96	29.68	20.00	50.80	28.92
35.25	89.53	41.86	24.25	61.59	29.98	20.25	51.43	29.28
35.50	90.17	42.15	24.50	62.23	30.29	20.50	52.07	29.64
35.75	90.80	42.45	24.75	62.86	30.60	20.75	52.70	30.00

36.00	91.44	42.78	25.00	63.50	30.91	21.00	53.34	30.37
36.25	92.07	43.05	25.25	64.13	31.22	21.25	53.97	30.73
36.50	92.71	43.34	25.50	64.77	31.53	21.50	54.61	31.09
36.75	93.34	43.64	25.75	65.40	31.84	21.75	55.24	31.45
37.00	93.98	43.94	26.00	66.04	32.15	22.00	55.88	31.81
37.25	94.61	44.23	26.25	66.67	32.46	22.25	56.51	32.17
37.50	95.25	44.53	26.50	67.31	32.77	22.50	57.15	32.54
37.75	95.88	44.83	26.75	67.94	33.08	22.75	57.78	32.90
38.00	96.52	45.12	27.00	68.58	33.38	23.00	58.42	33.26
38.25	97.15	45.42	27.25	69.21	33.69	23.25	59.05	33.62
38.50	97.79	45.72	27.50	69.85	34.00	23.50	59.69	33.98
38.75	98.42	46.01	27.75	70.48	34.31	23.75	60.32	34.34
39.00	99.06	46.31	28.00	71.12	34.62	24.00	60.96	34.70
39.25	99.69	46.61	28.25	71.75	34.93	24.25	61.59	35.07
39.50	100.33	46.90	28.50	72.39	35.24	24.50	62.23	35.43
39.75	100.96	47.20	28.75	73.02	35.55	24.75	62.86	35.79
40.00	101.60	47.50	29.00	73.66	35.86	25.00	63.50	36.15
40.25	101.24	47.79	29.25	74.29	36.17			
40.50	102.87	48.09	29.50	74.93	36.48			
40.75	103.51	48.39	29.75	75.56	36.79			
41.00	104.14	48.69	30.00	76.20	37.09			
41.25	104.78	48.98	30.25	76.83	37.40			
41.50	105.41	49.28	30.50	77.47	37.71			
41.75	106.05	49.58	30.75	78.10	38.02			
42.00	106.68	49.87	31.00	78.74	38.33			
42.25	107.32	50.17	31.25	79.37	38.64			
42.50	107.95	50.47	31.50	80.01	38.95			
42.75	108.59	50.76	31.75	80.64	39.26			
43.00	109.22	51.06	32.00	81.28	39.57			
43.25	109.86	51.36	32.25	81.91	39.88			
43.50	110.49	51.65	32.50	82.55	40.19			
43.75	111.13	51.95	32.75	83.18	40.49			
44.00	111.76	52.25	33.00	83.82	40.80			
44.25	112.40	52.54	33.25	84.45	41.11			
44.50	113.03	52.84	33.50	85.09	41.42			
44.75	113.67	53.14	33.75	85.72	41.73			
45.00	114.30	53.44	34.00	86.36	42.04			

Source: McArdle et al., 1981

CONVERSION CONSTANTS TO PREDICT PERCENT BODY FAT FOR YOUNG MEN

UPPER ARM			ABDOMEN			FOREARM		
Inches	cm	Constant A	Inches	cm	Constant B	Inches	cm	Constant C
7.00	17.78	25.91	21.00	53.34	27.56	7.00	17.78	38.01
7.25	18.41	26.83	21.25	53.97	27.88	7.25	18.41	39.37
7.50	19.05	27.76	21.50	54.61	28.21	7.50	19.05	40.72
7.75	19.68	28.68	21.75	55.24	28.54	7.75	19.68	42.08
8.00	20.32	29.61	22.00	55.88	28.87	8.00	23.32	43.44
8.25	20.95	30.53	22.25	56.51	29.20	8.25	20.95	44.80
8.50	21.59	31.46	22.50	57.15	29.52	8.50	21.59	46.15
8.75	22.22	32.38	22.75	57.78	29.85	8.75	22.22	47.51
9.00	22.86	33.31	23.00	58.42	30.18	9.00	22.86	48.87
9.25	23.49	34.24	23.25	59.05	30.51	9.25	23.49	50.23
9.50	24.13	35.16	23.50	59.69	30.84	9.50	24.13	51.58
9.75	24.76	36.09	23.75	60.32	31.16	9.75	24.76	52.94
10.00	25.40	37.01	24.00	60.96	31.49	10.00	25.40	54.30
10.25	26.03	37.94	24.25	61.59	31.82	10.25	26.03	55.65
10.50	26.67	38.86	24.50	62.23	32.15	10.50	26.67	57.01
10.75	27.30	39.79	24.75	62.86	32.48	10.75	27.30	58.37
11.00	27.94	40.71	25.00	63.50	32.80	11.00	27.94	59.73
11.25	28.57	41.64	25.25	64.13	33.13	11.25	28.57	61.08
11.50	29.21	42.56	25.50	64.77	33.46	11.50	29.21	62.44
11.75	29.84	43.49	25.75	65.40	33.79	11.75	29.84	63.80
12.00	30.48	44.41	26.00	66.04	34.12	12.00	30.48	65.16
12.25	31.11	45.34	26.25	66.67	34.44	12.25	31.11	66.51
12.50	31.75	46.26	26.50	67.31	34.77	12.50	31.75	67.87
12.75	32.38	47.19	26.75	67.94	35.10	12.75	32.38	69.23
13.00	33.02	48.11	27.00	68.58	35.43	13.00	33.02	70.59
13.25	33.65	49.04	27.25	69.21	35.76	13.25	33.65	71.94
13.50	34.29	49.96	27.50	69.85	36.09	13.50	34.29	73.30
13.75	34.91	50.89	27.75	70.48	36.41	13.75	34.91	74.66
14.00	35.56	51.82	28.00	71.12	36.74	14.00	35.56	76.02
14.25	36.19	52.74	28.25	71.75	37.07	14.25	36.19	77.37
14.50	36.83	53.67	28.50	72.39	37.40	14.50	36.83	78.73
14.75	37.46	54.59	28.75	73.02	37.73	14.75	37.46	80.09
15.00	38.10	55.52	29.00	73.66	38.05	15.00	38.10	81.45
15.25	38.73	56.44	29.25	74.29	38.38	15.25	38.73	82.80
15.50	39.37	57.37	29.50	74.93	38.71	15.50	39.37	84.16
15.75	40.00	58.29	29.75	75.56	39.04	15.75	40.00	85.52
16.00	40.64	59.22	30.00	76.20	39.37	16.00	40.64	86.88
16.25	41.27	60.14	30.25	76.83	39.69	16.25	41.27	88.23
16.50	41.91	61.07	30.50	77.47	40.02	16.50	41.91	89.59
16.75	42.52	61.99	30.75	78.10	40.35	16.75	42.52	90.95
17.00	43.18	62.92	31.00	78.74	40.68	17.00	43.18	92.31
17.25	43.81	63.84	31.25	79.37	41.01	17.25	43.81	93.66
17.50	44.45	64.77	31.50	80.01	41.33	17.50	44.45	95.02

17.75	45.08	65.69	31.75	80.64	41.66	17.75	45.08	96.38
18.00	45.72	66.62	32.00	81.28	41.99	18.00	45.72	97.74
18.25	46.35	67.54	32.25	81.91	42.32	18.25	46.35	99.09
18.50	46.99	68.47	32.50	82.55	42.65	18.50	46.99	100.45
18.75	47.62	69.50	32.75	83.18	42.97	18.75	47.62	101.81
19.00	48.26	70.32	33.00	83.82	43.30	19.00	48.26	103.17
19.25	48.89	71.25	33.25	84.45	43.63	19.25	48.89	104.52
19.50	49.53	72.17	33.50	85.09	43.96	19.50	49.53	105.88
19.75	50.16	73.10	33.75	85.72	44.29	19.75	50.16	107.24
20.00	50.80	74.02	34.00	86.36	44.61	20.00	50.80	108.60
20.25	51.43	74.95	34.25	86.99	44.94	20.25	51.43	109.95
20.50	52.07	75.87	34.50	87.63	45.27	20.50	52.07	111.31
20.75	52.70	76.80	34.75	88.26	45.60	20.75	52.70	112.67
21.00	53.34	77.72	35.00	88.90	45.93	21.00	53.34	114.02
21.25	53.97	78.65	35.25	89.53	46.25	21.25	53.97	115.38
21.50	54.61	79.57	35.50	90.17	46.58	21.50	54.61	116.74
21.75	55.24	80.50	35.75	90.80	46.91	21.75	55.24	118.10
22.00	55.88	81.42	36.00	91.44	47.24	22.00	55.88	119.45
22.25	56.52	82.34	36.25	92.07	47.57	22.25	56.51	120.80
22.50	57.15	83.26	36.50	92.71	47.89	22.50	57.15	122.15
22.75	57.79	84.18	36.75	93.34	48.22	22.75	57.78	123.50
23.00	58.42	85.10	37.00	93.98	48.55	23.00	58.42	124.85
			37.25	94.61	48.88			
			37.50	95.25	49.21			
			37.75	95.88	49.54			
			38.00	96.52	49.86			
			38.25	97.15	50.19			
			38.50	97.79	50.52			
			38.75	98.42	50.85			
			39.00	99.06	51.18			
			39.25	99.69	51.50			
			39.50	100.33	51.83			
			39.75	100.96	52.16			
			40.00	101.60	52.49			
			40.25	101.24	52.82			
			40.50	102.87	53.14			
			40.75	103.51	53.47			
			41.00	104.14	53.80			
			41.25	104.78	54.13			
			41.50	105.41	54.46			
			41.75	106.05	54.78			
			42.00	106.68	55.11			

Source: McArdle et al., 1981

CONVERSION CONSTANTS TO PREDICT PERCENT BODY FAT FOR OLDER MEN

BUTTOCKS			ABDOMEN			FOREARM		
Inches	cm	Constant A	Inches	cm	Constant B	Inches	cm	Constant C
28.00	71.12	29.34	25.50	64.77	22.84	7.00	17.78	21.01
28.25	71.75	29.60	25.75	65.40	23.06	7.25	18.41	21.76
28.50	72.39	29.87	26.00	66.04	23.29	7.50	19.05	22.52
28.75	73.02	30.13	26.25	66.67	23.51	7.75	19.68	23.26
29.00	73.66	30.39	26.50	67.31	23.73	8.00	23.32	24.02
29.25	74.29	30.65	26.75	67.94	23.96	8.25	20.95	24.76
29.50	74.93	30.92	27.00	68.58	24.18	8.50	21.59	25.52
29.75	75.56	31.18	27.25	69.21	24.40	8.75	22.22	26.26
30.00	76.20	31.44	27.50	69.85	24.63	9.00	22.86	27.02
30.25	76.83	31.70	27.75	70.48	24.85	9.25	23.49	27.76
30.50	77.47	31.96	28.00	71.12	25.08	9.50	24.13	28.52
30.75	78.10	32.22	28.25	71.75	25.29	9.75	24.76	29.26
31.00	78.74	32.49	28.50	72.39	25.52	10.00	25.40	30.02
31.25	79.37	32.75	28.75	73.02	25.75	10.25	26.03	30.76
31.50	80.01	33.01	29.00	73.66	25.97	10.50	26.67	31.52
31.75	80.64	33.27	29.25	74.29	26.19	10.75	27.30	32.27
32.00	81.28	33.54	29.50	74.93	26.42	11.00	27.94	33.02
32.25	81.91	33.80	29.75	75.56	26.64	11.25	28.57	33.77
32.50	82.55	34.06	30.00	76.20	26.87	11.50	29.21	34.52
32.75	83.18	34.32	30.25	76.83	27.09	11.75	29.84	35.27
33.00	83.82	34.58	30.50	77.47	27.32	12.00	30.48	36.02
33.25	84.45	34.84	30.75	78.10	27.54	12.25	31.11	36.77
33.50	85.09	35.11	31.00	78.74	27.76	12.50	31.75	37.53
33.75	85.72	35.37	31.25	79.37	27.98	12.75	32.38	38.27
34.00	86.36	35.63	31.50	80.01	28.21	13.00	33.02	39.03
34.25	86.99	35.89	31.75	80.64	28.43	13.25	33.65	39.77
34.50	87.63	36.16	32.00	81.28	28.66	13.50	34.29	40.53
34.75	88.26	36.42	32.25	81.91	28.88	13.75	34.91	41.27
35.00	88.90	36.68	32.50	82.55	29.11	14.00	35.56	42.03
35.25	89.53	36.94	32.75	83.18	29.33	14.25	36.19	42.77
35.50	90.17	37.20	33.00	83.82	29.55	14.50	36.83	43.53
35.75	90.80	37.46	33.25	84.45	29.78	14.75	37.46	44.27
36.00	91.44	37.73	33.50	85.09	30.00	15.00	38.10	45.03
36.25	92.07	37.99	33.75	85.72	30.22	15.25	38.73	45.77
36.50	92.71	38.25	34.00	86.36	30.45	15.50	39.37	46.53
36.75	93.34	38.51	34.25	86.99	30.67	15.75	40.00	47.28
37.00	93.98	38.78	34.50	87.63	30.89	16.00	40.64	48.03
37.25	94.61	39.04	34.75	88.26	31.12	16.25	41.27	48.78
37.50	95.25	39.30	35.00	88.90	31.35	16.50	41.91	49.53
37.75	95.88	39.56	35.25	89.53	31.57	16.75	42.52	50.28
38.00	96.52	39.82	35.50	90.17	31.79	17.00	43.18	51.03
38.25	97.15	40.08	35.75	90.80	32.02	17.25	43.81	51.78
38.50	97.79	40.35	36.00	91.44	32.24	17.50	44.45	52.54

38.75	98.42	40.61	36.25	92.07	32.46	17.75	45.08	53.28
39.00	99.06	40.87	36.50	92.71	32.69	18.00	45.72	54.04
39.25	99.69	41.13	36.75	93.34	32.91	18.25	46.35	54.78
39.50	100.33	41.39	37.00	93.98	33.14			
39.75	100.96	41.66	37.25	94.61	33.36			
40.00	101.60	41.92	37.50	95.25	33.58			
40.25	101.24	42.18	37.75	95.88	33.81			
40.50	102.87	42.44	38.00	96.52	34.03			
40.75	103.51	42.70	38.25	97.15	34.26			
41.00	104.14	42.97	38.50	97.79	34.48			
41.25	104.78	43.23	38.75	98.42	34.70			
41.50	105.41	43.49	39.00	99.06	34.93			
41.75	106.05	43.75	39.25	99.69	35.15			
42.00	106.68	44.02	39.50	100.33	35.38			
42.25	107.32	44.28	39.75	100.96	35.59			
42.50	107.95	44.54	40.00	101.60	35.82			
42.75	108.59	44.80	40.25	101.24	36.05			
43.00	109.22	45.06	40.50	102.87	36.27			
43.25	109.86	45.32	40.75	103.51	36.49			
43.50	110.49	45.59	41.00	104.14	36.72			
43.75	111.13	45.85	41.25	104.78	36.94			
44.00	111.76	46.12	41.50	105.41	37.17			
44.25	112.40	46.37	41.75	106.05	37.39			
44.50	113.03	46.64	42.00	106.68	37.62			
44.75	113.67	46.89	42.25	107.32	37.87			
45.00	114.30	47.16	42.50	107.95	38.06			
45.25	114.93	47.42	42.75	108.59	38.28			
45.50	115.57	47.86	43.00	109.22	38.51			
45.75	116.20	47.94	43.25	109.86	38.73			
46.00	116.84	48.21	43.50	110.49	38.96			
46.25	117.47	47.47	43.75	111.13	39.18			
46.50	118.11	48.73	44.00	111.76	39.41			
46.75	118.74	48.99	44.25	112.40	39.63			
47.00	119.38	49.26	44.50	113.03	39.85			
47.25	120.01	49.52	44.75	113.67	40.08			
47.50	120.65	49.78	45.00	114.30	40.30			
47.75	121.28	50.04						
48.00	121.92	50.30						
48.25	122.55	50.56						
48.50	123.19	50.83						
48.75	123.82	51.09						
49.00	124.46	51.35						

Source: McArdle et al., 1981

♦♦♦♦♦♦♦♦

APPENDIX V

RELATIVE FAT VALUES IN MALE AND FEMALE ATHLETES

Athletic Group or Sport	Sex	Age (yrs)	Height (cm)	Weight (kg)	Relative Fat %
Baseball	Male	20.8	182.7	83.3	14.2
		-	-	-	11.8
		27.4	193.1	88.0	12.6
Basketball	Female	19.1	169.1	62.6	20.8
		19.4	167.0	63.9	26.9
Centers	Male	27.7	214.0	109.2	7.1
Forwards		25.3	200.6	96.9	9.0
Guards		25.2	188.0	83.6	10.6
Canoeing	Male	23.7	182.0	79.6	12.4
Football	Male	20.3	184.9	96.4	13.8
		-	-	-	13.9
Defensive Backs		17-23	178.3	77.3	11.5
		24.5	182.5	84.8	9.6
Offensive Backs		17-23	179.7	79.8	12.4
		24.7	183.8	90.7	9.4
Line Backers		17-23	180.1	87.2	13.4
		24.2	188.6	102.2	14.0
Offensive Linemen		17-23	186.0	99.2	19.1
		24.7	193.0	112.6	15.6
Defensive Linemen		17-23	186.6	97.8	18.5
		25.7	192.4	117.1	18.2
Quarter Backs, Kickers		24.1	185.0	90.1	14.4
Gymnastics	Male	20.3	178.5	69.2	4.6
	Female	19.4	163.0	57.9	23.8
		20.0	158.5	51.5	15.5
		14.0	-	-	17.0
		23.0	-	-	11.0
		23.0	-	-	9.6
Ice Hockey	Male	26.3	180.3	86.7	15.1
		22.5	179.0	77.3	13.0
Swimming	Male	21.8	182.3	79.1	8.5
		20.6	182.9	78.9	5.0
	Female	19.4	168.0	63.8	26.3
Sprint	Female	-	165.1	57.1	14.6
Middle Distance	Female	-	166.6	66.8	24.1
Distance	Female	-	166.3	60.9	17.1
Tennis	Male	-	-	-	15.2
		42.0	179.6	77.1	16.3
	Female	39.0	163.3	55.7	20.3

Track and Field	Male	21.3	180.6	71.6	3.7
		-	-	-	8.8
Runners	Male	22.5	177.4	64.5	6.3
Distance	Male	26.1	175.7	64.2	7.5
		26.2	177.0	66.2	8.4
		40-49	180.7	71.6	11.2
		55.3	174.5	63.4	18.0
		50-59	174.7	67.2	10.9
		60-69	175.7	67.1	11.3
		70-75	175.6	66.8	13.6
		47.2	176.5	70.7	13.2
	Female	19.9	161.3	52.9	19.2
		32.4	169.4	57.2	15.2
Middle Distance	Male	24.6	179.0	72.3	12.4
Sprint	Female	20.1	164.9	56.7	19.5
	Male	46.5	177.0	74.1	16.5
Discuss	Male	28.3	186.1	104.7	16.4
		26.4	190.8	110.5	16.3
	Female	21.1	168.1	71.0	25.0
Jumpers and Hurdlers	Female	20.3	165.9	59.0	20.7
Shot-put	Male	27.0	188.2	112.5	16.5
		22.0	191.6	126.2	19.6
	Female	21.5	167.6	78.1	28.0
Volleyball	Female	19.4	166.0	59.8	25.3
		19.9	172.2	64.1	21.3
Weight Lifting	Male	24.9	166.4	77.2	9.8
Wrestling	Male	26.0	177.8	81.8	9.8
		27.0	176.0	75.7	10.7
		22.0	-	-	5.0
		23.0	-	79.3	14.3
		19.6	174.6	74.8	8.8
		15-18	172.3	66.3	6.9
		20.6	174.8	67.3	4.0

Source: Katch and McArdle (1973) and Wilmore et al. (1977)

♦♦♦♦♦♦♦♦

APPENDIX VI

SKINFOLD CALIPER TYPES

Harpenden Skinfold Caliper (www.topendsports.com)

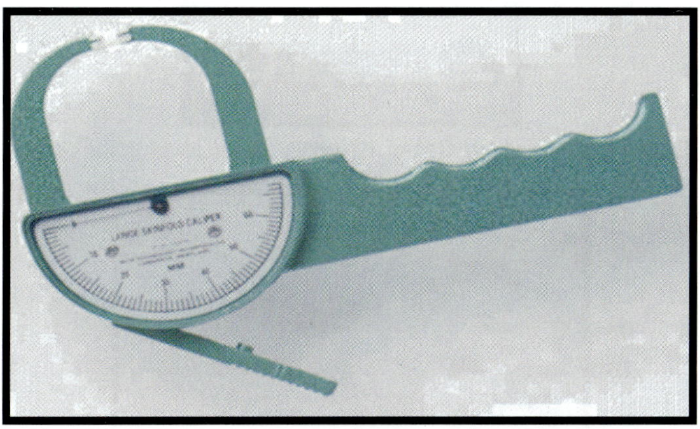

Lange Skinfold Caliper (www.exrx.net/Store/Other/Lange.html)

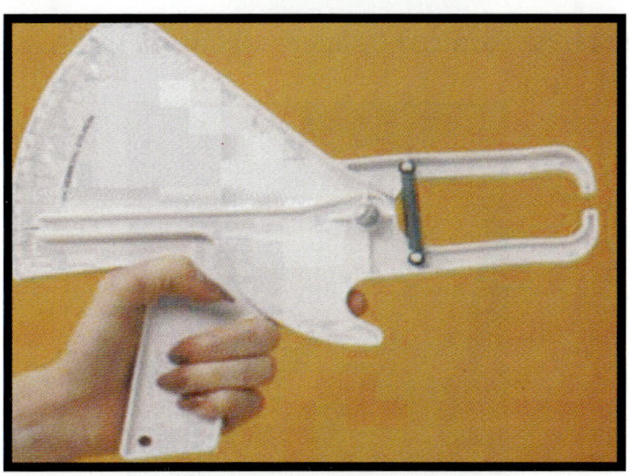

Slim Guide Skinfold Caliper (www.weider fitness.com)

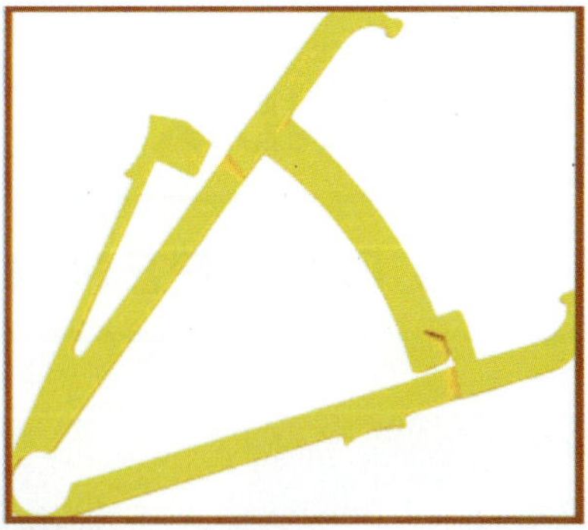

Accu-Measure Skinfold Caliper (www.first4shape.com/products-Accu-Measure-Fit)

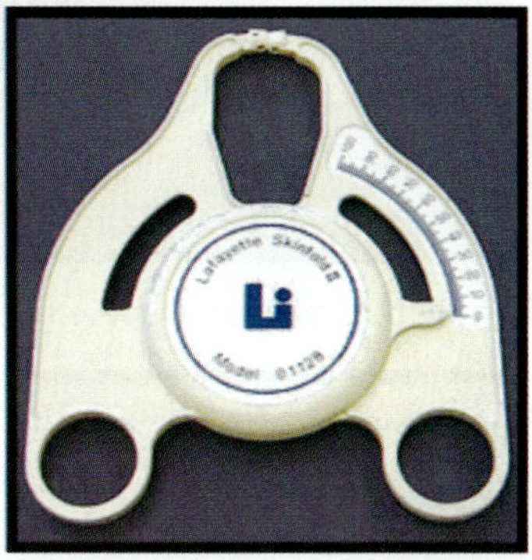

Lafayette Skinfold Caliper (www.lafayetteevaluation.com/)

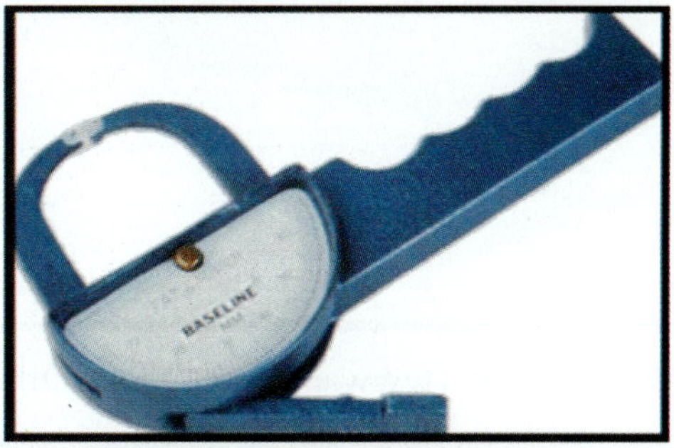

Baseline Skinfold Caliper (www.nexgenergo.com)

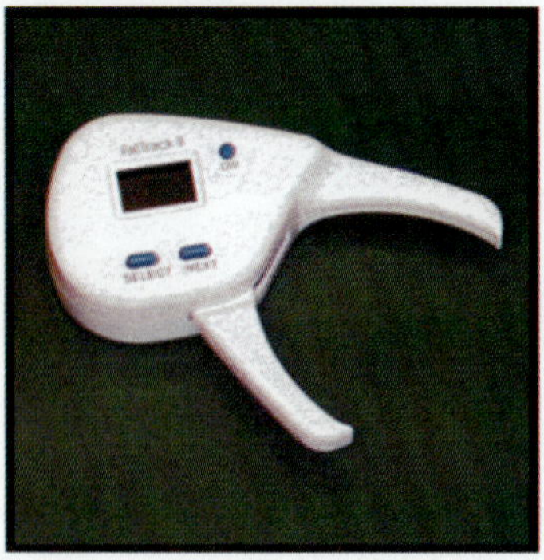

Fat Track Skinfold Caliper (www.creatinestore.co.uk/products/Fat-Track-Di)

APPENDIX VII

EQUIPMENTS

Lufkin Steel Tape (www.topendsports.com/testing/images/rulers.jpg)

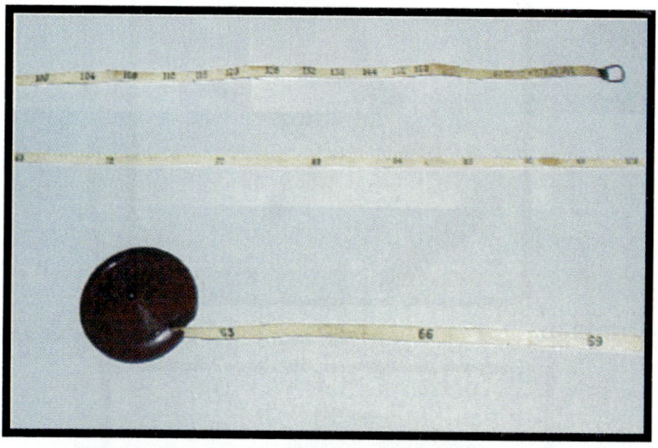

Metronome Tape (gwydir.demon.co.uk)

Circumference Measuring Ta pes (www.perspectiveent.com/tools.html)

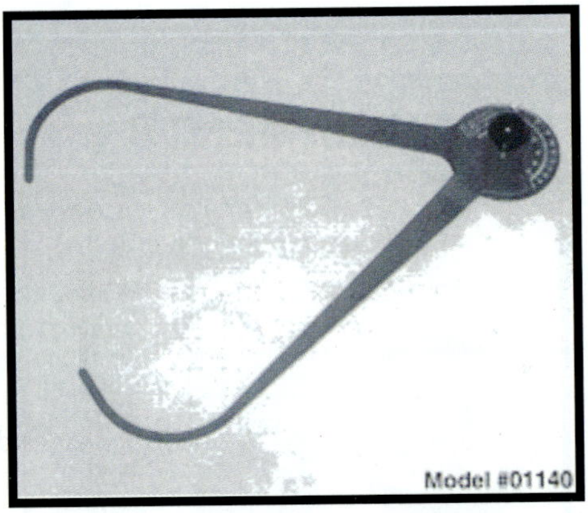

Chest Caliper (www.perspectiveent.com/tools.html)

Shoulder/Elbow Measure (www.topendsports.com/.../images/tape-measure.jpg)

Hand Dynamometer (m2.sourcingmap.com/smap/images/item/n/08b/ux_...)

Hand Dynamometer (www.komkare.com/images/dynam.jpg)

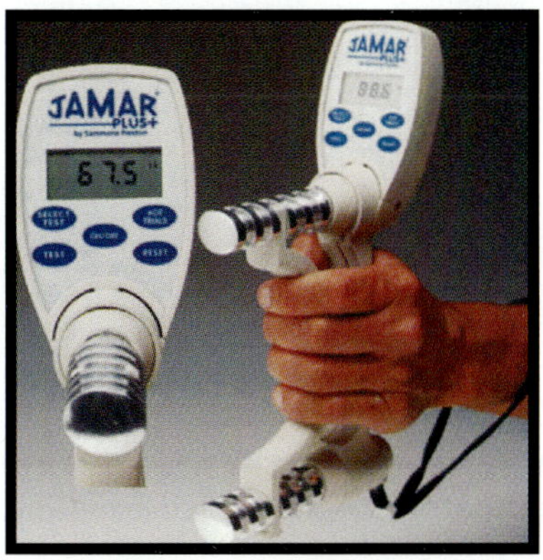

Digital Hand Dynamometer (healthinfousa.com/ebaylisting/jamard.jpg)

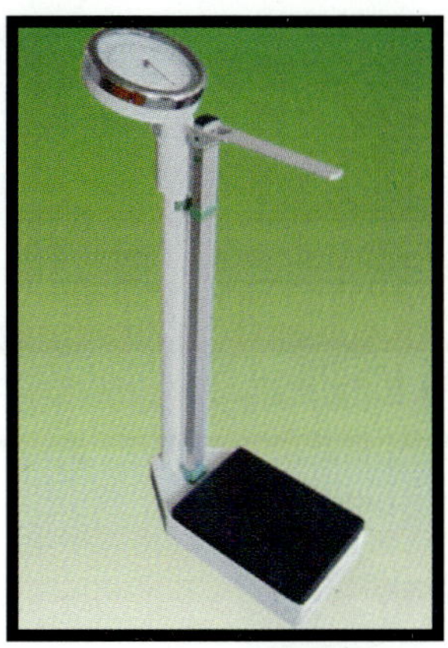

Weighing Scale (www.yuething.com.hk/images/ZT-120A.jpg)

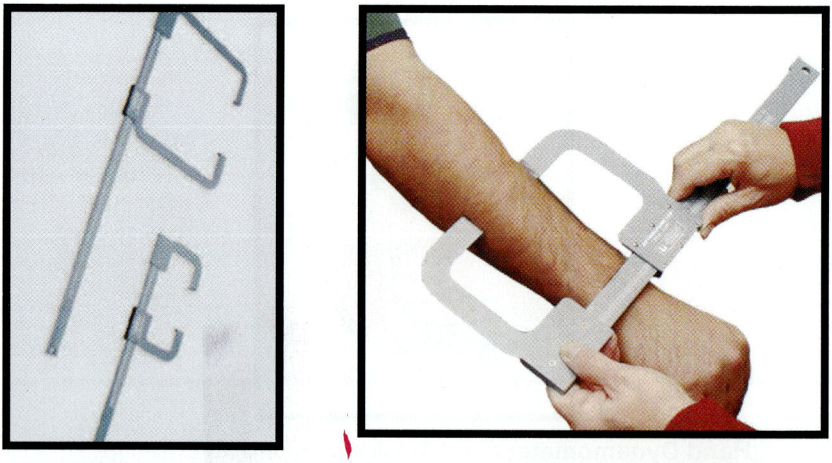

Small Anthropometer (www.si-instruments.com/files/catalog/Lafayett...)

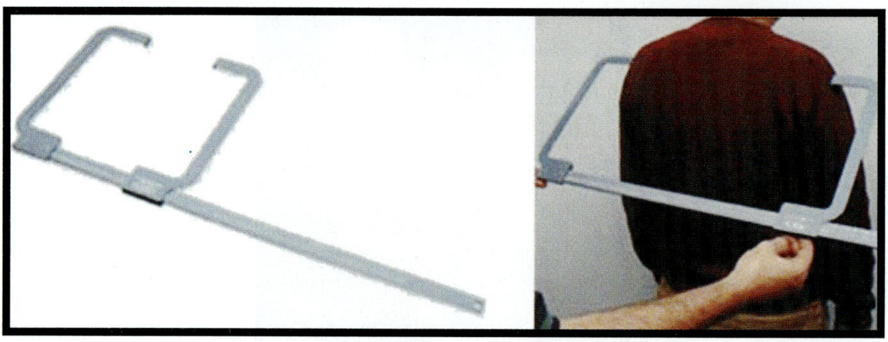

Large Anthropometer (www.perspectiveent.com/imgs/1290.jpg)

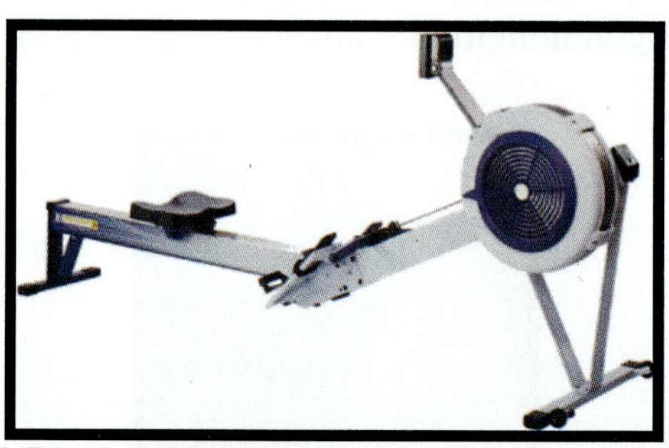

Concept 2 Rowing Machine (www.elitefitnessequipment.com)

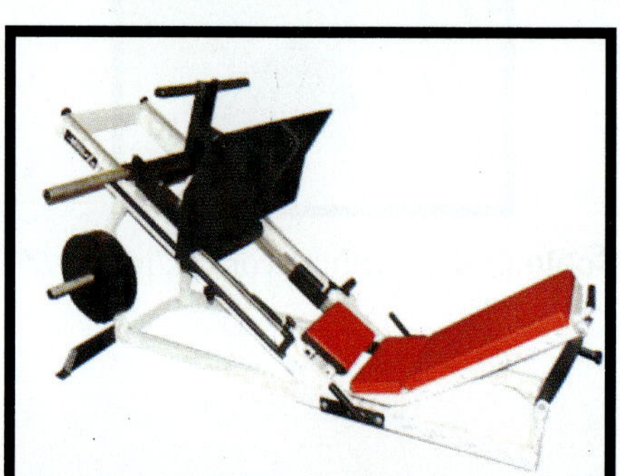

Leg Press Machine (venusfitness.net)

Knee Extension Machine (www.elitefitnessequipment.com/shop)

Leg Extension Machine (www.elitefitnessequipment.com)

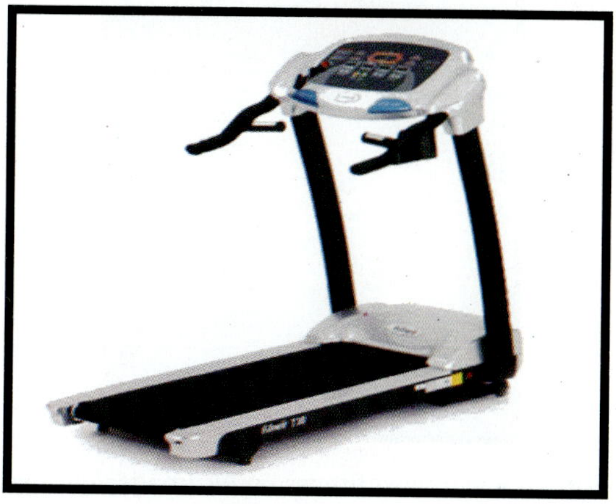

Treadmill (synaptoman.files.wordpress.com/.../treadmill. jpg)

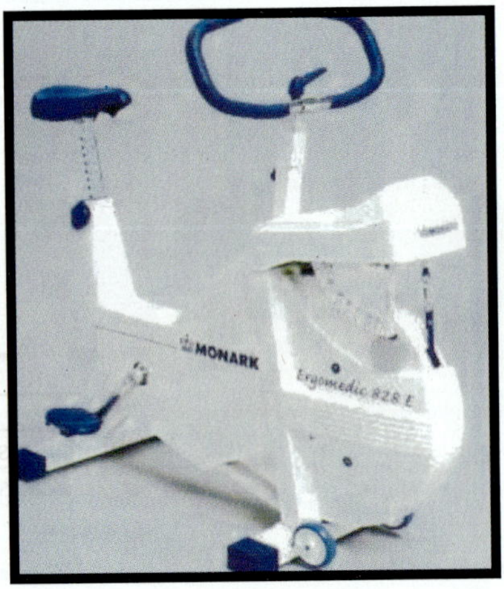

Bicycle Ergometer (porpax.bio.miami.edu/~cmallery/113/vo2max.htm)

Ergometer Cycle (www.comparestoreprices.co.uk/exercise-bikes)

Chinning Bar (www.intensefitness.co.uk/images/chinning_bar.jpg)

APPENDIX VIII

APPROXIMATE CONVERSIONS TO AND FROM METRIC MEASURES

Conversions to Metric Measures

When You Know	Multiply By	To Find
	Length	
Inches	2.5	Centimeters
Feet	30	Centimeters
Yards	0.9	Meters
Miles	1.6	Kilometers
	Area	
Square inches	6.5	Square centimeters
Square feet	9.09	Square meters
Square yards	0.8	Square meters
Square miles	2.6	Square kilometers
Acres	0.4	Hectares
	Mass/Weight	
Ounces	28	Grams
Pounds	0.45	Kilograms

Conversions from Metric Measures

When You Know	Multiply By	To Find
	Length	
Millimeters	0.04	Inches
Centimeters	0.4	Inches
Meters	3.3	Feet
Meters	1.1	Yards
Kilometers	0.6	Miles
	Area	
Square centimeters	0.16	Square inches
Square meters	1.2	Square yards
Square kilometers	0.4	Square miles
Hectares (10,000 m2)	2.5	Acres
	Mass/Weight	
Grams	0.035	Ounces
Kilograms	2.2	Pounds

Source: Nelson et al. (1994)

12 inches = 1 foot
3 feet = 1 yard
1760 yards = 1 mile
36 inches = 1 yard
Л (Paay) = 3.14 (22/7)

References

American College of Sports Medicine (ACSM). 2005. ACSM Guidelines for Exercise Testing and Prescription. 7th edition, Baltimore: Williams, and Wilkins.

American College of Sports Medicine.1995. From www.acsm.org/sportsmed.

Anderson, L., Dibble, M. V. and Turkki, P. R. et al.1982. Nutrition in Health and Disease, 17th Edition, Philadelphia, J. B. Lippincott Co.

archivosdemedicina.com/ojs/public/journals/12.

Arnot, R. and Gaines, C. 1984. Sports Talent.

Baechle, T. R. and Earle, R. W. 2000. Essentials of Strength Training and Conditioning. 2nd Edition, Champaigh, IL: Human Kinetics.

Balke, B. 1963. A Simple Field Test for the Assessment of Physical Fitness. Civil Aeromedical Research Institute Report No. 63-68. Oklahoma City Federal Aviation Agency.

Beashel, P. et al. 1997. The World of Sport Examined.

Behnke, A.R. and Wilmore, J.H. 1974. Evaluation and Regulation of Body Build and Composition. Englewood Cliffs, NJ: Prentice Hall.

Berg, R. Latin, R. W. and Baechle, T.R. 1992. Survey of Physical Fitness of NCAA Division I Football Players. NSCA J.

Bonora, E. Micciolo, R. et al.1995. Is It Possible to Derive a Reliable Estimate of Human Visceral and Subcutaneous Abdominal Adipose Tissue from Simple Anthropometric Measurements?. Metabolism. 44: 1617-1625.

Bouchard, C. Dionne, F. T. Simoneau, J. A. and Boulay, M. R.1992. Genetics of Aerobic and Anaerobic Performances. Exerc Sport Sci Rev.20:27-58; Bouchard, C. Shephard, R. J. Stephens, T. Sutton, J. R. and McPherson, B. D. (Eds.), Exercise Fitness and Health (pp.147-153). Champaign, IL: Human Kinetics).

3.bp.blogspot.com/_4VWEfGKtzp8/SfW4mGenTuI/AA...

Brennan, E.H. 1974. Development of a Binomial Involving Anthropometric Measurements for Predicting Lean Mass in Young Women. Masters Thesis. Incarnate Word College, San Antonio, Texas.

Brozek, J. et al., Densitometric Analysis of Body Composition: Revision of Some Quantitative Assumptions. Ann. N. Y. Acad. Sci. 1963. 110: 113-40.

Bruce, R.A. 1972. Multi-Stage Treadmill Test of Maximal and Sub Maximal Exercise. In: AHA: Exercise Testing and Training of Apparently Health Individuals: A Handbook for Physicians, New York.

Brzycki, M. Strength Testing: Predicting a One-Rep Max from Reps to Fatigue. JOPERD.1993.64: 88-90.

Bunc, V. And Dlouha, R. et al. 2000.Estimation of Body Composition by Multifrequency Bioimpedance Measurement in Children. IN: In Vivo Body Composition Studies. Annals New York Academy Sciences. 904: 203-204.

Burmeister, W. 1965. Potassium-40 Content as a Basis for the Calculation of Body Cell Mass in Man. Science. 148, 1336-1337.

Buskirk, E. R. 1974. Nutrition for the Athlete. Ryan, A. J. and Allman, F. L. (eds), Sports Medicine. Academic Press. 146, 149.

cdn-www.expertvillage.com/showImage.aspx?site...

ce-fit.net/images/core-abdominal-and-lower-ba...

Chu, D.A 1996.Explosive Power and Strength. Human Kinetics.

Conconi, F. et al. 1982. Determination of the Anaerobic Threshold by a Non-Invasive Field Test in Runners. Journal of Applied Physiology. 52: 869-873.

Cooper, K. H. 1968. A Means of Assessing Maximal Oxygen Intake. JAMA. 203:201-204.

Costill, D.L. King, D.S. Thomas, R. and Hargreaves, M. 1985. Effects of Reduced Training on Muscular Power in Swimmers. Physician and Sports Medicine.13(2):94-101.

Costill, D.L. 1986. Inside Running: Basics of Sports Physiology. Indianapolis: Benchmark Press.

Cureton, K. J. and Sparling, P. B. 1980. Distance Running Performance and Metabolic Responses to Running in Men and Women with Excess Weight Experimentally Equated. Med Sci Sports Exerc.12(4):288-94.

Danowski, T. S. (editor). 1964. Diabetes Mellitus: Diagnosis and Treatment. the American Diabetes Association, Inc. Chapter XVII. Therapy: Changing dietary concepts. Version of George, J. Hamwi. 73-78.

Davis, B. et al. 2000. Physical Education and the Study of Sport.

Dempster, P. and Aitkens, S. 1995. A New Air Displacement Method for the Determination of Human Body Composition. Med. Sci. Sports Exerc. 27:1692-1697.

Deurenberg, P. Weststrate, J. A. Seidell, J. C. 1991. Body Mass Index as a Measure of Body Fatness: Age-and Sex-Specific Prediction Formulas. Br. J. Nutrition. 65:105-114.

Duda, J. L 1989. Relationship between Task and Ego Orientation and the Perceived Purpose of Sport among High School Athletes. Journal of Sport and Exercise Psychology, 11:318-335.

Durnin, J.V.G.A. and Rahaman, M. M. 1967 the Assessment of the Amount of Fat in the Human Body from Measurements of Skinfold Thickness. Br. J. Nutr. 21: 681-689.

Durnin, J.V.G.A. and Womersley, J. 1974. Body Fat Assessed from Total Body Density and Its Estimation from Skinfold Thickness: Measurements on 481 Men and Women aged from 16 to 72 Years. Br. J. Nutr. 32: 77-97.

Edwards Sally In www.fitzones.com/members/Fitness/heartrate_zones.asp

en.wikipedia.org/wiki/Sport_psychology

en.mimi.hu/fitness/anaerobic_endurance.html

en.wikipedia.org/wiki/General_Fitness_Training

Eurofit Manual- For Flamingo Balance Test - http://www.ftvs.cuni.cz/katedry/kin/stochl/Eurofit_unifit_fitnessgram_sem4.pdf

Eurofit. 1993. Eurofit Tests of Physical Fitness. 2nd Edition, Strasbourg.

Ewald, G. and McKenzie, C. (editors). 1995. Manual of Medical Therapeutics, 28th Edition. Little, Brown And Company.30 ("Hamwi method").

Fields, D. A. Goran, M. I. and McCrory, M. A. 2002. Body-Composition Assessment via Air-Displacement Plethysmography in Adults and Children: A Review. Am. J. Clin. Nutr. 75:453-467.

Fox And Haskell Formula from http://en.wikipedia.org/wiki/Heart_rate

Frisancho, A. 1974. Triceps Skinfold and Upper Arm Muscle Size Norms for Assessment of NutritionalStatus.Am.J.Clin.Nutr.27:1052-1058.

Frisancho, A. R. 1981. New Norms of Upper Limb Fat and Muscle Areas for Assessment of Nutritional Status. Am. J. Clin. Nutr. 34: 2540-2545.

Frisancho, A. R. and Flegel, P. N. 1983. Elbow Breadth as a Measure of Frame Size for US Males and Females. Am. J. Clin. Nutr.37:311-14.

Frisancho, A.R. 1990. Anthropometric Standards for the Assessment of Growth and Nutritional Status. The University of Michigan Press.

Fuchs, R. J. Theis, C. F. and Lancaster, M. C. 1978. A Nomogram to Predict Lean Body Mass in Men. Am. J. Clin. Nutr. 31: 673-678.

Gallagher, D. And Visser, M. et al. 1996. How useful is Body Mass Index for Comparison of Body Fatness across Age, Sex, and Ethnic Origins? Am. J. Epidemiology. 143: 228-239.

Garrow, J. S. and Webster J. 1985. Quetelet's Index (W/H2) as a Measure of Fatness. Int. J. Obesity. 9:147-153.

Gilbert, B. Forbes, James. Gallup. and Hursh, John. B. 1961. Estimation of Total Body Fat from Potassium-40 Content. Science 13, 133 (3446)101-102.

Ginn, E. 1993. The Application of the Critical Power Test to Swimming and Swim Training Programmes. National Sports Research Centre.

Ginn, E. 1993. Critical Speed and Training Intensities for Swimming. Australian Sports Commission.

Goldman H. I. and Becklake, M. R. 1959. Respiratory Function Tests: Normal Values of Medium Altitudes and the Prediction of Normal Results. Am. Rev. Respir. Dis.79:457-67.

Guedes, D. P.1985. Estudo da gordura corporal atraves da mensuracao dos valores de densidade corporal e da espessura de cutaneas em universitarios [dissertacaol]. Universidade Federal de Santa maria. In de Fonseca, P. H. S. Marins, J. C. B. de Silva, A. T. 2007.

gwydir.demon.co.uk

Equations for the Estimation of Body Density in Professional Soccer Players. Rev. Bras. Med. Esporte. 13(2):135-138.

Hall, L.K. 1977. Anthropometric Estimations of Body Density of Women Athletes in Selected Athletic Activities. Doctoral Dissertation, The Ohio State University. In Fox, E.L. and Close, N.A. (eds), Sports Physiology, 2nd Edition, 1983, Saunders College Publishing.

Hall, J. G. Froster-Iskenius, U. G. and Allanson, J.E. 1989. Handbook of Normal Physical Measurements. Oxford University Press.

healthinfousa.com/ebaylisting/jamard.jpg

Hickson, R.C. Foster, C. Pollock, M.L. Galassi, T.M. and Rich, S. 1985. Reduced Training Intensities And Loss Of Aerobic Power, Endurance, And Cardiac Growth. J Appl Physiol. 58(2):492-9.

Hodgdon, J.A. and Friedl, K. 1984. Development of the DoD Body Composition Estimation Equations. Technical Document No. 99-2B. Naval Health Research Center, San Diego, California.

Hodgdon, J.A. and Beckett, M.B. 1984. Prediction of Percent Body Fat for U.S. Navy Men from Body Circumferences and Height. Report No 84-11. Naval Health Research Center, San Diego.

Hodgdon, J.A. and Beckett, M.B. 1984. Prediction of Percent Body Fat for U.S. Navy Women from Body Circumferences and Height. Report No 84-29. Naval Health Research Center, San Diego.

Houmard, J.A. Costill, D.L. Mitchell, J.B. Park, S.H. Hickner, R.C. and Roemmich, J.N. 1990. Reduced Training Maintains Performance in Distance Runners. Int. J. Sports. Med. 11(1):46-52.

Houmard, J.A. Scott, B.K. Justice, C.L. and Chenier, T.C. 1994. The Effects of Taper on Performance in Distance Runners. Med. Sci. Sports. Exerc.26(5):624.

http://en.wikipedia.org/wiki/Physical_fitness_test

http://en.wikipedia.org/wiki/Cooper_test

http://en.wikipedia.org/wiki/Harvard_Step_Test

http://www.brianmac.co.uk/eval.htm

Hume, R. 1966.Prediction of Lean Body Mass from Height and Weight. J. Clin. Path.19:389-391.

i.ehow.com/.../4617210/84891-main_Full.jpg

images.teamsugar.com/.../12981/03_2008/squat.jpg

International Standards for Anthropometric Assessment.2001. Published by the International Society for the Advancement of Kinanthropometry (ISAK).

Jackson, A. S., and Pollock, M. L. 1978. Generalized Equations for Predicting Body Density of Men. Br. J. Nutr. 40: 497-504.

Jackson, A. S., Pollock, M. L. and Ward, A.1980. Generalized Equations for Predicting Body Density of Women. Medicine and Science in Sports and Exercise. 12:175-182.

James, W.P.T. 1976. Research on Obesity. London. Her Majesty's Stationery Office. (ISBN 0-11-4500347).

Johnson, B.L. and Nelson, J.K. 1986. Practical Measurements for Evaluation in PE. 4th Edition.

Jumps Decathlon Tables: Grouping of Decathlon Disciplines. By Woolf, A. Ansley L. and Bidgood, P. 2007. J. Quantitative Analysis in Sports. 3(4):1-13.

Karvonen. Retrieved fromhttp://en.wikipedia.org/wiki/Heart_rate and home.xnet.com/~nowlin/heartrate.htm

Katch, F.I. and McArdle, W. D.1973. Prediction of Body Density from Simple Anthropometric Measurements in College-Age Man and Women. Hum. Biol. 45(3):445-55.

Katch, F.I. and McArdle, W.D. 1983. Nutrition, Weight Control and Exercise", 2nd Edition, Lea And Febiger, U.S.A.

Keys, A. Brozek, J. et al. 1950. The Biology of Human Starvation. Minneapolis: University of Minnesota Press.

Kilne, G. et al. 1987. Estimation of VO2 max from a One Mile Track Walk, Gender, Age and Body Weight. Med. Sci. Sports Exerc. 19:253.

Ledesma, A. (Angel). Personal Communication. From angel.ledesma@nutripac.com.mx.

Leger, L.A. and Lambert, J. 1982. A Maximal Multistage 20m Shuttle Run Test to Predict VO2 max. Eur. J. Appl. Physiol. 49:1-5.

Lohman, T. G. 1981. Skinfolds and Body Density and Their Relation to Body Fatness: A Review. Hum. Biol. 53(2):181-225.

Londeree and Moeschberger Retrieved from http://en.wikipedia.org/wiki/Heart_rate

m2.sourcingmap.com/smap/images/item/n/08b/ux_...

Marriott, B. M. and Grumstrup-Scott, J. (eds) 1992. Body Composition and Physical Performance. Applications for the Military Services. National Academy Press. Washington, DC.

Maud PJ, Schultz BB (1989) Norms for the Wingate Anaerobic Test with Comparison to another Similar Test. Res. Q. Exerc. Sport. 60:144-151.

McArdle, W.D. et al. 1981. Exercise Physiology, Lea and Febiger.

McArdle, W.D. Katch, F.I. and Katch, V.L. 2000. Essentials of Exercise Physiology: 2nd Edition. Philadelphia, PA: Lippincott Williams & Wilkins.

McCrory, M.A. Gomez, T.D. Bernauer, E.M. and Mole, P.A. 1995. Evaluation of a New Air Displacement Plethysmograph for Measuring Human Body Composition. Med. Sci. Sports. Exerc27:1686-1691.

McWhirter, J.P. and Pennington, C. R.1994. Incidence and Recognition of Malnutrition in the Hospital.BMJ.308:945-948.

media.summitmedicalgroup.com/.../xabdstra.jpg

Melina, R. M. Hamill, P. V. V. And Lameshow, S. 1973. National Center for Health Statistics: Selected Body Measurements of Children 6-11 years: US. Vital and Health Statistics, Series 11 (123) [DHEW Publication No. (HSM) 73-1605].

Miller et al Retrieved from http://en.wikipedia.org/wiki/Heart_rate

National Center for Health Statistics (NCHS). 1987. Anthropometric Reference Data and Prevalence of Overweight, US 1976-80. Vital and health statistics, Series 11, No. 238 (DHHD Pub. No. PHS, 87-1688.

Nelson, J. K. Moxness, K. E. et al. Mayo Clinic Diet Manual. 1994. 7th Edition. St. LOUIS Mosby-Yearbook.

Oja, P. Tuxworth, B. (eds).1995. Eurofit for Adults: Assessment of Health-Related Fitness. Finland: Council of Europe Publishing.1-13.

Pandya, N. C. and Shah, C. S. 1988. Logarithmic Tables. 10th Edition, Charotar Publication House, Anand, Gujarat.

Pollock, M.L. 1973. Quantification of Endurance Training Programs. Exercise and Sport Sciences Reviews. 1:155-188.

porpax.bio.miami.edu/~cmallery/113/vo2max.htm

Pouliot, M.C. Despres, J.P. Lemieux, S. Moorjani, S. Bouchard, C. Tremblay, A. Nadeau, A. and Lupien, P.J.1994. Waist Circumference and Abdominal Sagittal Diameter: Best Simple Anthropometric Indexes of Abdominal Visceral Adipose Tissue Accumulation and Related Cardiovascular Risk in Men and Women. Am. J. Cardio. 73: 460-468.

Quadrathlon Tables (1992).Athletics Coach - Vol 26 No 1 page 29.

Robinson, J.D. and Lupkiewicz, S.M. et al. 1983. Determination of Ideal Body Weight for Drug Dosage Calculations. Am. J. Hosp. Pharm. 40: 1016-1019.

Rosin, R. and Shulov, A. 1961. Estimation of Total Body Fat from Potassium-40 Content. Science. 133: 1918.

Ruff, C.B. Jamison, P.J. 2002. Weight for Trunk Frame Size: An Alternative Index for Fitness In Populations of Varying Body Proportions. Am. J. Phys. Anthropol. 34 (Supplement): 134.

Ruff, C. 2002. Variation in Human Body Size and Shape. Annu. Rev. Anthropol. 31: 211-232.

Schweigert, D. 1996. Normative Values for Common Preseason Testing Values: NCAA Division II Women's Basketball. NSCA J. 18(6):7-10

Segal, K.R. van Loan, M. et al. 1988. Lean Body Mass Estimation by Bioelectrical Impedance Analysis: A Four-Site Cross-Validation Study. Am. J. Clin. Nutr. 47: 7-14.

Sharkey, B. J. and Gaskill, S. E. 2007. Fitness and Health. 6th Edition, Human Kinetics.

Siri, W.E. 1961. Body Composition from Fluid Spaces and Density: Analysis of Methods. In Techniques for Measuring Body Composition. 1994. Washington DC: National Academy of Sciences. Br. J. Nutr. 71(6): 89.

Sprint Bounding and the Sprint-Bound Index. 1992. NSCA Journal, 14(4):18-21.

static.howstuffworks.com/gif/core-abdominal-a...

Swain, et al. 1994. Target HR for the Development of CV Fitness. Medicine & Science in Sports & Exercise, 26(1):112-116.From: http://www.brianmac.demon.co.uk/vo2max.htm

synaptoman.files.wordpress.com/.../treadmill. jpg

The Physical Fitness Specialist Certification Manual. 1998. The Cooper Institute for Aerobics Research, Dallas TX. Printed in Advance Fitness Assessment & Exercise Prescription, 3rd Edition, Vivian. H. Hayward.

Thorland, W. G. Johnson, G. O. Tharp, G. D. Housh, T. J. and Cisar, C. J. 1984. Estimation of Body Density in Adolescent Athletes. Hum. Biol. 56(8):439-48.

training.runinthesun.com/endurance_training.asp

VanItallie, T.B. and Yan, M.U. et al.1990. Height-Normalized Indices of the Body's Fat Free Mass and Fat Mass: Potentially Useful Indicators of Nutritional Status. Am. J. Clin. Nutr. 52: 953-959.

von Dobeln, W. 1959. Anthropometric Determination of Fat-Free Body Weight. Acta Medica Scandinavica.165: 37-40.

venusfitness.net

Wilmore, J.H. Behnke, A.R. 1970. An Anthropometric Estimation of Body Density and Lean Body Weight in Young Women. Am. J. Clin. Nutr. 23: 267-274.

Wilmore, J. H. et al. 1977. Body Physique and Composition of the Female Distance Runner. Ann. NY Acad. Sci. 301, 764 – 776.

Wilmore, J.H. and Costill, D.L. 2005. Physiology of Sport and Exercise. 3rd Edition. Champaign, IL: Human Kinetics.

Wright, H.F. Dotson, C.O. and Davis, P.O. 1980. An Investigation of Assessment Techniques for Body Composition of Women Marines. US Navy Medicine. 71: 15-26.

www.am-i-fat.com/body_frame_size.html

www.astm.org/Standards/D6829.htm

www.auxguidanceskills.info/.../swimmer.jpg

www.backtobasicstoys.com/images/2596.jpg

www.comparestoreprices.co.uk/exercise-bikes

www.creatinestore.co.uk/products/Fat-Track-Di

wwwdelivery.superstock.com/WI/223/1612/Previe.

www.efeld.com/images/phd/trunk_synergy.gif

www.e-lacrosse.com/2006/yeager/sbj.gif

www.elitefitnessequipment.com/shop

www.exrx.net/Store/Other/Lange.html

www.first4shape.com/products-Accu-Measure-Fit

www.fitgolf.com/files/2008/12/bridge-with-leg..

www.fitnessfactory.com/images/Item/190m.jpg

www.intensefitness.co.uk/images/chinning_bar.jpg

www.komkare.com/images/dynam.jpg

www.lafayetteevaluation.com/

www.leehayward.com/bodyfat_test.htm

www.medindia.net/patients/calculators/framesize1.asp

www.msu.edu/~kraftjoh/fitness.html. Accessed 11/03/2003.

www.mycaloriemanager.co.uk/images%5Crunn.jpg

www.myfit.ca/shuttlerun.jpg

www.nexgenergo.com

www.ncpad.org/.../Spina/TrunkRotation.jpg

www.nlm.nih.gov/medlineplus/ency/imagepages/17182.htm

www.nutritionalassessment.english.azm.nl/algoritme+na/onderzoek/

www.pcis.net/gagne/fitness/Entry.html. Accessed 11/07/2003

www.perspectiveent.com/imgs/1290.jpg

www.signonsandiego.com/news/health/fitness/20

www.si-instruments.com/files/catalog/Lafayett...

www.specialolympics.org/Special+Olympics+Public+Website/English/...and. ../Strength+Training+and+Conditioning.htm -

www.sport-fitness-advisor.com/fitnesstests.html

www.theage.com.au/ffximage/2006/03/21/cycling...

www.thefitmap.co.uk/exercise/tests/flexibility/flexion/hip.htm

www.thefitmap.co.uk/exercise/tests/strength/core/ncf.htm

www.thermacare.com/.../lower_trunk_rot.gif

www.thesportjournal.org/.../shuttle%20run.jpg

www.topendsports.com/.../abdominal-strength.gif

www.topendsports.com/.../images/home-sit-ups.gif

www.topendsports.com/testing/balance.htm

www.topendsports.com/testing/reactime.htm

www.topendsports.com/testing/images/rulers.jpg

www.topendsports.com/.../images/tape-measure.jpg

www.uksport.gov.uk/.../runtest1bomcmain.jpg

www.verticaljumpmanual.com/wp-content/uploads..

www.weiderfitness.com

www.yuething.com.hk/images/ZT-120A.jpg

Yuhasz, M.S. 1974. Physical Fitness Manual, London Ontario, University of Western Ontario.

Zoladz Retrieved from http://en.wikipedia.org/wiki/Heart_rate and home.xnet.com/~nowlin/heartrate.htm

♦♦♦♦♦♦♦♦